WAS THE CAT IN THE HAT BLACK?

WAS THE CAT IN THE HAT BLACK?

The Hidden Racism of Children's Literature,
and the Need for Diverse Books

Philip Nel

OXFORD
UNIVERSITY PRESS

OXFORD
UNIVERSITY PRESS

Oxford University Press is a department of the University of Oxford. It furthers the University's objective of excellence in research, scholarship, and education by publishing worldwide. Oxford is a registered trade mark of Oxford University Press in the UK and certain other countries.

Published in the United States of America by Oxford University Press 198 Madison Avenue, New York, NY 10016, United States of America.

First issued as an Oxford University Press paperback, 2019

Library of Congress Cataloging-in-Publication Data
Names: Nel, Philip 1969– author.
Title: Was the cat in the hat black? : the hidden racism of children's literature, and the need for diverse books / Philip Nel.
Description: Oxford University Press : New York, NY, 2017.
Identifiers: LCCN 2016045070 | ISBN 9780190635077 (hardback : alk. paper) | ISBN 9780190932879 (paperback : alk. paper)
Subjects: LCSH: Children's literature, American—History and criticism. | Race in literature. | Racism in literature.
Classification: LCC PN1009.5.R32 N47 2017 | DDC 810.9/9282—dc23
LC record available at https://lccn.loc.gov/2016045070

CONTENTS

CONTENTS

ACKNOWLEDGMENTS

Special thanks to those whose work and advice I have benefited the most from: Robin Bernstein, Zetta Elliott, Cat Keyser, Cameron Leader-Picone, Michelle Martin, Ebony Elizabeth Thomas, and Karin Westman.

For offering suggestions and lending expertise, my thanks to: Michelle Abate, Melissa Adams-Campbell, Megan Montague Cash, Clémentine Beauvais, Natalia Cecire, Nina Christensen, Sarah Park Dahlen, Anna Mae Duane, Debra Dudek, Gerald Early, Brigitte Fielder, Amy Greer, Jerry Griswold, Marah Gubar, Daniel Hade, Erica Hateley, Jennifer Hughes, Cheryl Klein, Eric Lott, Beth Marshall, Christopher Myers, Don Pease, Scott Peeples, Debbie Reese, Teya Rosenberg, Lori Sabian, and Lara Saguisag.

For assistance in the pursuit of images and permissions, thanks to Bruce Tabb and Randy Sullivan (University of Oregon Libraries); Eric Reynolds and Paul Baresh (Fantagraphics); Kate Hart; Hannah Ehrlich (Lee & Low Books, Inc.); Margot Abel and Deborah Pope (The Ezra Jack Keats Foundation); Mary Sullivan (Penguin USA); Emily Dowdell (Peachtree Publishers); Alex Bradshaw (Penguin

Random House UK); Carey Schroeter (Allen & Unwin); Vanthi Pham (ObeyGiant.com); Loren Spivack; Kate Hart; Charles Cohen; Naomi Wood; Joe Sutliff Sanders; Olga Holownia; Farah Mendlesohn; Kari Sperring; Jaclyn Dolamore. For lending their aesthetic expertise when I needed it, thanks to: Megan Montague Cash, Mark Newgarden, Mervi Pakaste, and Dan Warner.

A hearty thanks to all those in Eric Lott's group at the Futures of American Studies Seminar, June 2010: Ashley Carson Barnes, Alex Black, Todd Carmody, Alex Corey, Brigitte Fielder (again!), Michele Fazio, Erica Fretwell, Jack Hamilton, Elissa Underwood Marek, Marty Northrop, Jonathan Senchyne, and John Charles Williamson. Additional thanks go to Michelle Turgeon at Washington University (in St. Louis), for suggesting the notion of the Cat in the Hat as a biracial ambassador.

The idea for the title chapter (and thus the book) began when Anita Silvey mentioned that Annie Williams was African American. My thanks to her, and to Hollins University's Francelia Butler Children's Literature Conference, at whose invitation I presented the first version of the title chapter, back in 2008.

For his patronage, thanks to the late Alvin Buenaventura (1976–2016): his generosity helped underwrite the sabbatical year during which this book was my central focus. While we're on the subject, thanks to Kansas State University for the aforementioned sabbatical and for partially funding the travel to conferences at which this work was presented. Thanks to the conferences that granted me a venue in which to develop these chapters: the American Studies Association (2008, 2012, 2014–2016), Australasian Children's Literature Association for Research (2014), Children's Literature Association (2012, 2014, 2015), and the International Research Society for Children's Literature (2011, 2013). Thanks, also, to the many people and institutions who invited me to present this when it was still a work in progress: University of Antwerp (Vanessa Joosen), DePauw University (Claudia Mills), Washington University (Gerald Early), College of Charleston (Scott Peeples), Dartmouth (Donald Pease), and Hollins (Leslie Wessel, Ellen Malven, and Amanda Cockrell).

Thanks to Carl Bromley, Zakia Henderson-Brown, and their colleague (whose name I regrettably failed to note) at the New Press for talking about the book with me. It especially helped me rethink the title chapter. Thanks, too, to New York University Press's Eric Zinner, with whom I have been talking about this book for several years now. I appreciate your support!

And, of course, a big thanks to Oxford University Press' Sarah Humphreville for her enthusiastic embrace of this book, and to Brendan O'Neill for his support. The two anonymous readers of this manuscript offered the most helpful comments I've received on any publication in my nearly two decades as an academic. I thank them heartily—I've benefited a great deal from their advice. Thanks, also, to the third anonymous reader who, in his or her review of the fourth and fifth chapters, led me to useful quantitative data I've incorporated. An enthusiastic thanks to OUP's Lucas Heinrich for his clever cover. Thanks to project manager Prabhu Chinnasamy for overseeing the book's final phases. Finally, thanks to copy-editors Johanna Baboukis and Raji Nirmal for their efforts in capitalization-consistency, typographical-errata-elimination, and general flaw-fixing.

I continue to find it strange that George Nicholson (1937–2015), who supported this project, is not around to see it published—or to discuss future projects, or to meet for lunch whenever I'm in New York. Yet I also feel extremely lucky to have found a new advocate and friend in InkWell Management's Stephen Barbara. He's thorough, strategic, patient, and supportive. Come what may, I know that Stephen has my back. Thank you, Stephen!

ACKNOWLEDGMENTS

The final thanks (added to this paperback) goes to my research assistant Catherine Williams for diligently organizing a representative sample of some of the data discussed in this edition's new Afterword.

Introduction

Race, Racism, and the Cultures of Childhood

Fifty years after the civil rights movement, we have a new civil rights crusade—the Black Lives Matter movement, inspired by the 2013 acquittal of seventeen-year-old Trayvon Martin's murderer, and galvanized by the 2014 Ferguson protests against police brutality. Fifty years after Nancy Larrick's famous "All-White World of Children's Books" (1965) asked where were the people of color in literature for young readers, the We Need Diverse Books™ campaign is asking the same questions. These two phenomena are related. America is again entering a period of civil rights activism because racism is resilient, sneaky, and endlessly adaptable. In other words, racism endures because racism is structural: it's embedded in culture, and in institutions. One of the places that racism hides—and one of the best places to oppose it—is books for young people.[1]

In her oft-cited article, Larrick lamented that "nonwhite children are learning to read and to understand the American way of life in books which either omit them entirely or scarcely mention them." These omissions damage the child of color, and may harm White children even more: "Although his light skin makes him one of the world's minorities, the white child learns from his books that he is the kingfish. There seems little chance of learning the humility so urgently needed for world cooperation, instead of world conflict, as long as children are brought up on gentle doses of racism, through their books."[2]

A half-century later, readers and creators of children's books are still asking why non-White characters are so scarce—most famously, Walter Dean Myers and Christopher Myers in *The New York Times* on March 16, 2014. Noting that books impart values and "explore our common humanity," Walter Dean Myers asked, "What is the message when some children are not represented in those books?" His son Christopher observed that because "children of color are at best background characters, and more often than not absent" from children's books, "when kids today face the realities of our world, our global economies, our integrations and overlappings, they all do so without a proper map. They are navigating the streets and avenues of their lives with an inadequate, outdated chart, and we wonder why they feel lost." These questions—raised by the Myerses, many others, and the We Need Diverse Books campaign (also launched in 2014)—are but the most visible examples of the "race" problem in children's literature.[3]

While young people's books have in the past fifty years made meaningful progress in representing people of color, the growth of multicultural books for children has flatlined (fig. I.1). In the last dozen years, the percentage of children's literature featuring people of color has stayed fairly constant, from 13 percent (in 2002) to 15 percent (in 2015) of the total number of children's books published annually, even though half of US school-age children are now people of color. (I say "fairly constant" because the number fluctuates— 11 percent in 2004, 13 percent in 2008, 8 percent in 2013—but has never risen above 15 percent.) So. Why are we still asking versions of Nancy Larrick's question? In this book, I offer a few answers.[4]

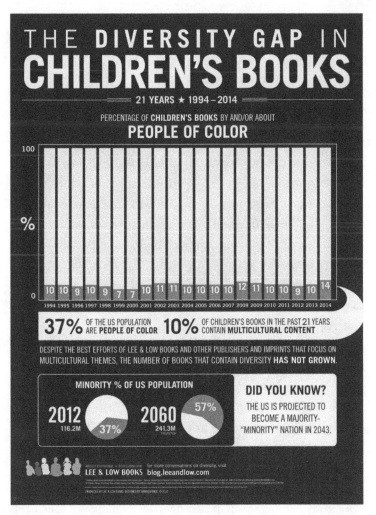

Figure I.1. Lee & Low Books, "The Diversity Gap in Children's Books 1994–2014." Copyright © 2015, Lee & Low Books.

DENIAL, COLOR-BLIND RACISM, AND CHILDREN'S CULTURE

One answer lies in the literature itself. The cultures of childhood play a prominent role in replicating prejudice. As Robin Bernstein has noted, "discredited racial ideology" sneaks into children's culture under the "cloak of innocence," and once there, continues to seep into the culture. *Was the Cat in the Hat Black?*, then, is a book about what happens when race gets displaced, re-coded, hidden. It is about how racist ideologies persist in the literature and culture of childhood, frequently in ways that we fail to notice on a conscious level. It is about how race is present especially when it seems to be absent.[5]

A present absence also points to the efficiency of structural racism, which tends to do its dirty work beyond public view, fueled as much by unconscious racial assumptions as by conscious ones. You do not need to be Donald Trump or David Duke to participate in the work of racism. As Karen Fields and Barbara Fields write, racism is "not an emotion or a state of mind, such as intolerance, bigotry, hatred or malevolence." It is, instead, "first and foremost a social practice, which means that it is an action and a rationale for action, or both at once." The Fields's line "an action and a rationale for action" neatly underscores how racism is routine and unacknowledged, unconscious and continually reimagined, a belief that feels like a truth. In other words, racism does not require overt statements of prejudice—say, Mr. Trump's allegation that most Mexicans are criminals, drug dealers, or rapists. However, the "widespread and mistaken belief that racial animus is necessary for the creation and maintenance of racialized systems of social control" is, as Michelle Alexander says, "the most important reason that we, as a nation, have remained in deep denial."[6]

Though denial conceals structural racism from all people, it particularly afflicts those who do not feel the pernicious effects of these "racialized systems of social control"—those who have never been followed by security as they walk through a department store, whose relatives have never been denied the right to vote, who have never needed to ask a White friend to hail a cab for them, who have never been refused a bank loan because of their race, who have never had mug shots of members of their racial group used for target practice. Structural racism often remains unseen to those who know that, when they take a literature course or go to a film or play a video game, they will see people racially similar to them represented in a positive light. Structural racism lurks at the edges of visibility for people who have never been asked "What are you?" or "Why do you sound White?" or been asked to speak for their entire racial group. In other words, White people—the people who hold nearly all positions of power in children's publishing, and who write the vast majority of children's books—are much less likely to see structural racism.[7]

Indicative of the ways in which denial does its work, you likely *knew* much of what you read in the previous paragraph, and yet you also might not *dwell* much on these facts. We often simultaneously know and do not know about the suffering of others. To borrow Stanley Cohen's succinct explanation, "Denial may be neither a matter of telling the truth nor intentionally telling a lie. . . . There seem to be states of mind, or even whole cultures, in which we know and don't know at the same time. Perhaps this was the case with those villagers living around the concentration camp?" Perhaps this is the case with Americans living in a deeply racist society? Or, for that matter, perhaps this is the case with a children's book industry in which only 3 percent of creators are people of color and yet 50 percent of school-age children are ethnic minorities? People know . . . but they don't *know*.[8]

In other words, it's not that individuals within the children's book industry *consciously intend* to act in ways that sustain institutional racism. It's rather that the system tends to prevent its participants from attaining a full awareness of their role in perpetuating its values. Children's publishing advances its own version of what Eduardo Bonilla-Silva calls "color-blind racism," a more subtle but just as pernicious justification for racial injustice. As he says,

> Compared to Jim Crow racism, the ideology of color blindness seems like "racism lite." Instead of relying on name calling (niggers, Spics, Chinks), color-blind racism otherizes softly ("these people are human, too"); instead of proclaiming God placed minorities in the world in a servile position, it suggests they are behind because they do not work hard enough; instead of viewing interracial marriage as wrong on a straight racial basis, it regards it as "problematic" because of concerns over the children, location, or the extra burden it places on couples.

This style of racism may be more genteel than Jim Crow, but, Bonilla-Silva points out, "it is extremely effective in preserving systemic advantages for whites and keeping people of color at bay." Publishers advance color-blind racism via the language of business—by, say, alleging that a Native American author's work will not sell, or claiming that a Korean American author's protagonist is too similar to another Asian American protagonist, or that perhaps an African American might instead pursue a historical novel because there is not much of a market for African American fantasy. The rhetoric is different, but its effect is the same. As Bonilla-Silva writes, in naturalizing systems of inequality, "color-blind racism serves today as the ideological armor for a covert and institutionalized system in the post-Civil Rights era."[9]

Color-blind racism's ideological armor also means that Whites and non-Whites understand racism in quite different ways. Whites tend to view racism as personal; non-Whites know that racism is structural. As Michael Omi and Howard Winant write, "Non-white students . . . see racism as a system of power," while White students "tend to locate racism in color consciousness and find its absence in color-blindness." In other words, Whites often think of racism as using a racist slur, but fail to consider the more pervasive, institutional kind. In contrast, people of color accurately "see the centrality of race in history and everyday experience." This is one reason why the occasional presence of non-White people within children's books has not fundamentally transformed racialized structures of power. It is also a reason why children's literature needs to dramatically increase not just the presence of people of color, but the variety of their lived experiences. It's why children's publishing needs more editors of color who recognize diverse stories as publishable. It's why we're still asking versions of Nancy Larrick's question, and why people like the award-winning writer and educator Zetta Elliott have turned to self-publishing to get their stories out to the young readers who need them.[10]

STRUCTURES OF RACISM IN THE CULTURES OF CHILDHOOD

Describing her childhood reading experience, Elliott admits, "I learned early on that only white children had wonderful adventures in distant lands; only white children were magically transported through time and space; only white children found the buried key that unlocked their own private Eden." Novelist Chimamanda Ngozi Adichie remembers "The strangeness of seeing oneself distorted in literature—and indeed not seeing oneself at all—was part of my own childhood." Writer and professor Kiese Laymon recalls being more drawn to "American blues, soul, and hip-hop" than to books, "because most American literature . . . did not create an echo. Most American literary classics were not courageous, imaginative, or honest enough to imagine our people or our experiences as parts of its audience." All of these award-winning authors of color were born in the 1970s—Elliott in Canada, Laymon in Mississippi, and Adichie in Nigeria. Their experiences are recent. They're all of my generation—indeed, slightly younger than I am.[11]

Born in Massachusetts in 1969, I never had to look for people of my race in the books I read. I took for granted that books would feature White characters. The possibility of their absence occurred to me only rarely—such as when I read Ezra Jack Keats's *The Snowy Day* (1962). Peter (the book's protagonist) was the first literary child of color I met, and the first character of color I identified with (fig. I.2). As I was, Peter is a contemplative, curious boy. He makes snow angels, explores his neighborhood, discovers that his feet can make different kinds of tracks in the snow, pretends to be a mountain climber, and often feels more comfortable in the company of his imagination than in the company of other children. His race and urban neighborhood differed from my own, but he otherwise seemed just like me. That I could experience his race as incidental rather than as revelatory (as, say, a rare character who shared my skin color) was a mark of my privilege as a White child. So is the fact that I was never deterred from reading by a library full of books that did not depict me or my experiences. Finally, not once in my childhood did I feel the trauma of experiencing racism—because, though it was all around me, it was never directed *at* me.

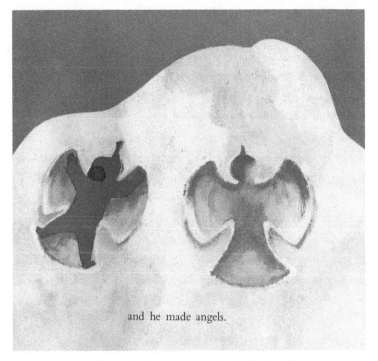

and he made angels.

Figure I.2. Ezra Jack Keats, *The Snowy Day* (1963): Peter makes snow angels. Reprinted courtesy of the Ezra Jack Keats Foundation.

In contrast, the National-Book-Award winning author Jesmyn Ward (born 1977) recalls the sharp injuries of the racism—both casual and overt—that she endured. One White classmate told "nigger jokes," another asked, "Why don't you put some nigger braids in my hair?," and a group of White students taunted her by "joking about lynching." She felt "so depressed I was silenced, because the message was always the same: *You're Black. You're less than White.* And then, at the heart of it: *You're less than human.*" Satirist and entrepreneur Baratunde Thurston (also born 1977) recalls being on a camping trip "somewhere in Virginia," with his mother and friend Reggie. While the two boys were "playing alone in the nearby lake," a "little white boy approached us from the shore and loudly announced, 'There's niggers in the water! Look at the niggers!'" Having met each other through karate class, he and Reggie "conferred on whether or not to use our combined karate skills to kick this little racist's ass," but decided that "the Who-Knows-Where Woods of Probably, Virginia" wasn't the safest place for a fight. So, he says, "In that moment, the black pride I absorbed in my home was balanced by the embarrassment, rage, paranoia, and self-restraint that often accompanies blackness in the outside world of America."[12]

Though I saw many instances of racism in childhood, since I was never on the receiving end, they were at most confusing and quite often forgettable. Of all of them, I remember my racist doll most clearly. Golly was one of my stuffed animals, whom I called "fellows," allegedly because, seeing them lined up along the foot of my bed, my mother remarked, "That's a funny-looking bunch of fellows you have there." It's an appropriate term. I was a shy child, and these fellows were my friends, each with a unique personality—except for Golly. Gary (a dog whose name was an anagram of his *gray* color) was friendly, and a little boisterous in a doglike way. Teddy and Panda were my close friends and confidants. In contrast, Golly was none of the above. Golly's face was a blank mask, the doll's gender indeterminate, and its humanity doubtful.

That I saw this racist doll as unconnected to race or even human beings exemplifies how racism can hide in plain sight, but it also offers some insight into what children see or don't see. As an adult, I look at Golly, and the racial caricature makes me queasy; I feel ashamed at having grown up with a racist doll. As a child, I looked at Golly and saw only Golly—a claim that illustrates the efficient invisibility of ideology. The idea that I "saw only Golly" neatly conceals the fact that I was, unawares, absorbing messages about race and power, and that, in its otherness, this doll was affirming my own

Whiteness as normal. Then, I had no sense that this doll was derived from minstrelsy, or was something that I should not be harboring. Golly was just Golly. When I got a second Golly, which (like the first) was a handmade gift from a South African relative, I remember thinking: *Oh. Now I have two of my least favorite fellows.*

I regularly hugged and cuddled Panda and Teddy. They slept by my side each night. I tolerated the Gollies. If all the fellows were invited to a party, then the Gollies would of course be included. It would have been rude to omit them. But that's it. They were invited out of obligation, not affection. With their black faces, bright red lips, and manic grins, the Gollies lived in internal exile among the better-loved fellows. They were more things than friends.

Their thingness, however, may explain why I responded as I did. Distinguishing between objects and things, Robin Bernstein writes, "An object becomes a thing when it invites people to dance." If, as Bernstein suggests, a doll is a "scriptive thing," then my Gollies prompted certain "meaningful bodily behaviors," revealing a "*script* for a performance." This does *not* mean that all who played with a Golly would interact in precisely the same way, but rather that the doll invites certain kinds of play, and that children can accept, reject, or revise those invitations. For me, my Gollies largely elicited polite indifference. I didn't play with either Golly much. I never even gave the second Golly a name of its own. Though soft, my Gollies didn't inspire me to cuddle them (fig. I.3).[13]

However, my mother (who grew up in 1940s South Africa) *did* cuddle her childhood Golly. Werner Sollors (a child of 1940s Germany) has a similar memory of his childhood doll, Maxi—a black-faced, big-eyed woolen doll his mother knitted for him. In his *The Temptation of Despair* (2014), Sollors includes a photo of himself at age five hugging Maxi, which, he says, "suggests a friendly relationship to a maternally and lovingly created image of blackness

Figure I.3. Photograph of author with Golly, at home in Lynnfield, Mass., USA, c. 1972. Photo: author.

in my early childhood." As soft, "lovingly created" dolls, Golly and Maxi do script cuddling.[14]

Growing up in Massachusetts in the 1970s, I resisted that script because I found my Gollies a bit creepy, even grotesque. On one level, I may have been unconsciously responding to the ugliness of the racial caricature. Golly is short for "Golliwog," whose history dates to Florence Kate Upton's children's book *The Adventures of Two Dutch Dolls and a Golliwogg* (1895). Upton was born in Flushing, New York, but at age fourteen—after her father's death—moved with her mother and sisters back to England. (Her parents were English.) The character was based on a blackface minstrel doll she had played with as a child in the United States. The book and the dolls were very popular in the United Kingdom, inspiring greeting cards, dolls, puzzles, perfume, jewelry, Claude Debussy's "Golliwogg's Cakewalk" (1908), and much more. A pop-culture phenomenon in the United Kingdom, the Golliwogg soon migrated to South Africa, where it was comparably popular, and to the United States, where it met only modest success. As the Jim Crow Museum of Racist Memorabilia explains, it is "the least known of the major anti-black caricatures in the United States."[15]

Given the doll's relative obscurity in the United States, blaming my cool response to the Gollies entirely on some unconscious awareness of their racist content is far too tidy an answer. The Gollies were not only other because they were grotesque; they were also other because they were Black. Growing up in an all-White Massachusetts town, I had no friends or even acquaintances of color. Though there were then public policies promoting desegregation, America in the 1970s was—as it is now—a highly segregated place. I lacked friends of color until high school, a Connecticut prep school that made some effort to attract non-White students. My experience was not and is not unusual. The Public Research Institute recently reported that a full 75 percent of Whites have "entirely white social networks without any minority presence."[16]

CONFRONTING THE "IMAGE LIBRARIES" OF CHILDHOOD

The Golly is not an anomalous artifact of South Africa's influence on my childhood. (My parents and extended family are South African.) It is not an isolated example of how racist culture crosses borders. It embodies racism's pervasiveness. A book from my childhood library, *Walt Disney's Story Land* (Golden Press, 1974) includes Joel Chandler Harris's "De Tar Baby," "Adapted from the Motion Picture 'Song of the South,'" featuring characters talking in "Black" dialect. Of books that remain in print today, the *Asterix* comics, by

René Goscinny and Albert Uderzo (1959–1979) and Uderzo solo (1980–2009), feature racial caricatures of most non-White characters: Native Americans in *Asterix and the Great Crossing* (1975), and Africans in *Asterix and Cleopatra* (1965). Random House's Yearling imprint not only keeps Lynne Reid Banks's *The Indian in the Cupboard* series (1980–1998) in print, but in 2010 relaunched them with new cover designs. More subtly, the influence of blackface minstrelsy lingers on in Raggedy Ann, Mickey Mouse, Bugs Bunny, and the Cat in the Hat. Racism's legacy is particularly tenacious in children's literature and culture.[17]

When I've brought my Gollies into class for discussions of racist children's culture, I've half-jokingly described the experience as a "visit to the island of racist toys." But they're not an island. They're the ocean. Though now called "Native Americans" instead of "Indians" (as they were in my youth), Playmobil's depiction of non-White peoples traffics in stereotypes: in its toys, Native Americans *all* live in tepees and wear headdresses, and the sole "African/African American" family comes with a basketball. Or *came* with one. Playmobil recently discontinued this family. Very often, even imperfect representations of non-White people can be scarce. The "Black" version of the toy is either hard to find or simply doesn't exist.

None of this is to deny the significant progress in the past forty years. From Diana Ross and Michael Jackson in *The Wiz* (1978) to Seychelle Gabriel in *The Legend of Korra* (2012–2014), from Virginia Hamilton's *M. C. Higgins, the Great* (1974) to Jacqueline Woodson's *Brown Girl Dreaming* (2014), children's culture has developed a greater number and more diverse representations of non-White people. While there is also a wide range of aesthetic quality and a limited range of genre diversity, filmic and literary representations of people of color have nonetheless come a long way since the days of Stymie (Matthew Beard) and Buckwheat (Billie Thomas) in *Our*

Gang (aka *The Little Rascals*, 1922–1944), Prince Bumpo in Hugh Lofting's *Doctor Dolittle* (1920), and the Indians in J. M. Barrie's *Peter and Wendy* (popularly known as *Peter Pan*, 1911). In African American children's literature alone, Hamilton, Woodson, Langston Hughes, Arna Bontemps, Mildred Taylor, Muriel Feelings, Tom Feelings, Julius Lester, Walter Dean Myers, Christopher Myers, Kadir Nelson, Rita Williams-Garcia, and many others have brought nuanced, complex, fully realized characters of color into books for young people. Katharine Capshaw's, Michelle Martin's, and Rudine Sims Bishop's histories of African American children's literature not only chronicle the groundbreaking work of these writers and artists who have challenged the all-White world of children's literature. They also delineate the many types of resistance, from personal to institutional, that these creative pioneers faced. (Their scholarship has been vital for this book, especially the fifth chapter, which addresses structural racism in the publishing industry.)

For those who find it far-fetched to fault racism in children's culture (and popular culture more broadly) for the persistence of racist attitudes, I would argue that the racially charged images we encounter as children stay with us, often in ways we are not aware. As Christopher Myers writes, such images "linger in our hearts, vast 'image libraries' that color our actions and ideas, even if we don't recognize them on a conscious level. The plethora of threatening images of young black people has real-life effects." Writing those words just after Trayvon Martin's murderer was found not guilty, Myers added, "I wondered: if the man who killed Trayvon Martin had read *The Snowy Day* as a kid, would it have been as easy for him to see a seventeen-year-old in a hoodie, pockets full of rainbow candies and sweet tea, as a threat? What might have been different if images of round-headed Peter and his red hood and his snow angels were already dancing in his head?" (fig. I.4).[18]

Figure I.4. Shepard Fairey, *Trayvon Martin*: created for *Ebony Magazine* (2012). Courtesy of Shepard Fairey/ObeyGiant.com.

While encountering a few non-stereotypical representations may not fundamentally alter the psyches of people raised in our racism-saturated culture, I nonetheless endorse Myers's optimism. If young people grow up encountering a *much* wider range of books, toys, movies, and video games featuring protagonists of color, then this abundance of varied representations might help to counter the Gollies, the Uncle Remuses, and all the other racist tropes embedded in the culture we consume. What we learn as children shapes our worldview so profoundly because, when we are small, we are still in the process of figuring out who we are and what we believe. For this reason, children's toys, books, and culture are some of the most important influences on who we become—and on what biases we harbor . . . or don't harbor.

AMERICAN EXCEPTIONALISM IN THE AGE OF OBAMA

Racism in American children's literature and culture has not receded into the past because America has yet to reckon with how central racist oppression is to American history and identity. As Susan Sontag pointed out in 2003, the United States has a Holocaust Memorial Museum and even an Armenian Genocide Museum, but "there is no Museum of the History of Slavery—the whole story, starting with the slave trade in Africa itself, not just selected parts, such as the Underground Railroad—anywhere in the United States." The reason for this absence, she suggests, is that slavery

> is a memory judged too dangerous to social stability to activate and create. The Holocaust Memorial Museum and the future Armenian Genocide Museum and Memorial are about what didn't happen in America, so the memory-work doesn't risk arousing an embittered domestic population against authority. To have a museum chronicling the great crime that was African slavery in the United States of America would be to acknowledge that the evil was *here*. Americans prefer to picture the evil that was *there*, and from which the United States—a unique nation, one without any certifiably wicked leaders through its entire history—is exempt. That this country, like every other country, has its tragic past does not sit well with the founding, and still all-powerful, belief in American exceptionalism.

While there *are* counterhistories to these myths of American exceptionalism, they lack the prominence of the Holocaust Memorial Museum.[19]

As David Amsden noted in 2014, "Slavery is by no means unmemorialized in American museums, though the subject tends to be lumped in more broadly with African-American history." The National Voting Rights Museum—which opened in 1993—does locate evil here in the United States, and provides some of the memory-work that Sontag calls for. The National Civil Rights Museum opened in 1991, Ferris State University's Jim Crow Museum of Racist Memorabilia in 1996, the National Underground Railroad Freedom Center in 2007, and the Smithsonian National Museum of African American History and Culture in September 2016. In December 2014, the Whitney Plantation opened its doors to the public for the first time: as far as I know, it is the *sole* plantation devoted to telling the story of slavery, and the closest thing the United States has to a National Slavery Museum. However, it is located in Wallace, Louisiana. The National Voting Rights Museum is in Selma, Alabama; the Jim Crow Museum is in Big Rapids, Michigan; the National Underground Railroad Freedom Center is in Cincinnati, Ohio. In contrast, the Holocaust Memorial Museum and Armenian Genocide Museum are both in Washington, D.C. While there are sound historical reasons to locate the National Voting Rights Museum in a city where people fought for those rights and to tell the story of slavery *on* a plantation, it's telling that there is no such museum in the US capital, the only US city where residents—50 percent of whom are Black and 10 percent of whom are Hispanic—have no voting representatives in Congress. The Smithsonian National Museum of African American History and Culture's location in Washington does identify African Americans' central place in the history of America, but it also de-emphasizes the American government's crimes against humanity. The museum (which opened in 2016) does have exhibits on slavery, but it is *not* a museum devoted to this subject; as its website indicates, its three central themes are history, community, and culture. Why not resistance, history, and culture? Or resistance, pride, and culture? For that matter, why did it take this long to get such a museum? As Amsden points out,

> Forty-eight years after World War II, the United States Holocaust Memorial Museum opened in Washington. A museum dedicated to the Sept. 11 terrorist attacks opened its doors in Lower Manhattan less than 13 years after they occurred. One hundred and fifty years after the end of the Civil War, however, no federally funded museum dedicated to slavery exists, no monument honoring America's slaves.

Despite the counter-narratives, that "founding, and still all-powerful, belief in American exceptionalism" persists.[20]

Exemplifying the subtle ways that exceptionalism is both ingrained and ignored, children's books about American slavery are harder to find than children's books about the Holocaust—even though there are only slightly more children's books about the Holocaust than there are about American slavery. A January 2015 Amazon.com search for "children's books slavery historical fiction" yielded 464 titles; an Amazon.com search for "children's books Holocaust historical fiction" yielded 512 titles. But Amazon's website amplifies this otherwise modest disparity. In the "Historical Fiction" section of the "Children's Books/Literature & Fiction" list, Amazon gives "Holocaust" its own category, but not "slavery." (Its other categories are: "Africa," "Ancient Civilizations," "Europe," "Exploration & Discoveries," "Medieval," "Military & Wars,"

"Prehistory," "Renaissance," and "United States.") Children's books about US slavery do appear in the "United States" and "Africa" sections, but the structure of Amazon's menus elides slavery's central importance. Similarly, the much more thoughtfully organized resources from the University of Wisconsin's Cooperative Children's Book Center—which actively tracks books by and about people of color—include only "Holocaust" in its index of subjects. It does not include Slavery, Racism, Race, or the American Civil War. CCBC does provide several multicultural lists, and Amazon.com has that category, too. However, the structures of both websites elide one of the most important crimes of American history.[21]

Since Barack Obama's candidacy and election (twice), exceptionalism initially coalesced around words like "post-racial" and "color-blind"—as if, magically, his ascent foretold the end of racism in the United States. Children's books about the forty-fourth president spin versions of this myth, some with a greater sense of complexity and nuance than others. Two of the better and most popular ones, Nikki Grimes and Bryan Collier's *Barack Obama: Son of Promise, Child of Hope*, and Jonah Winter and A. G. Ford's *Barack* (both from 2008), imply that, by embracing his biracial background, Obama is able to transcend race. Though this is dangerously wrong, it reflects the optimism that surrounded his election, and follows a tradition of picture books that offer heroic portraits of African Americans. These children's books do for Obama what Doreen Rappaport and Bryan Collier's *Martin's Big Words* (2001) did for Dr. Martin Luther King, Jr., or Hildegarde Hoyt Swift and Lynd Ward's *North Star Shining* (1947) and Lucille Clifton and Don Miller's *The Black BC's* (1970) did for Joe Louis, Harriet Tubman, and many others. The Obama books also do what children's literature has done since the founding of the Republic, seeking to transform a president's biography into myth, fitting his life into preexisting national narratives.

Mason Weems's *The Life of George Washington* (1808) invented the cherry tree story; similarly, these more recent books promote the notion of racially transcendent Obama, a bridge between diverse communities.[22]

Until the final year or so of his presidency, Obama's rhetoric frequently positioned himself in precisely this way—so it's no surprise that dramatic retellings of his life do the same. Indeed, one might argue that his successes *depended* upon his ability to deliver a biography that can be mapped onto American exceptionalism. As he often said, "in no other country on earth is my story even possible." However, as President Obama knew (and as the election of Donald Trump later confirmed), neither he nor the country has moved "beyond race." In both of his national elections, Obama garnered a minority of the White vote—43 percent in 2008 and 39 percent in 2012. His victories rested on the huge majorities he received in the Asian vote (62 percent and 73 percent), the Hispanic vote (67 percent and 71 percent), and the African American vote (95 percent and 93 percent).[23]

Beyond voting patterns, racial disparities persist throughout American life. According to the Bureau of Labor Statistics, in the second quarter of 2016 (the most current statistics available, as this is being written), the unemployment rate for Blacks was 8.3 percent, Hispanics 5.6 percent, Whites 4.2 percent, and Asians 3.8 percent. In 2009, the median household incomes of Blacks and Latinos were, respectively, $38,269 and $40,000. But the median household income of Whites was $61,280. Structural inequalities permeate every area of life in America, from education to health care to the justice system. Race matters. As Eduardo Bonilla-Silva writes, Obama's presidency has "accelerate[d] the pace toward *symbolic* unity without the nation enacting the social policies needed for all of us to be truly 'all Americans.'" In fact, as Michelle Alexander notes, America's racially based caste system depends on "black exceptionalism": "Black success stories lend credence to the notion that anyone, no matter how poor or how black you may be, can make it to the top, if only you try hard enough."[24]

Inasmuch as Obama's rise allowed some to opine that his election signaled the end or at least diminishment of racism, it has merely strengthened the "common wisdom" that social progress inevitably accompanies temporal progress. In the world of children's books, this belief removed the sense of urgency that nurtured and sustained the development of multicultural—especially African American—children's literature in the 1970s, 1980s, and 1990s. This is one reason why the percentage of school-age children of color is four to five times the percentage of books published annually that feature people of color. This disparity between diverse children's books and the diverse children who need them is especially worrying, particularly given the often unacknowledged resilience of racism in the culture at large.

NOSTALGIA AS IDEOLOGY

Adults often fail to acknowledge the racism in beloved books, toys, films, or games from their childhoods because doing so would complicate their affective relationship with their memories. Racial stereotypes safely hide in children's literature and culture because nostalgia can mystify ideology. To admit racist content in cherished memories unsettles not only adults' nostalgia, but their sense of themselves. The logic goes like this: (1) Good people do not like racist things. (2) I like this book (or film, or game). (3) Therefore, this book (or film, or game) is not racist. Some corollaries invoked in support of the "not racist" claim include the following. (A) History excuses my taste: we didn't know any better back then. (B) Why does everything have to be politically correct? (C) Well, it's complicated.

That last corollary isn't wrong. It *is* complicated, but complexity shouldn't be deployed as an alibi for racism. Part of what makes *Charlie and the Chocolate Factory* and *Huckleberry Finn* complicated is that they are both racist and beloved, both racist and beautiful, both racist and revered classics. As chapters one and two explore in more detail, enduring cultural works can be—and often are—both.

Part of the work of this book is to encourage readers of all ages to admit these mixed feelings. Just as affect can mystify ideology, affect can also reveal ideology. That is, nostalgia for a racist item can suppress critical engagement. However, anger, shock, or sadness can activate an analytical encounter. We need to create the spaces in our classrooms and homes for the emotional experiences that inspire reflection.

In those spaces, we need to dismantle the defensive apparatus that Robin DiAngelo calls "White Fragility." One reason that White people resist admitting racist content in beloved childhood texts is that, to borrow DiAngelo's terms,

> White people in North America live in a social environment that protects and insulates them from race-based stress. This insulated environment of racial protection builds white expectations for racial comfort while at the same time lowering the ability to tolerate racial stress, leading to what I refer to as White Fragility. White Fragility is a state in which even a minimum amount of racial stress becomes intolerable, triggering a range of defensive moves. These moves include the outward display of emotions such as anger, fear, and guilt, and behaviors such

as argumentation, silence, and leaving the stress-inducing situation. These behaviors, in turn, function to reinstate white racial equilibrium.

Those Whites (such as Alan Gribben, discussed in chapter 2) who defend *Huckleberry Finn* by downplaying or minimizing racism's centrality often do so out of a lack of what DiAngelo calls "racial stamina." They "have not had to build the cognitive or affective skills or develop the stamina that would allow for constructive engagement across racial divides." Unable to reflect upon or acknowledge their complicity in sustaining structures of racism, such Whites discredit, dismiss, or evade charges that a book they love is also a book that perpetuates stereotypes.[25]

In its drive to uncover what Clare Bradford calls "strategies of elision" and the ways in which texts "enact a repression of memory," *Was the Cat in the Hat Black?* is a parallel project to her *Unsettling Narratives: Postcolonial Readings of Children's Literature* (2007). As Bradford's book does, mine also explores how past power dynamics inhere in present ones. Where *Unsettling Narratives* attends to the politics of colonialism, *Was the Cat in the Hat Black?* instead zeroes in on the ways in which racism persists in the cultures of childhood and the culture industry—both of which of course intersect with the marginalization of the colonized. While most of the racism my book exposes is more subtle than that documented in Donnarae MacCann's *White Supremacy in Children's Literature: Characterizations of African Americans, 1830–1900* (1998), I share her interest in challenging institutional racism. As McCann writes, "When institutional forms of racism were weakened, as in the overthrow of legal slavery, they were often reconstituted in different configurations. People are the cogs in institutional machines, and if prejudice is a permanent fixture in the mind, progressive change will be tenuous at best." The work of decoupling prejudice from people's thought processes begins in childhood, with books that and teachers who work to arrest the development of racism.[26]

THE CHAPTERS, THE STRUCTURES

Because racism inheres in social structures, it can go unnoticed by those with the privilege to ignore it. This book aims not only to make racism legible to those who have the luxury of not noticing, or who have simply become habituated to its pervasiveness. It intends to help all people more effectively oppose this persistent social disease. Since structural racism is everywhere, this book could easily have thirty chapters—or fifty. The rationale behind my five principal areas of focus is to look at discrete, different manifestations of structural racism in the world of children's books: the subtle persistence of racial caricature, how anti-racist revisionism sustains racist ideas, racial invisibility as a form of racism, racial erasures via whitewashed young adult book covers, and genre-coded institutional discrimination within the publishing industry.

The first chapter—"The Strange Career of the Cat in the Hat; or, Dr. Seuss's Racial Imagination"—introduces the book's titular visual trope, and explores how children's literature conceals its own racialized origins. I read *The Cat in the Hat* as racially complicated, inspired by blackface caricature and actual people of color. Considering the Cat's racial complexity is a form of desegregation, recognizing non-White ancestors' continued presence in canonical children's literature. The book takes its title from this chapter because Seuss's Cat serves as one example of how racism hides openly—indeed, thrives—in popular culture for young people.

The second chapter, "How to Read Uncomfortably: Racism, Affect, and Classic Children's Books," examines how "cleaning up" now-objectionable stereotypes in iconic children's books instead enacts a more insidious kind of propagandizing. Attempts to erase racism from Mark Twain's *Huckleberry Finn*, Hugh Lofting's *Doctor Dolittle*, Roald Dahl's *Charlie and the Chocolate Factory*, and P. L. Travers's *Mary Poppins* do not get rid of racist ideologies; they do make them less obvious, and thus more difficult to resist. Instead of depriving young readers of the opportunity of affectively engaging with racist children's literature, we might—I argue—teach them how to cope with offensiveness. Teaching the original versions of these books can help young people targeted by racism learn how to direct their anger, instead of internalizing it and compounding the injury. It can also make White readers aware of racism's pervasiveness and their own racially embodied selves.

"Whiteness, Nostalgia, and Fantastic Flying Books: William Joyce's Racial Erasures vs. Hurricane Katrina"—the third chapter—considers the most pervasive but least examined type of structural racism in children's literature: the absence of non-White characters from places where we might expect to see them. A case study for this phenomenon, William Joyce's *The Fantastic Flying Books of Mr. Morris Lessmore* (an electronic book app [2011] that became an Oscar-winning animated short [2011] and a picture book [2012]) exemplifies what Jerome McCristal Culp Jr. calls "The Woody Allen Blues": the mistaken belief that if you do not represent Black characters, then your work cannot be racist. Just as Allen's film *Manhattan* (1979) has *no* characters of color, so Joyce's *Morris Lessmore* has no African Americans. Yet Hurricane Katrina, a primary inspiration for the story, killed over twice as many African Americans as it did Whites. *Morris Lessmore*, however, focalizes its narrative through the White titular character, and aestheticizes the structural inequalities that the storm made visible. The beauty of Joyce's technological marvel deflects attention away from the Whiteness that sustains it and all allegedly timeless stories (as critics claimed *Morris Lessmore* was). Unmarked Whiteness reads as "universal," transcending time and place. Situating *Morris Lessmore* in the contexts of Joyce's larger body of work and other child-centered culture about Hurricane Katrina, this chapter argues that his imaginative, nostalgic vision subtly reinscribes early-twentieth-century ideologies of race, while effacing the history dependent upon them.

The fourth chapter, "Don't Judge a Book by Its Color: The Destructive Fantasy of Whitewashing (and Vice-Versa)," examines the common marketing practice of "whitewashing," the growing resistance to it, and how this struggle maps a form of institutional exclusion in young adult literature. Believing that readers won't buy young adult fantasy and science-fiction novels with a person of color on the cover, American publishers put a White face on the dust jacket for a story with a non-White protagonist. Focusing on Cindy Pon's *Silver Phoenix*, Justine Larbalestier's *Liar*, Jacyln Dolamore's *Magic under Glass*, and Rae Carson's *The Girl of Fire and Thorns*, the chapter argues that visually changing the character's race has several effects, including altering a novel's racial politics, and promoting Whiteness as normative. Illustrating the lasting damage of market economics' color-blind logic, whitewashed covers hide characters of color from readers of color.

The fifth and final chapter, "Childhoods 'Outside the Boundaries of Imagination': Genre Is the New Jim Crow," argues that, in contemporary children's publishing, genre functions as a form of segregation, restricting non-White children to only certain types of stories. Editors' claims that a manuscript is or is not marketable cloaks racially based genre assumptions in the "objective" language of business, and becomes a self-fulfilling prophecy—perpetuating what Christopher Myers calls the "apartheid of literature." Not only are people of color dramatically underrepresented in children's literature, but market logics dictate that "acceptable" Blackness remain only within certain genres—primarily biography, realism, and historical fiction. Restricting children of color to specific imaginary spaces further impairs the imaginations of young readers of color, suggesting that, say, fantasy, science fiction, and dystopian novels are primarily for White children. To expose genre's racial borders, this chapter constructs a history of gaps in representation, marking the places where "decolonizing the imagination" (to use Zetta Elliott's term) can and must begin.[27]

To avoid being a book that only diagnoses a problem, the "Conclusion: A Manifesto for Anti-Racist Children's Literature" offers a multi-part remedy. It proposes changes in publishing, teaching, funding, and writing that, if undertaken, would combat racism in children's books. While the conclusion does not have all the answers to such a deeply systemic problem, it does chart a path forward, offering nineteen concrete suggestions on how we might act.

NOT ERASING RACE

For a couple of years, the working title for this book was *Erasing Race in Children's Literature*—a phrase intended to evoke the ways in which race gets displaced, submerged, or otherwise marginalized in discussions of children's books. I abandoned that title because the goal is to make visible the structures that sustain racism in both the books and the publishing industry. I want to highlight how

Whiteness's racially "unmarked" status institutionalizes a children's literature apartheid, and to propose changes to the ways we produce, read, and teach literature for young people. As Paula Connolly notes, "As literature teaches each successive generation what race means, it also teaches children what their function is in terms of race, citizenship, and personhood."[28]

As originally conceived, this book was to be a global study of racism in children's literature. Research quickly convinced me that doing the subject justice required a sharper focus. Two factors led me to focus primarily on anti-Black racism, and on representations of African Americans in books for young people. First, despite the centrality of race-based slavery in American history and the long shadow it continues to cast, portrayals of American life frequently elide or minimize the impact of both slavery and its legacy. We often hear, for example, that America is a "nation of immigrants," even though the US population includes the descendants of kidnapped Africans and of the Native Americans who already lived here. Second, of all minority children's literatures in the United States, African American children's literature has the longest history and the largest body of work. The book thus draws fewer examples from children's literature featuring Native Americans, Latino/as, or Asian Americans. In its discussion of (mostly) anti-Black racism and African American characters, *Was the Cat in the Hat Black?* offers a theoretical and practical intervention, applicable beyond its (admittedly) narrow data set. In other words, the book's mode of analysis aspires to be a model for making visible and challenging the varieties of racism in children's literature and culture.[29]

An icon of children's literature, *The Cat in the Hat* illuminates how images from the past continue to haunt the present, and discarded racial ideas linger on. Seuss's famous feline shows that constructions of Whiteness depend on constructions of Blackness not just in classic American literature, but in classic children's stories. The Cat's story begins over sixty years ago, when three people stood in a Boston elevator: an African American elevator operator, Dr. Seuss, and a White publisher who was about to ask Seuss to write a book that would help children learn to read.[30]

Chapter 1

The Strange Career of the Cat in the Hat; or, Dr. Seuss's Racial Imagination

One spring day in 1955, Dr. Seuss and William Spaulding—director of Houghton Mifflin's educational division—stepped into the publisher's elevator at 2 Park Street in Boston. The two men had met in Washington during the Second World War, and Spaulding now thought Seuss could help him solve the crisis in American education. Rudolf Flesch's *Why Johnny Can't Read—and What You Can Do about It* (1955) and John Hersey's *Life* magazine article "Why Do Students Bog Down on First 'R'?" (1954) both claimed that Johnny and Susie were not learning to read because the Dick and Jane primers were boring. Hersey even proposed that Dr. Seuss write a better primer. With that in mind, Spaulding summoned Seuss to Boston.[1]

As they rode the elevator up to Spaulding's office, Seuss noticed that the elevator operator was—as Seuss's biographers tell us—an elegant, petite woman who wore white gloves and a secret smile. They don't mention that her name was Annie Williams, nor do they say that she was African American. When the two men had dinner later that evening, Spaulding asked Seuss directly: "Write me a story that first-graders can't put down!" He insisted that the book's vocabulary be limited to 225 different words, but was confident that Seuss could write a better primer.[2]

When Seuss sketched this book's feline protagonist, he gave him Mrs. Williams's white gloves, her sly smile, and her color. However, she is but one Black influence on Seuss's most famous character. One source for that red bow tie is Krazy Kat, the black, ambiguously gendered creation of biracial cartoonist George Herriman. Seuss, who admired what he called "the beautifully insane sanities" of *Krazy Kat*, also draws upon the traditions of minstrelsy—an influence that emerges first in a minstrel show he wrote for his high school. The Cat in the Hat is thus racially complicated, inspired by blackface performance, racist images in popular culture, and at least one real African American.[3]

Considering the Cat's racial complexity serves as an act of desegregation, acknowledging the "mixed bloodlines" (to borrow Shelley Fisher Fishkin's phrase) of canonical children's literature. Tracking the evolution of Seuss's racial imagination, the Cat's influences exemplify how children's literature conceals its own racialized origins. The Cat in the Hat's many ancestors unmask how racist tropes continue to circulate within children's culture—typically, in ways that audiences and creators do not fully recognize.[4]

SEUSS'S POLITICAL EVOLUTION: FROM EARLY STEREOTYPES TO OPPOSING PREJUDICE

Decades before the birth of his Cat in the Hat, racial caricature was a normal part of Theodor Seuss Geisel's childhood. D. W. Griffith's acclaimed film *Birth of a Nation* (1915), released the month Geisel turned eleven, offered a popular, racist depiction of the Civil War and Reconstruction. Indeed, Griffith's classic helped establish the dominant cultural narrative of that history, a White suprema-cist revisionism in which White Southerners are victims, the Ku Klux Klan are heroes, and African Americans are foolish and ani-malistic. In Seuss's early twenties, *The Jazz Singer* (1927), the first feature-length "talking picture," starred Al Jolson in blackface. One of Geisel's favorite childhood books, Peter Newell's *The Hole Book* (1908), follows a bullet's comically disruptive journey through its pages, including one where a Black mammy points to the hole in the watermelon, and addresses, in dialect, a group of wide-eyed Black children: "'Who plugged dat melon?' mammy cried,/As through the door she came./'I'd spank de chile dat done dat trick/Ef I could learn his name'" (fig. 1.1). Seuss remembered this book so well that sixty years after reading it, he could still quote its opening verse by heart. The popular culture of the early twentieth century embedded racist caricature in Geisel's unconscious, as an ordinary part of his visual imagination.[5]

Figure 1.1. Peter Newell, *The Hole Book* (1908). Public Domain. Image courtesy Morse Department of Special Collections, Hale Library, Kansas State University.

So it is not surprising that such caricature emerges in his work—that he wrote "Chicopee Surprised" and acted in it in blackface, at Springfield High School. In this production, seventeen-year-old Ted Geisel performed as one of the members of the jazz quartet, and as one of the blackfaced "end men." Seuss's early cartoons also offer abundant examples of minstrel-like figures, among many other stereotypes. A 1923 issue of *Jack-o-Lantern*, Dartmouth College's humor magazine (of which he was editor), had a Ted Geisel cartoon in which two thick-lipped Black boxers face off. Playing on the fact that one has a slightly lighter skin tone, the caption reads, "Highball Thompson wins from Kid Sambo by a shade"—with a labored pun on "shade." For a 1928 issue of *Judge*, he drew carnival-goers throwing baseballs at a Black man's head, while the man's wife berates him: "Out sportin' again, are yo', nigger? Jest wait 'til I lay hands on yo' tonight." A 1929 issue of the same magazine offers Seuss's "Cross Section of the World's Most Prosperous Department Store," in which a White salesman directs a White customer to choose one of two dozen monkey-faced Black men. The sign above them reads, "Take Home a High-Grade Nigger for Your Woodpile!"[6]

Readers of Dr. Seuss's children's books may be appalled by the grotesque caricature in his early work. Heinous images like these are all too common in the art of Seuss and his contemporaries. Charles Cohen points to a non-Seuss cartoon in *College Humor* (which also ran Seuss's cartoons), in which a caricatured African American stands with hands tied behind his back, and, referring to the noose around his neck, says, "Say, boss, put that under my other ear. I've got a boil on this side." As Cohen points out, the humor in Seuss's "black" cartoons never derives from lynching. For Seuss, racist caricature was acceptable; murder was not. This is not to excuse the harm done by the stereotypes in his cartoons. Rather, it is to suggest

that his work from the 1920s and 1930s participates in typical caricature of the period.[7]

Somewhat less typical is Seuss's repudiation of these attitudes
during the Second World War, when he returns to the "woodpile" metaphor, but removes the racist caricature and adds criticism of racist discrimination in hiring. In a July 1942 cartoon, a
White man hangs a sign reading "No Colored Labor Needed"
on a woodpile labeled "War Work to Be Done"; meanwhile, one
African American says to another, "There seems to be a white man
in the woodpile!" (fig. 1.2). The vastness of the pile conveys clearly

Figure 1.2. Dr. Seuss, "There seems to be a white man in the woodpile." *PM*, July
8, 1942. From the Oolongblue Collection of Charles D. Cohen, DMD.

that *all* labor is needed. During the war, Seuss's early 1940s political cartoons criticize both prejudice against African Americans and anti-Semitism, but deliver abundant stereotypes of people of Japanese ancestry. Here, too, however, Seuss would move away from stereotypes. Serving in the US Army's Information and Education Division, he wrote a military training film, *Your Job in Japan* (1945), which General MacArthur considered too sympathetic to the Japanese and so prevented it from being shown. Seuss and his first wife Helen also co-wrote the documentary *Design for Death* (1947), portraying the Japanese as victims of centuries of class dictatorship.[8]

By the time he was writing *The Cat in the Hat*, Seuss had started speaking out against stereotyping. In a 1952 essay, he pointedly critiques racist humor. Though children's laughter is "giddy" and "unfettered," as children grow up they learn the "conditioned laughter" of adults: "You began to laugh at people your family feared or despised—people they felt inferior to, or people they felt better than. . . . [Y]ou were supposed to guffaw when someone told a story which proved that Swedes are stupid, Scots are tight, Englishmen are stuffy and the Mexicans never wash." As a result, "Your laughs were beginning to sound a little tinny" and "Your capacity for healthy, silly, friendly laughter was smothered." According to Seuss, jokes that mock an entire group of people do not create healthy laughter, nor emotionally healthy people.[9]

Seuss had also begun writing stories that take a critical look at power and its misuse. His anti-Fascist parable "Yertle the Turtle" (in which Yertle is a version of Hitler) appeared in *Redbook* in April 1951, with the revised version published as a book in 1958. Inspired by his opposition to anti-Semitism, Seuss wrote "The Sneetches," first published in *Redbook* in July 1953. Seuss was so sensitive to prejudice that the revised version of the story almost did not become a book. When a friend told him it "was anti-Semitic," Seuss put "The Sneetches" aside. Fortunately, Random House sales manager (and, later, president) Robert Bernstein persuaded him that the story did have an effective anti-discrimination message. Seuss then finished the book, which was published in the fall of 1961. Published the same year as *Brown vs. Board of Education*, Seuss's *Horton Hears a Who!* (1954) presents the Whos' smallness as an arbitrary mark of difference for which they are unfairly penalized. At the time, the *Des Moines Register* interpreted Horton's refrain, "A person's a person, no matter how small" as "a rhymed lesson in protection of minorities and their rights."[10]

HIDDEN IN PLAIN SIGHT: THE PERSISTENCE OF RACIAL STEREOTYPES IN SEUSS'S WORK

Yet during the same decade that he is writing anti-racist children's books and *The Cat in the Hat*, racial caricature continues to appear in Seuss's art. In *If I Ran the Zoo* (1950), Gerald McGrew proposes going to "the African Island of Yerka" to "bring back a tizzle-topped Tufted Mazurka." The Tufted Mazurka—a "canary with quite a tall throat"—sits on a perch carried by two African men. Suggesting a kinship with animals, the two nearly naked Africans have tufts on their heads that resemble the tuft on the bird's. Their faces, each adorned with a nose ring, seem to come straight out of Seuss's early cartoons. His "Africa—Its Social, Religious, and Economical Aspects" (March 1929) also shows round-bellied, wide-eyed Black men. More or less subtle stereotyping emerges elsewhere in his 1950s work. As Michelle Abate has suggested, Seuss's depiction of the Grinch echoes nineteenth-century caricatures of the

Irish. Samuel R. Wells's *New Physiognomy; or Signs of Character as Manifested Through Temperament and External Forms* (1866) ran F. A. Chapman's illustration of Florence Nightingale as the epitome of "Anglo-Saxon maidenhood," contrasting it with "Bridget McBruiser" as an example of Irish depravity (fig. 1.3). Her mouth and eyes resemble those of the Grinch, whose book appeared the same year as *The Cat in the Hat*. Any influence of stereotyping here is more subtle than *If I Ran the Zoo*'s visit to "the mountains of Zomba-ma-Tant/With helpers who all wear their eyes at a slant," but the Grinch's face suggests that, even as Seuss wrote books designed to challenge prejudice, he never fully shed the cultural assumptions he grew up with. As Barthes, Foucault, Williams, and others have reminded us, this is how ideology works. It's insidious, learned unconsciously, and influences us without our being aware of it. As Barthes writes in *Mythologies* (1957/1972), "French toys *literally* prefigure the world of adult functions," preparing "the child

Fig. 747. – FLORENCE NIGHTINGALE.   Fig. 748.—BRIDGET MCBRUISER.

Figure 1.3. Bridget McBruiser, from Samuel R. Wells's *New Physiognomy; or Signs of Character as Manifested Through Temperament and External Forms* (1866).

to accept them all, by constituting for him, even before he can think about it, the alibi of a Nature which has at all times created soldiers, postmen, and Vespas." Children's books function much in the way that toys do. They "reveal the list of all the things the adult does not find unusual: war, bureaucracy, ugliness, Martians." And racist stereotypes.[11]

Toys and children's books are especially adept at—to borrow a phrase from Robin Bernstein's *Racial Innocence* (2011)—mystifying "racial ideology by hiding it in plain sight." As Bernstein says, "children's culture has a special ability to preserve (even as it distorts) and transmit (even as it fragments) the blackface mask and styles of movement, which persist not only in Raggedy Ann and the Scarecrow but also in the faces and gloved hands of Mickey Mouse and Bugs Bunny." To her list, we can add the Cat in the Hat. In many ways, Seuss's twentieth-century black cat matches Eric Lott's description of the nineteenth-century blackface minstrel: both are ambivalent figures, "with moments of resistance to the dominant culture as well as moments of suppression," and they emerge during a struggle over the rights of Blacks in America. Six months after *The Cat in the Hat*'s March 1957 publication, that struggle made headlines when President Eisenhower sent in the 101st Airborne, integrating Little Rock Central High School, despite protests from Governor Orval Faubus and his allies. Seuss, who supported integration, mentions this conflict in "How Orlo Got His Book," a fanciful story of the Cat's origins, published in November 1957. The reason that Orlo can't or won't read, Seuss says, is that "every book he is able to read is far beneath his intellectual capacity." Thanks to television, Orlo, at six years old, "has seen more of life than his great-grandfather had seen when he died at the age of 90": "When he twists the knobs of his television set, he meets everyone from Wyatt Earp to Governor Faubus."[12]

THE CARICATURE IN THE HAT

Dr. Seuss did not write *The Cat in the Hat* as a fable of integration, but the book does dramatize a conflict between White children and a black cat whose character and costume borrow from blackface performance. The Cat's umbrella (which he uses as a cane) and outrageous fashion sense link him to Zip Coon, that foppish "northern dandy negro." His bright red floppy tie recalls the polka-dotted ties of blackfaced Fred Astaire in *Swing Time* (1936, fig. 1.4) and of blackfaced Mickey Rooney in *Babes in Arms* (1939). His red-and-white-striped hat brings to mind Rooney's hat in the same film. These garish costumes signal the Cat's and the blackface character's aspiration to and unawareness of bourgeois acceptability. As William

Figure 1.4. Fred Astaire as Lucky Garnett, during the "Bojangles of Harlem" number, *Swing Time* (directed by George Stevens, 1936).

Mahar says of the minstrel character Zip Coon, the Cat is "a pretender, a charlatan, a confidence man who is sincere and ignorant of the values associated with social station or power." He falsely claims that he knows this middle-class household's rules: "Your mother/ Will not mind at all if I do." But we, the two children, and the fish all know that she *would* mind. Seuss's narrator invites us to laugh at the Cat's preposterous claims. "I can fan with the fan/As I hop on the ball! But that is not all./Oh, no./That is not all," says the Cat, just before he falls from the ball and lands "on his head."[13]

The Cat's minstrel ancestry reveals Seuss's racial unconscious, indicating how his imagination resuscitated and revised early twentieth-century stereotypes. The medium in which Seuss works is partly to blame here. Seuss's energetic, calligraphic style of cartoon art—the fact that his drawings speak via the vocabulary of cartooning, a medium Scott McCloud has described as "amplification through simplification"—necessarily foregrounds elements of caricature. The Cat's displays of what Sianne Ngai calls "animatedness" amplify the caricature even further. As she writes, "animatedness foregrounds the degree to which emotional qualities seem especially prone to sliding into *corporeal* qualities where the African American subject is concerned, reinforcing the notion of race as a truth located, quite naturally, in the always obvious, highly visible body." The Cat embodies his emotional experience: his facial expressions and bodily movements render his feelings as legible as the book's reading-primer text. If, as Ngai suggests, "the mouth functions as a symbolically overdetermined feature in racist constructions of blackness," the Cat's open mouth also ties him to racial stereotypes: it is open in thirteen out of its eighteen appearances. In the animated cartoon version (1971, teleplay and lyrics by Dr. Seuss), animatedness becomes an even clearer racial embodiment when the Cat spreads his white-gloved hands out to his sides, and opens his mouth wide to sing, "I'll never see my darling/moss-covered three-handled family grudunza anymore." On the final word, he folds his hands, and delivers a look of pathos. His affect and gestures echo those of Al Jolson singing "Mammy" in *The Jazz Singer*. During the "Cat, hat" song, the Cat's white-gloved gestures and expressive mouth also recall the black-face performer, even if his claim to inhabit a variety of nationalities and ethnicities—French, Spanish, German, Eskimo, Russian, Scots, Swiss, Irish, Dutch—severs the link between the Cat and any specific group of people. As Ngai argues, "while animatedness . . . reinforc[es] the historically tenacious construction of racialized subjects as exces-sively emotional, bodily subjects, they might also . . . highlight anima-tion's status as a nexus of contradictions with the capacity to generate unanticipated social meanings and effects." Similarly, the Cat's ani-matedness both creates a racialized subjectivity and complicates his role in the narrative.[14]

His debt to blackface minstrelsy is comparably complicated. Restoring the Cat's racialized ancestry produces ambiguous results, both oppressive and emancipatory. If the Cat is a black-face performer, come to entertain the White children, then his performance is many things—grotesque, unsettling, both blur-ring boundaries and affirming them. On the one hand, the Cat is a merrily transgressive force who *should* be in the house. Until he walks in, the children live in a bland, static world—bored out of their minds, doing "nothing at all." Sally and her brother often seem more intrigued than frightened by their visitor. While the fish complains, they watch the Cat's juggling act, look at his bright red box with interest, and smile as they shake hands with Thing One and Thing Two. Not until page 45 of this sixty-one-page book does either child object, and only within the final ten pages does the boy at last take action. If the Cat makes them anxious, he also arouses their interest.[15]

On the other hand, the fish is right when he says to the Cat: "You SHOULD NOT be here/when our mother is not." This black cat is creating chaos in this White family's home. Recalling the long cultural history of representing people of color as animals, he is an animal impersonating a human, dressed to the nines and pretending to be a member of the class and race to which he aspires. Inasmuch as their clothes and language emphasize performance, the efforts of the blackface character—and of the Cat—may highlight race and class as social constructs. Yet, if their acting suggests that social class and race are roles, it also invites us to laugh because they cannot perform these roles convincingly. A blackface caricature and the Cat falter in their performances because they are essentially different, essentially other. Performance alone cannot transport them across these boundaries. Their failed mimicry solicits our laughter.[16]

The effects of this laughter are as ambiguous as the blackface minstrel himself. As Lott says, the blackface character both strives to and fails to conceal the material predicament of African Americans: attempting to forget history, it proffered the myth of the happy plantation slave, but it also "flaunted" the facts of enslavement, serving as an "uncomfortable reminder" of it. Seuss's Cat offers a mid-twentieth-century parallel, evoking the varied and contradictory images of African Americans in popular media of the 1950s. Read one way, the Cat is an entertainer, singing and dancing like Sammy Davis, Jr. in the Broadway show *Mr. Wonderful* (1956). The Cat arrives to serve as the day's entertainment, bringing "good games," "new tricks," and "FUN-IN-A-BOX." Standing atop the box and tipping his hat, the Cat is a merry emcee, introducing the performing Things. Later works featuring the Cat emphasize his role as showman: in the original script for the TV special *The Grinch Grinches the Cat in the Hat* (1982), he is the Things' impresario, managing their nightclub act. In *The Cat in the Hat Comes Back* (1958), the Cat's hat is like a car full of circus clowns, holding far more than its small space could possibly contain: twenty-six Little Cats, and Voom. However, read a second way, the Cat's performance fails to conceal the threat of violence. Not just a smiling song-and-dance man (or cat), the Cat in the Hat embodies unrest: he unsettles the social order, bending the rake, scaring the fish, and unleashing two Things who both knock the wind out of Sally and knock over a vase, lamp, books, and dishes. In his subversive aspect, the Cat evokes media images of violence associated with the civil rights movement. Though he is initiating the violence (rather than practicing nonviolent civil disobedience and receiving a violent response from Whites), his disruptive presence serves as a reminder of African Americans' struggle for human rights. He is entertainer, warning, and provocateur.[17]

At his most provocative, the Cat embraces the blackface character's willingness to flout the rules to which he is expected to conform. Likening the minstrel performer to the Bohemian, Lott quotes T. J. Clark's description: "The Bohemian caricatured the claims of bourgeois society. He took the slogans at face-value; if the city was a playground he would play; if individual freedom was sacrosanct then he would celebrate the cult twenty-four hours a day; *laissez-faire* meant what it said." Seuss's Cat behaves much as Clark's Bohemian does. Shortly after Sally's brother complains "How I wish/We had something to do!" the Cat enters and—perhaps punning on the "thing" in "something"—brings Thing One and Thing Two. In the animated television special, the Cat further exploits this literalism. The fish orders him "Out! And take those Things with you!" Feigning misunderstanding, the Cat replies, "Take the things? But whoever heard of a house without things in it?" His game in the book, too, is to take the children's wishes all too literally. Responding to their need for fun, the Cat always introduces his mischief as "fun": "These

Things will not bite you./They want to have fun." And, earlier, "we can have/Lots of good fun, if you wish,/With a game that I call/UP-UP-UP with a fish!" In the tradition of the Bohemian and the blackface performer, the Cat invokes bourgeois notions of fun in order to question them.[18]

The most subversive aspect of the caricature implied by Seuss's Cat is that, unlike the blackface performer and the racial caricature elsewhere in Seuss's own work, the Cat's racial category is *not* his defining feature, as it is for the Black characters on the African Island of Yerka, or for those "helpers who all wear their eyes at a slant" in *If I Ran the Zoo*. That book and Seuss's other bestiary books— *Scrambled Eggs Super!* (1953), *On Beyond Zebra!* (1955), *If I Ran the Circus* (1956), *Dr. Seuss's Sleep Book* (1962), and so on—all depend on an exoticized other. When Seuss sticks to fantasy, these others seem to float free from any specific race, ethnicity, or nationality. Greater knowledge of early twentieth-century stereotypes might well unearth other caricatures lurking beneath the surface of Seuss's art, but these at least appear benign. The High Gargel-orum, from *On Beyond Zebra!*, are tall floppy-footed, thumb-twiddling creatures: as their name suggests, they have collars where they gargle. The Hoodwink, from *If I Ran the Circus*, has a basket-shaped hood, and a punny name. If these have roots in cruel caricature, that ancestry has been effectively concealed: they seem purely fantastical. However, when Seuss veers toward the real, he moves toward stereotypes. In *Scrambled Eggs Super!*, Ali of the Mt. Strookoo Cuckoos scenes looks like a standard-issue Seuss adult plus a beard and a turban. Though the depiction could be worse, he is nonetheless purely a figure of fun: as he flees persecution by allies of the Mt. Strookoo Cuckoos, this gullible Arab invites laughter. Ali may be a milder caricature than the Africans from Yerka or those slant-eyed helpers, but he is a caricature just the same.[19]

INFLUENCE AND AMBIGUITY: THE CAT'S OTHER
RACIALIZED ANCESTORS

These images appear in his work because Seuss was a cultural sponge. He absorbed everything he saw and reflected these influences in his work: the Indian-brand motorcycles of Springfield, Massachusetts; the acacia trees of Kenya; the architecture of Antonio Gaudí; the art of Picasso, M. C. Escher, Rube Goldberg, and Palmer Cox; and stereotypes of women and people of color. The complex mixture of images and ideas shaped Dr. Seuss the artist, and Theodor Geisel the man. Even as he wrote books designed to challenge prejudice, he never fully shed the cultural assumptions he grew up with, and was likely unaware of the ways in which his visual imagination replicated the racial ideologies he consciously sought to reject.

Even if Seuss were conscious of how popular visual culture had shaped his racial imagination, it would be nearly impossible to disentangle the many strands of influence. The Cat in the Hat's Black ancestors are not all suffused with racial caricature. Certainly, some are. Contributing to the Cat's dark coloring and strengthening his ties to blackface performance, one likely ancestor is directly associated with minstrelsy: Harry S. Miller's song, "The Cat Came Back" (1893), a "COMIC NEGRO ABSURDITY" which tells of an old yellow cat who will not leave Mister Johnson's home and, subsequently, will not leave several other places. As the refrain says, the "cat came back for it wouldn't stay away." In the 1893 sheet music, the lyrics are all in an imitation Black dialect: "Dar was ole Mister Johnson, he had troubles ob his own;/He had an ole yaller cat that wouldn't leave its home./He tried eb'ry thing he knew to keep de cat away;/Eben sent it to de preacher, an' he tole for it to stay." Though Seuss never mentions "The Cat Came Back," his sequel *The Cat in the Hat Comes Back* (1958) echoes its title, his Cat stories bear strong narrative similarities to the tale of the cat in the song (both are pesky cats who are hard to get rid of), and its prevalence in pop culture makes it likely that Seuss would have known it.[20]

Yet other Black influences are less obviously invested in racial caricature. For instance, a definite musical forebear of the Cat in the Hat is the jazz or swing musician as "cat," an African American slang term that dates to the early 1930s. J. E. Lighter's *Historical Dictionary of American Slang* cites five references from that decade, from a 1931 song by Hezekiah Jenkins to a 1937 *New Yorker* article that stated, "Dance musicians are known as *cats*." In 1938, this term inspired the Cat in the Hat's earliest known ancestor (in Seuss's work) and the first Seussian cat who walks upright—a clarinet-playing cat in Seuss's illustrations for "What Swing Really Does to People." This article, by the White clarinet-playing jazz musician Benny Goodman, describes the "new language" of "swing music," including the fact that the "musicians are 'cats.'" The idea of the Cat in the Hat as jazzman returns three decades later in *The Cat in the Hat Songbook* (1967), published the same year that Disney's *The Jungle Book* caricatured jazz musicians as apes during the musical number "I Wanna Be Like You." Seuss's Cat lacks the overt caricature of Disney's apes, but he does mime playing a trombone during lyrics that recall the term "be-bop": "I can beep a beeper. Beep, beep, beep!/I can boop a booper. Boop, boop, boop!/So, if you need a fellow who can boop and beep,/I'm the boop-boop booper that you need!/Beep, beep!/Plunk, plunk!/Strum, strum!/Boop, boop, plink!" If the expressive movements of his arms and hands recall Ngai's racialized "animatedness," the Cat's words here make him sound like a bop musician—or, possibly, a beatnik?[21]

Minstrel, musician, beatnik. The Cat is as ambiguous and complex as his array of racialized ancestors. *Krazy Kat*, a likely source for the Cat's red bow tie, embodies that racial complexity. George

Herriman, *Krazy Kat's* creator, had African ancestry, but he allowed himself to be read as Greek, and always wore a hat (presumably to hide his curly hair). As Ian Lewis Gordon suggests, Krazy Kat's malleable universe may have been inspired by "Herriman's life as a mixed race individual living in a world where people were forced to be black or white." In some of the strips, Herriman's characters switch their colors, literally playing with race as a construct. In an October 1921 sequence, a bag of flour turns Krazy from black to white; soot turns Ignatz mouse from white to black (fig. 1.5). When they meet, neither one recognizes the other, highlighting both how race shapes perception and the folly of that way of seeing. The folly is the punch line: they may not recognize each other, but the color-switching does not confuse the reader. That said, as Jeet Heer points out, the black-white binary remains: "*Krazy Kat* doesn't upturn the division between black and white, but gives us a fresh ironic perspective on it." Herriman, incidentally, hid his biracial ancestry so thoroughly that although his 1880 birth certificate marks his race as "colored," his 1944 death certificate identifies him as "Caucasian." The ambiguity of his own complexion allowed him to elude the classification into which he was born, and highlights the social constructedness of race.[22]

Like Krazy Kat, the Cat in the Hat is a protean figure, and his transformative capabilities both resist and participate in American racism. In *The Cat in the Hat Comes Back*, the Cat gives birth to twenty-six Little Cats—which either re-genders him as feminine, or (since his progeny spring, Zeus-like, from his head) does not. Read in the context of his blackface minstrel ancestry and Seuss's own earlier cartoons, the Cat's prodigious procreative abilities tie him to the myth of African Americans' allegedly abundant sexuality, a trope Seuss exploits in a 1929 cartoon. A Black minister addresses a Black mother and her five children: "Sorry, sister, but you can't

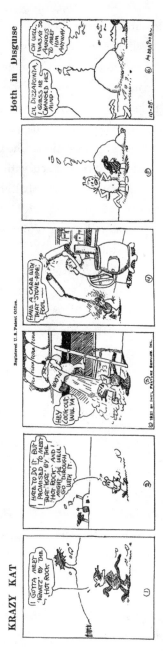

Figure 1.5. George Herriman, *Krazy Kat*, October 25, 1921. Image courtesy of Fantagraphics Books.

get wholesale baptizin' rates unless you got a minimum of twelve chillun.'" She replies, "Well, pawson, duck these five kids now, and give me credit for seven mo' in the future." On the other hand, the Cat's continuous and changing performance works against this racist essentialism by highlighting his endless revisions of himself. He is as versatile as the minstrel performer who danced, told jokes, sang songs, acted in skits, and did impersonations. The Cat plays games, juggles, impersonates respectability, and acts with fellow performers Thing One, Thing Two, and the twenty-six Little Cats. Further complicating color, the Cat is in one respect the visual inverse of a blackface performer: instead of being a White man with a Black face, he is a black cat with a white face.[23]

In this sense, the Cat should be read as a mixed-race character. Interpreting him as a biracial ambassador to the children's home both establishes the Cat's color as a faux-genetic "fact" and underscores the social constructedness of race. That is, on the one hand, his artistic DNA combines Black and White influences; on the other, reading the Cat as Black highlights the longstanding American legal and social tendency to "read" anyone with Black ancestry as Black. Barack Obama is often spoken of as the nation's first African American president when, as the child of a Black Kenyan father and a White Kansan mother, he really is *both* that *and* the nation's first multiracial president. The Cat is the creative progeny of a White Massachusetts-born father (Seuss) and a culture saturated with racial stereotypes. In a Houghton Mifflin elevator on that spring day in 1955, an imagination steeped in blackface performance transformed the white-gloved, brown-skinned Mrs. Williams into the white-gloved, black-and-white-skinned (or -furred?) Cat in the Hat.

Possibly, the Cat's white face—and mixed race—creates an ambiguity that prevents readers from seeing his roots in blackface performance. Certainly, the Cat's color does vary: sometimes he appears whiter, and sometimes he appears blacker. He has a darker face and body on the original cover to *The Cat in the Hat Songbook* (1967), and is darker still in the plastic toy created by Revell in 1960 (fig. 1.6). The orange background of the Houghton Mifflin school edition of *The Cat in the Hat* creates a sharper contrast with the Cat, also highlighting his blackness. On the other hand, the original Cat in the Hat plush dolls from the early 1960s (fig. 1.7) gave the Cat black arms and legs but a white torso and face, making him whiter than he appears in *The Cat in the Hat* or *The Cat in the Hat Comes Back*. I would argue, though, that his shifting color is not the primary reason that people fail to see the Cat's

Figure 1.6. Cat in the Hat plastic toy, made by Revell, 1960. From the Oolongblue Collection of Charles D. Cohen, DMD.

Figure 1.7. Cat in the Hat plush doll, made by Impulse, 1961–1966. From the Oolongblue Collection of Charles D. Cohen, DMD.

cultural roots. People don't see the blackface ancestry of the Cat for the same reason that they don't see the blackface ancestry of Bugs Bunny, Mickey Mouse, or the Scarecrow. These images are so embedded in the culture that their racialized origins have become invisible. As Robin Bernstein says, "when a racial argument is effectively countered in adult culture, the argument often flows stealthily into children's culture [where] the argument appears racially innocent. This appearance of innocence provides a cover under which otherwise discredited racial ideology survives and continues, covertly, to influence culture." This is why contemporary readers don't see the Cat in the Hat's racialized ancestry, and why he is able to be read as White.[24]

RACE, REPRESENTATION, AND POWER:
DESEGREGATING AMERICAN
CHILDREN'S LITERATURE

Or, rather, the Cat is *usually* able to be read as White. Three satirical works featuring the Cat highlight his ancestry in blackface performance and African American culture, and suggest that his racialized origins have remained legible—even if only unconsciously—to some readers of his story. In Robert Coover's "The Cat in the Hat for President" (1968), the Cat's role as a popular if unqualified presidential candidate frequently relies upon racialized images of African Americans. Like the blackface performer, Coover's version of the Cat juggles, sings, does tricks, and makes people laugh. He embodies America, his "floppy striped Hat, [a] parody of Uncle Sam's." And he is oversexed: As his campaign begins to spiral out of control, he carries "a stiff red peenie through all the churches in Indianapolis." Drawing on images of White supremacist terrorism of African Americans, Coover has a Mississippi lynch mob kill the Cat. The mob skins him, roasts him, and then eats him—producing a hallucinogenic vision of the Cat as America. Their "vision was all red, white, and blue, shot through with stars, bars, and silver bullets," as the "whole hoopla of American history stormed through [their] exploded minds." Echoing Ralph Ellison's reading of minstrelsy (on which more in a moment), this Cat is emphatically American—and racially Black.[25]

Alan Katz and Chris Wrinn's *The Cat NOT in the Hat! A Parody by Dr. Juice* (1996) also highlights the color of Seuss's Cat (fig. 1.8). Imagining the Cat in the Hat as O. J. Simpson, this book includes such lines as "One knife? Two knife? Red knife. Dead wife." After Simpson is arrested, the book depicts him shackled to a football, getting fingerprinted: "Juice gave in/And in a blink/They dipped

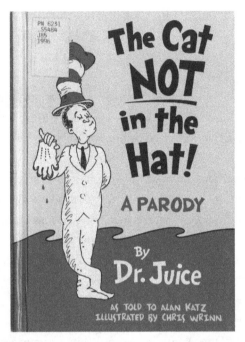

Figure 1.8. Alan Katz and Chris Wrinn, *The Cat NOT in the Hat! A Parody by Dr. Juice* (1996). Image courtesy of the Library of Congress.

his all-star hands in ink./They snapped his photo, front and side./ And said, 'Big man, you will be tried!' " The book mocks the lawyers on both sides, the media coverage, and the verdict. In the estimation of *The Cat NOT in the Hat!*, the Cat is a Black criminal who has evaded the law—an interpretation that Seuss's estate did not like. Dr. Seuss Enterprises sued for copyright infringement, and won in a ruling that has become a landmark in copyright law. According to the court, *The Cat NOT in the Hat* merely mimicked Seuss's style to retell the Simpson case; it did not hold that style "up to ridicule," and so was not parody. Distribution of the book was suppressed. The sole extant copy is in the Library of Congress.[26]

Perhaps because he published it via his own Free Market Warrior Publications, Loren Spivack's *The Cat and the Mitt by Dr. Truth* (2012) evaded the scrutiny of Dr. Seuss Enterprises: readers purchased it by mail, or directly from Spivack at conservative political events. Replacing Sally and the narrator with Franklin Delano Roosevelt and Theodor Geisel, *The Cat and the Mitt* casts a grinning President Obama in the role of the Cat in the Hat, and Governor Romney in the role of the fish (fig. 1.9). Spivack's Obama, whose hat is a black Soviet *ushanka* (complete with hammer-and-sickle insignia), embodies the caricature promoted by Fox News from 2008 to 2012. The fictional Obama and Dem 1 and Dem 2 (caricatures of Nancy Pelosi and Harry Reid) "Tore up the constitution/And then gave it a kick!" The book's Obama avatar is creating a government-run healthcare system with "Death Panels" that will kill Grandma; the actual Obama's successful bailout of the auto industry is here a failure, designed only to entice lazy union voters. Bowing in greeting to Japanese Emperor Akihito or Saudi Arabian King Abdullah, Obama (in *The Cat and the Mitt*'s estimation) shows his willingness to "grovel to dictators/And bow to their kings./ Who cares about dignity?/I'll just kiss their rings." The book's artist accompanies this last allegation with Leandro Martins Moraes's illustration of President Obama bowing to three dictatorial heads of state, two of whom he had never met: Iranian President Mahmoud Ahmadinejad and North Korean Premier Kim Jong-un (the third, Venezuelan President Hugo Chavez, did meet Mr. Obama in 2009). The book also argues that Obama himself is as megalomaniacal as any dictator, giving him such lines as "I'll build myself up/And make America small," "I'm their messiah, you see," and "I'm their socialist king!" Depicting the first US president of African descent as incompetent and duplicitous, the book's words and pictures not only evoke the blackface antecedents of Seuss's Cat but also a range

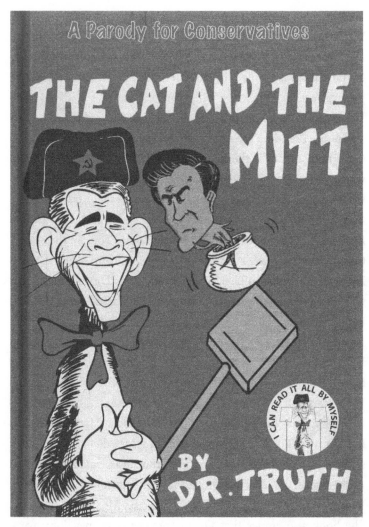

Figure 1.9. Loren Spivack, *The Cat and the Mitt by Dr. Truth*. Art direction by Patrick Fields (2012). According to Spivack, the book's title is *The New Democrat*, but was published with this title as "a special edition we made once and sold for just 3 months in 2012 during the election campaign."

of racist stereotypes that have been used to discredit Obama. (To name but two visual examples: in February 2009, the *New York Post*'s Sean Delonas depicted the president as a dead ape; in 2010, the Brazilian cartoonist Carlos Latuff portrayed Obama as both a slave and an Uncle Tom.)[27]

The Cat and the Mitt, *The Cat NOT in the Hat*, and "The Cat in the Hat for President" all bring the racial subtext of *The Cat in the Hat* to the fore, indicating that some readers in 2012, 1996, and 1968 perceived the racialized ancestry of Seuss's Cat. Although there is no record of readers in 1957 interpreting the Cat in racial terms, considering his cultural roots makes visible four ways in which American picture books have been a battleground in the fight against racism. First, as Michele Martin has shown, the 1950s were a turning point for African Americans in children's literature. The beginnings of the civil rights movement shaped the generation of "authors and illustrators whose work has been the mainstay of African American children's literature since the 1960s, such as Jerry Pinkney, Tom Feelings, Julius Lester, Leo and Diane Dillon, Eloise Greenfield, and Virginia Hamilton." Further, as Martin, Katharine Capshaw, Rudine Sims Bishop, and Julia Mickenberg have documented, children's literature has been and continues to be a site where artists and writers debate race, representation, and civil rights. From E. W. Kemble's virulently racist *A Coon Alphabet* (1898) to Lucille Clifton's positive, Afrocentric *The Black BC's* (1970); and from books that directly tackle racism, like Margret and H. A. Rey's *Spotty* (1945) or Langston Hughes's *First Book of Negroes* (1952) to books that model affirmative images of African Americans, like Ezra Jack Keats's *The Snowy Day* (1962) or Bryan Collier's *Uptown* (1999), books for children have entered contemporary political arguments about race. Recognizing the Cat in the Hat's ancestry in both African American culture and blackface performance allows us to move Seuss's most iconic character from the periphery to the center of these arguments. His color and the conflicting ways of reading that color locate him at the heart of debates about segregation.[28]

Second, just as recognizing how Black voices shaped Mark Twain's *Huckleberry Finn* helps, in Shelley Fisher Fishkin's estimation, to desegregate American literature, so understanding how Black voices and blackface created Seuss's *Cat in the Hat* assists us in desegregating children's literature. As Fishkin puts it, "No one would attempt to write a segregated history of American music, but the history of American literature has, for the most part, been a segregated enterprise: White writers come from White literary ancestors, Black writers from Black ones. It is time to acknowledge the very mixed bloodlines on both sides." Similarly, it is time to acknowledge those "mixed bloodlines" in both literature for children and popular culture. Seuss's work is not only heir to that of Lewis Carroll, Edward Lear, and Hilaire Belloc; it is also heir to that of E. W. Kemble (in its stereotypes) and Langston Hughes (in challenging those same stereotypes). Furthermore, Seuss did not only inspire the White children's-book creators Lane Smith, Jack Prelutsky, and Sandra Boynton. He also inspired Filipina-American cartoonist Lynda Barry; African American rappers Kool Moe Dee, who learned to rap from Muhammad Ali's self-promotional rhymes and *How the Grinch Stole Christmas!*, and RUN-DMC, who name-check Seuss in "Peter Piper" ("Dr. Seuss and Mother Goose both did their thing"); and White funk-rockers the Red Hot Chili Peppers, who recorded *Yertle the Turtle* as a rap on their 1985 album *Freaky Styley*. We can better perceive this complicated, interracial mixture if we remain open to the ways in which White and non-White cultures influence each other, and if we acknowledge that one of the most iconic characters in American children's literature and culture—who for over half a century has taught children to read—is in many ways a character of mixed racial heritage.[29]

The third reason to consider the Cat's racial history is that in the 1950s, readers of children's literature saw animal characters as distinctly racialized. In both racist and anti-racist children's literature, differences between animals have a long history of representing differences between (or similarities among) races. In 1959, racist Southerners accused Garth Williams's *The Rabbits' Wedding* (1958)—in which a white rabbit marries a black rabbit—of promoting integration, and demanded that the book be removed from libraries. In Alabama, State Senator E. O. Eddins said, "This book should be taken off the shelves and burned"; Alabama public libraries removed the book from the open shelves of the children's section, and put it on a closed shelf "reserved for works on integration . . . (circulation by special request only)." In Florida, Orlando *Sentinel* columnist Henry Balch called *The Rabbits' Wedding* "the most amazing evidence of brainwashing I've run across recently." He wrote, "As soon as you pick up the book, you realize these rabbits are integrated. One of the techniques of brainwashing is conditioning minds to accept what the brainwashers want accepted." He sent copies of his column to every state legislator. Ms. Evaline Schunk, head of juvenile services at the Orlando Public Library, called Balch's criticism "'a ridiculous thing,' and said that the city's six copies of the book would remain on the shelves." The controversy became a media phenomenon, appearing in *Time, Newsweek, Life,* and the *New York Times.*[30]

Fourth, considering the politically charged context of *The Cat in the Hat*'s publication, as well as the more outspoken politics of Seuss's other works, the book offers a powerful metaphor for thinking about race and nation. Borrowing from American iconography, the minstrel and the Cat both dramatize the moral contradictions at the heart of the republic. As Ralph Ellison wrote of the minstrel, "His costume made use of the 'sacred' symbolism of the flag—white and red striped pants and coat and with stars set in a field of blue for a collar—but he could appear only with his hands gloved in white and his face blackened with burnt cork or greasepaint." For Ellison, writing in 1958, this costume effaced the identity of the performer, reducing "the humanity of Negroes . . . to a sign," and aiding the White person's self-delusion "over the true interrelatedness of blackness and whiteness." But the trappings of minstrelsy are also key to American identity, because they suggest possibility: "Masking is a play upon possibility and ours is a society in which possibilities are many. When American life is most American it is apt to be most theatrical." Blackface minstrelsy, then, is American in that it both oppresses and liberates, denies identity and creates the possibility for new identities.[31]

Seuss's Cat functions in parallel ways. His costume, too, is peculiarly American—the Cat's red-and-white-striped hat and red bow tie recall Uncle Sam. Shira Wolosky suggests that "the Cat sports a stovepipe hat and bowtie based in Uncle Sam cartoons, where they in fact originated in earlier Geisel drawings and ads." While that's not exactly a "fact," at least one of Seuss's wartime cartoons does suggest his Uncle Sam as an antecedent to the Cat: A January 1942 cartoon shows Seuss's top-hatted bird (representing Uncle Sam) looking askance at Nazi subs pouring into his bathtub (fig. 1.10); in a parallel image, *The Cat in the Hat Comes Back* finds the Cat contending with a pink ring in the bathtub. In other wartime cartoons, the top-hatted figure represents other ideas (Japan in one, the America First organization in another), but—those images aside—the Cat's red-and-white-striped hat is a very American image, and has been embraced as such. As in Coover's "The Cat in the Hat for President," the Cat is "all red, white, and blue."[32]

To paraphrase Ellison's reading of blackface minstrelsy, Seuss's black Cat also masks the contradictions of American democracy in 1957. The Cat's ability to adapt his claims to meet the children's

Figure 1.10. Dr. Seuss, "Latest modern convenience: hot and cold running subs." *PM,* Jan. 22, 1942. From the Oolongblue Collection of Charles D. Cohen, DMD.

expectations makes him a character of possibility—even if he cannot always deliver what he seems to promise. As a response to the *Why Johnny Can't Read* crisis, the Cat offered the hope that his exciting poetic narrative would make literacy available to all American children. As the *Saturday Review*'s Helen Masten noted, thanks to *The Cat in the Hat,* "children are going to have the exciting experience of learning that they *can* read after all." Clifton Fadiman called the book "the most influential first-grade reader since McGuffey," the first primer that "actually amuses the tot, and so persuades him that reading is a worthwhile experience." Reviewers were quick to hail the Cat as a great reading teacher, embodying the "I Can Read It All By Myself" slogan added both to his book and to all subsequent volumes in Random House's Beginner Books series. However, despite *Brown v. Board of Education* (1954) three years before, schools and libraries remained segregated in most Southern states. Black students did not have access to the same materials White students had. Even though the Houghton Mifflin school edition was reasonably priced at $1.60 (in contrast with Random House's $2.00 trade edition), a school with fewer resources could not afford new books. In the documentary *Freedom Summer* (2014), Anthony Harris illustrates precisely this point when he recalls his experiences as one of the African American children educated in activist-run "Freedom Schools" in Mississippi during the summer of 1964: "In the public schools, where I was in school, I had never heard of Dr. Seuss. It was at Freedom School where we not only read the story of the Cat in the Hat, but we acted it out." If the Cat represents all American children's right to literacy, he also masks a separate but unequal educational system.[33]

An embodiment of the discrepancy between the ideals and the realities of America in the 1950s, the Cat reflects the decade's conflict between advocates of civil rights and proponents of segregation. As Mary L. Dudziak notes, desegregation became a postwar imperative because foreign news coverage of American racism repeatedly embarrassed a country that, as part of its anti-Communist foreign policy, sought to position itself as a moral beacon for freedom and democracy. The *Brown* decision thus gave the US government a great propaganda weapon: "After *Brown*, the State Department could blame racism on the Klan and the crazies. They could argue that the American Constitution provided for effective social change. And, most importantly, they could point to the *Brown* decision as evidence that racism was at odds with the principles of American democracy." However, just as *Brown* did not end American racism, neither did Seuss's progressive impulses liberate his own racialized imagination. Blackface's legacy lives on in the character of the Cat, and racial stereotypes continue to emerge in Dr. Seuss books— despite the fact that Ted Geisel was a liberal Democrat whose anti– poll tax cartoons appeared two decades before the Twenty-Fourth Amendment made poll taxes illegal, and that the first version of his anti-prejudice fable "The Sneetches" appeared a year before the *Brown* decision. In this sense, Seuss's works from the 1950s reflect the ideological battle between segregationists and anti-segregationists then unfolding in the courts, on the streets, and throughout the educational system.[34]

SEUSS AND THE CAT, THEN AND NOW

In a photo probably taken in November or December 1957, Dr. Seuss is seated at a table, signing books (fig. 1.11). A multiracial group of children and some adults crowds around Seuss, as if he were the Second Coming of Santa Claus. On display behind him are copies of his most recent books: *How the Grinch Stole Christmas!* (published October 1957) and *The Cat in the Hat* (March 1957). In front of him are his bestiary books that depend upon exoticized others—*If I Ran the Zoo, Scrambled Eggs Super!, If I Ran the Circus,* and *Horton Hears a Who!* While Dr. Seuss signs books behind her, an African American girl, holding a Seuss book—likely just signed by the man himself—offers a wide grin to the camera. This scene of innocent adoration masks the books' political subtexts. The photo conveys an image of a multicultural America where all children have access to literacy, liberty, and the pursuit of happiness.

Seuss's activist children's books reach toward this ideal, but the complex relationship between his liberal Democratic politics and his visual style creates work that quietly preserves what it ostensibly

Figure 1.11. Dr. Seuss signing books, c. November 1957. From Philip Nel, *The Annotated Cat: Under the Hats of Seuss and His Cats* (Random House, 2007).

opposes. Emerging at a crucial juncture in Seuss's development as a political artist, *The Cat in the Hat* carries both the unconscious stereotyping of his earliest work and the progressive goals of his mature work. As threat and liberator, blackface performer and reading teacher, object of ridicule and force to be reckoned with, the Cat is ambiguous, both crossing and affirming boundaries. This ambiguity is at the heart of debates not only about Blackness but also about children's literature, racial identity, and American democracy in the 1950s and today.

Racial caricature's overt and covert presence in Seuss's work is key to understanding not just his moral and artistic legacies but the ways in which America's past persists in its present. However, Dr. Seuss Enterprises—the corporate entity that oversees the licensing and production of all things Seuss—would prefer to keep Seuss's racial problems silent. When I wrote the Seuss biography for the official *Seussville* website, I was asked to cut any mention of the Japanese and African American stereotypes, even though my narrative framed these cartoons in a positive way. Pointing to his later anti-racist books, I wrote that "Considered across his career, however, Seuss's stereotypes soften or disappear over time." That wasn't acceptable to Random House. Since I wanted to be paid for my work, I cut where I was asked to cut. A few years later, when I published the article version of this chapter, Dr. Seuss Enterprises refused my requests to include *all* images for which they claim copyright. I had published five articles and two books on Seuss, and one of those was a Random House book; Dr. Seuss Enterprises had never previously denied my requests. So, I asked why, in this case, they had. I received no answer, but suspect that the reason lies in the desire to ignore the complicated legacy of race in Seuss's work.

Beyond explaining why no images from Seuss's books appear in this chapter, my interactions with Dr. Seuss Enterprises underscore corporations' interest in sanitizing the past. I quite understand why a publisher or literary estate would want to represent an artist's work in the best possible light: they don't want to damage the brand, hurt sales, or otherwise compromise the commercial viability of their property. After all, the only reason any images from Disney comics appear in the classic *How to Read Donald Duck* (1971; English translation, 1975) is that authors Ariel Dorfman and Armand Mattelart did not seek permission from the Walt Disney Company. However, the failure to discuss a work honestly—denying the complex truths of Seuss, Disney, race, and imperialism—helps sustain the structures of racism in children's literature and culture. To borrow Robin DiAngelo's words, "A continual retreat from the discomfort of authentic racial engagement results in a perpetual cycle that works to hold racism in place." If we are ever to break this cycle, we need to experience that discomfort. Reading racist classics of children's literature can help us initiate those uncomfortable but necessary conversations.[35]

Chapter 2

How to Read Uncomfortably

Racism, Affect, and Classic Children's Books

Just as popular characters like the Cat in the Hat, Mickey Mouse, and Bugs Bunny naturalize their minstrel origins, so bowdlerized versions of classic children's books normalize the racism that revisionists aspire to expunge. The wish both to preserve the work of literature and to excise its offensive parts are what Kenneth Kidd aptly labels "progressive censorship, the censorship of materials that are racist, sexist, homophobic, or otherwise out of line with contemporary social and ethical mores." Though of course we do not want books' stereotypes to infect developing young minds, attempts to remove racism from literature has a range of consequences, some of them intended by the bowdlerizers, but many more of them not. In this chapter, I explore the disparate, sometimes contradictory, consequences of trying to keep children "safe" from racial stereotypes. Attempts to erase racism are interesting failures, displacing and refiguring ideologies of race. As Toni Morrison says, "The act of enforcing racelessness in literary discourse is itself a racial act."[1]

CENSORING CHILDREN'S BOOKS

Out of the many bowdlerized children's books, this chapter focuses primarily on four popular ones: Mark Twain's *Adventures of Huckleberry Finn* (1885, rev. 2011), Hugh Lofting's *Doctor Dolittle* (1920, rev. 1988), P. L. Travers's *Mary Poppins* (1934, rev. 1967 and 1981), and Roald Dahl's *Charlie and the Chocolate Factory* (1964, rev. 1973). Alan Gribben's revision of Twain is the most famous of these, not because it is the most recent, but because *The Adventures of Huckleberry Finn* is a "classic"—a term which, on its own, refers to a classic book for grown-ups. The uproar over Gribben's version focused almost exclusively on *The Adventures of Huckleberry Finn*, even though his NewSouth edition revises both *Huck Finn* and *The Adventures of Tom Sawyer* (1876)—both of which were at the time of their publication considered "boys' books" *and* capital-"L" Literature (for adults).[2]

In response to Gribben's edition, which replaces "nigger" with "slave" and "Injun" with "Indian," *The New York Times* was "horrified" and predicted that "most readers . . . will be horrified too." Legal scholar Jonathan Turley said "such editing of a great literary work" was "nothing short of shameful and shocking." NYU education professor Diane Ravitch felt "offended by the prospect that Mark Twain's classic work will be expurgated, rewritten by someone who wants to shield readers from the book's original language." Those were just the critics on the left. As *RightPundits* blogger Shannon Bell wrote, "One of the great novels of all time is about to be neutered" because "Removing the 'n' word from *Huckleberry Finn* will instantly remove much of what makes the novel so great."[3]

I will return to the underlying assumptions of some of those responses later in the chapter, but for now I want to stress that the absence of any uproar over the altered *Tom Sawyer* underscores the cultural acceptability of bowdlerizing children's books. Cleaning up offensive books for young readers is so common a practice that it typically happens without comment. The 1988 edition of Hugh Lofting's *Doctor Dolittle* removes all references to skin color, and Prince Bumpo no longer wishes to be White—Polynesia instead tricks him through hypnosis. In 1973, Roald Dahl revised his *Charlie and the Chocolate Factory*: instead of African pygmies (fig. 2.1), the Oompa-Loompas became small white people from Loompaland (fig. 2.2). P. L. Travers rewrote the "Bad Tuesday" chapter of *Mary Poppins* twice—in 1967, to remove the dialect from the people of various ethnicities they meet as they travel around the world, and, in 1981, to remove these people and replace them with animals. Polar Bears replace Eskimos, a Hyacinth Macaw replaces the "negro" family, a Panda replaces the old "Mandarin" Chinese man, and a Dolphin and her son replace Chief Sun-at-Noonday and the "Indian boy." Nothing on any of these three books' covers indicates that they

Figure 2.1. Joseph Schindelman, illustration of Oompa-Loompas, from chapter 15 of Roald Dahl's *Charlie and the Chocolate Factory*, 1964. Illustrations by Joseph Schindelman, copyright © 1964, renewed 1992 by Joseph Schindelman; from *Charlie and the Chocolate Factory* by Roald Dahl. Used by permission of Alfred A. Knopf, an imprint of Random House Children's Books, a division of Penguin Random House LLC. All rights reserved.

Figure 2.2. Joseph Schindelman, illustration of Oompa-Loompas, from chapter 15 of Roald Dahl's *Charlie and the Chocolate Factory*, 1973. Illustrations by Joseph Schindelman, copyright © 1964, renewed 1992 by Joseph Schindelman; from *Charlie and the Chocolate Factory* by Roald Dahl. Used by permission of Alfred A. Knopf, an imprint of Random House Children's Books, a division of Penguin Random House LLC. All rights reserved.

have been edited. Within, the chapter title "Bad Tuesday (Revised version)" offers *Mary Poppins*'s sole admission of alteration, and an afterword by Christopher Lofting (the author's son) acknowledges changes to "a few minor references" in *Doctor Dolittle* because they "were never intended by the author to comment on any ethnic group" and "are not an integral part of the story." The current edition of *Charlie and the Chocolate Factory* offers no indication that the book's contents are at all different. Even the copyright page offers only "Text copyright © Roald Dahl, 1964."[4]

RACIAL INNOCENCE

People feel comfortable revising children's books because, on a deep level, many of us still believe in the innocent child, a powerful set of ideas promoted by Locke, Rousseau, and Wordsworth—ideas underwriting nineteenth-century social reform movements that banned child labor and led to the creation of free public education. Though the concept of childhood innocence has done a lot of good, it has done a fair bit of harm, too. As Marah Gubar reminds us, to equate childhood with innocence is to idealize an unsustainable, negative state in which "the child replaces the Noble Savage as a human ideal, a stance that entails valuing nature and instinct over art, intelligence, and acquired knowledge." The problem of trying to enforce innocence is that, as they grow up, children gain experience and knowledge. Some of those experiences will hurt; some of that knowledge will make them sad. If we exclude troubling literary works from the discussion, then children will face pain, bigotry, and sorrow on their own. As Herb Kohl reminds us, "It is not developmentally inevitable that children will learn how to evaluate with sensitivity and intelligence what the adult world presents them. It is our responsibility, as critical and sensitive adults, to nurture the development of this sensibility in our children." Further, he notes, critical reading can be a source of both pleasure and power: "children quickly come to understand that critical sensibility strengthens them. It allows them to stand their ground. . . . It is a source of pleasure as well—of the joy that comes from feeling that one is living according to conviction and understanding."[5]

A second problem with the innocent child is that, as Robin Bernstein has eloquently argued, she or he is invariably raced as White: "White children became constructed as tender angels while black children were libeled as unfeeling, noninnocent nonchildren." Though Bernstein's *Racial Innocence* focuses on nineteenth- and early-twentieth-century children's culture, children of color in contemporary America still face standards of judgment that are much more severe than those faced by White children. To paraphrase

Gary Younge, racism has stolen Black childhood. As he notes, "the penalty for being 'young and irresponsible' is not the same for everyone." For instance, "Black and white youth . . . use marijuana at about the same rate, but black youths are nearly four times as likely to be arrested for it." As Michelle Alexander reveals, "A report in 2000 observed that among youth who have never been sent to a juvenile prison before, African Americans were more than six times as likely as whites to be sentenced to prison for *identical* crimes." Thanks to the unequal way in which laws are applied, Black young people constantly have to prove why they should not be shot or jailed. To put this another way, young White people are innocent until proven guilty, but young people of color are guilty until proven innocent. Indeed, young Black people are often shot dead, with no trial at all. According to a 2014 study of FBI data, police are twenty-one times more likely to shoot Black teens than they are White teens.[6]

ERASING RACE TO KEEP CHILDREN SAFE?

The racism that creates these bleak statistics begins in childhood. So, why not excise racism from classic children's books? Advocates of bowdlerizing or banning these novels correctly point to the powerful role that the original versions of *Charlie and the Chocolate Factory* and *Doctor Dolittle* have played in dehumanizing people of color. As New York librarian Isabelle Suhl wrote in 1968, "what justification can be found by anyone—and I ask this particularly of those adults who still defend Lofting—to perpetuate the racist Dolittle books? How many more generations of black children must be insulted by them and how many more white children allowed to be infected with their message of white superiority?" Racist texts can inflict real psychic damage on children of all races, but the child who is a member of the targeted group sustains deeper wounds than the child who is not. The racial ideologies of Dahl, Lofting, Travers, and Twain all but ensure that children who are (and have historically been) the targets of prejudice will suffer in ways that White children will not. The White child who encounters the n-word or Prince Bumpo or an Oompa-Loompa has the unearned privilege of not seeing people of her or his race being stereotyped. That said, as Suhl notes, such books damage White children, too, conveying to them that they are more important, and that dominating people of color is acceptable. Prejudice harms different groups in different ways, and its harmful effects are not distributed equally. Even assigning such a text risks reinforcing structural racism.

Indeed, there is a case to be made for removing racist books from grade-school curricula. Julius Lester has admitted that he is "grateful that among the many indignities inflicted on me in childhood, I escaped *Huckleberry Finn*." He adds that, "as a black parent," he sympathizes "with those who want the book banned, or at least removed from required reading lists in schools. While I am opposed to book banning, I know that my children's education will be enhanced by not reading *Huckleberry Finn*." John H. Wallace goes even further, arguing that *Huckleberry Finn* "should not be used with children. It is permissible to use the original *Huckleberry Finn* with students in graduate courses of history, English, and social science if one wants to study the perpetuation of racism." We could develop this line of reasoning further, and argue that the best way to hasten the decline of a racist classic—and thus the racism it may propagate—is not to teach it at all, at any level.[7]

However, ignoring the symptoms does not cure the disease. It is more risky to ban racist books outright, or to use only the bowdlerized versions. It is a less risky choice to teach these books critically, helping students see the ways in which they reinforce racism, engaging them in difficult and painful, but sadly necessary conversations. Here's why. American children become racialized subjects very early in life. Children of color also tend to become *aware* of their racialized subjectivity early on. In W. E. B. Du Bois' famous account (1903), "the Veil" descends for him in childhood, when a classmate refuses his visiting card. This failed exchange inaugurates his sense of "double-consciousness, this sense of always . . . measuring one's soul by the tape of a world that looks on in amused contempt and pity." In an equally famous work from a generation later, the speaker of Countee Cullen's "Incident" (1925) recalls a six-month visit to Baltimore, at the age of eight. All he remembers is the moment that another child "poked out/His tongue, and called me, 'nigger.' " To turn to a more recent example, Jacqueline Woodson's National Book Award–winning verse memoir *Brown Girl Dreaming* (2014) speaks of "the stores downtown,/ [where] we're always followed around/just because we're brown." Memoirs, fiction, and poetry by people of color offer countless other examples of children of color grappling with racial prejudice at a young age.[8]

Though White American children also become racialized subjects early in life, they are more typically oblivious to the ways in which race shapes their lives. As Peggy McIntosh has pointed out, unearned advantages tend to remain invisible to those who have them. But from their earliest days, American children inhabit racial—and racist—social structures that shape the ways they see themselves and others, that distribute power and opportunity unequally, and that continue to affect them covertly and overtly throughout their lives. Children—especially children of color— notice this difference, even if they may not be able to fully articulate what they understand. If White children are going to stop perpetuating racism (whether accidentally or intentionally), they will need to recognize racial injustice. If children of color are going to survive in America, they will need to learn how to respond to racism.

Learning how to respond is especially important in the wake of Donald Trump's election to the US presidency, which has made overt racism more socially acceptable than it has been in decades. During his campaign, teachers reported an increase in racist bullying and harassment. Children learn from their elders. When Trump said that Mexicans were criminals, and Muslims should be banned from entering the United States, White children learned to repeat those ideas on the playground. One Oregon K-3 teacher reported that her Black students were "concerned for their safety because of what they see on TV at Trump rallies." A teacher from a middle school with a large population of African American Muslims said that her "students are terrified of Donald Trump. They think that if he's elected, all black people will get sent back to Africa." These are not isolated examples. They represent a trend. According to the Southern Poverty Law Center's 2016 study, *The Trump Effect*, "Over two-thirds (67 percent) of educators reported that young people in their schools— most often immigrants, children of immigrants, Muslims, African Americans and other students of color—had expressed concern about what might happen to them or their families after the election." The Trump candidacy and presidency has required *all* good teachers to learn how to discuss racism in the classroom.[9]

As Brigitte Fielder noted after I presented a version of this chapter at a conference, "The decision to talk about racism is a position of privilege." I mention this because some people reading this book may question the wisdom of talking about racism with young children. Most people who raise this question will be White. Since children of color face racism from their earliest days, the adults in their lives do not have the choice of whether to discuss racism with them. The subject will come up, and responsible adults will also bring it up, in the hopes of improving the children's safety. Parents tell their Black children (especially their sons), "only walk in the street with one boy at a time" because "if it's three or more, you're a mob. That's how they [the police] will see you." They tell them never to ask the police for help. They tell them to be unfailingly polite with police officers. They say: "Don't run or they'll shoot you." As Ta-Nehisi Coates writes in *Between the World and Me* (2015), a letter to his son and a powerful meditation on race in contemporary America,

> you are a black boy, and you must be responsible for your body in a way that other boys cannot know. Indeed, you must be responsible for the worst actions of other black bodies, which, somehow, will always be assigned to you. And you must be responsible for the bodies of the powerful—the policeman who cracks you with a nightstick will quickly find his excuse in your furtive movements.

Or, as Coates says earlier in the book, "the police departments of your country have been endowed with the authority to destroy your body. . . . The destroyers will rarely be held accountable. Mostly they will receive pensions." For the safety of children of color, their parents or guardians *need* to talk with them about racism. In contrast, White children—safely ensconced in the privilege of their own Whiteness—face little risk of bodily harm from the threat of racism, whether or not adults discuss it with them. However, if parents of White children fail to talk with their children about racism, then they are allowing White privilege to remain unacknowledged and thus the social structures of prejudice to go unchecked.[10]

For most of its history, the United States has been a White supremacist police state. As Michael Omi and Howard Winant remind us, "For most of its existence both as a European colony and as an independent nation, the U.S. was a *racial dictatorship*." After the Civil War, there was "the brief egalitarian experiment of Reconstruction," after which "followed almost a century of legally sanctioned segregation and denial of the vote." Though the Civil Rights Act (1964) and Voting Rights Act (1965) toppled barriers to voting and legal segregation, obstacles to political participation and equal opportunity persist today. As Michelle Alexander's *The New Jim Crow* persuasively demonstrates, "More black men are imprisoned today than at any other moment in our nation's history. More are disenfranchised today than in 1870, the year the Fifteenth Amendment was ratified prohibiting laws that explicitly deny the right to vote on the basis of race." In the last few years, the US Supreme Court has eviscerated the Voting Rights Act; states with Republican legislatures have passed voter I.D. laws, combating the nonexistent problem of "voter fraud," and disenfranchising those who tend not to vote for them (people of color, younger voters, etc.); Donald Trump, running as a White supremacist, became president of the United States; "Stand Your Ground" laws have become the new legal lynching, allowing Whites to kill Blacks with impunity (Trayvon Martin is the most famous victim). Across the country, police murder unarmed Black boys (most famously, Michael Brown, in Ferguson), men (Eric Garner in New York City), women (Rekia Boyd in Chicago), and girls (Aiyana Stanley-Jones in Detroit). So, in US classrooms and homes, Americans should not be teaching the lie of American exceptionalism, and then, later, after young people have either swallowed the lie or begun to realize that they've been lied to, telling them truth. The founding myth of America is freedom from tyranny, but the reality is tyranny—slavery, genocide, exploitation, and other crimes that official histories prefer to keep silent.[11]

EVERYONE DID *NOT* THINK THAT WAY

Children's books can break that silence. Reading the un-bowdlerized classics of children's literature can help young people understand that racism is not anomalous. It is embedded in the culture, and defended by cultural gatekeepers. *Doctor Dolittle*—by a British-born author who lived half his life in the United States, and whose second *Dolittle* book won the Newbery Medal—can teach us this fact and help debunk the everyone-thought-that-way-then argument. Advancing precisely this logic in defense of the novel, Jerry Griswold argues that it is "reckless" to label as racist the scene in which Prince Bumpo wishes to be White: "Lofting did not rise above his times," he concludes. Defending the same scene, Nancy Springer argues that "white men of that era regarded themselves as superior to blacks, and Lofting was no exception. Any author is necessarily a product of his or her time." We should "not attempt to impose today's standards on the past." There are so many assumptions packed into phrases like "his times," "the past," and "today's standards." These words efface *whose* times, *whose* past, and *whose* standards. I'll hazard a guess that during "his times," Africans saw themselves as more fully human than Lofting's books present them. In "Signposts on the Road Less Taken," an article that should be required reading for all English teachers, Robin Bernstein shows why the that's-what-everyone-thought-back-then argument is a weak one: "In the 1850s, some people held radically egalitarian beliefs, while others espoused white supremacy. The same is true today. What has changed is less the array of thinkable thoughts than the proportion of people espousing each belief. . . . But the full set of racial beliefs has remained relatively stable." As she shows us, this "relative stability of the range of racial beliefs is important because it refutes a progressive narrative of history that falsely implies that history is inevitable." All people in Lofting's times did *not* hold the same beliefs. To defend Lofting's racism on the grounds that everyone was then racist colludes with White supremacist narratives, excusing White people's ignorance in the past without acknowledging the harm done to real people in both past and present.[12]

Defending his bowdlerized version of *Huckleberry Finn*, Alan Gribben argues that when the novelist "was growing up in Hannibal, Missouri, his views on slavery were in keeping with those of his fellow villagers" but that, as an adult, he made "an unreserved turnabout from his younger attitudes." Indeed, Gribben argues, "he presumably would have been quick to adapt his language [in *Tom Sawyer* and *Huckleberry Finn*] if he could have foreseen how today's audiences recoil at racial slurs in a culturally altered country." To the that's-what-everyone-thought-back-then argument, Gribben adds, first, Twain's change of heart—presumably unaware that including this point actually undercuts his "everyone thought that way" claim. Next, Gribben offers an imaginary 176-year-old Mark Twain editing his novel for contemporary readers. Save for the invention of a posthumous (zombie?) Samuel Clemens revising his work, the rest of Gribben's argument simply recapitulates Twain's own claims about the novel. However, as Jonathan Arac pointed out a decade before Gribben's bowdlerized edition, such allegations are suspect. During his 1895–1896 lecture tour, Twain said, "In those old slave-holding days the whole community was agreed as to one thing—the awful sacredness of slave property." However, as Arac notes, what Twain "calls the 'whole community' excludes slaves" and those Whites who opposed slavery. Gribben's "fellow villagers" also excludes slaves and abolitionists. Furthermore, if we can agree that by 1895–1896, a sixty-year-old author has gained some distance "from his younger attitudes," then Gribben's claim that "Twain would ultimately make an unreserved turnabout from his younger attitudes" also collapses into wishful thinking—the kind of wishful thinking that, as Arac persuasively argues, has enabled the book's hypercanonization as a classic American novel that (via its alleged anti-racism) absolves America of its racism. Gribben's strange defense of *Huckleberry Finn* participates in this endeavor, myopically ignoring the ample contrary evidence in both Twain's life and the novel.[13]

That many otherwise thoughtful people insist on defending *Huckleberry Finn* as an anti-racist book indicates how pervasive that interpretation is, and how necessary it is to challenge it. It is hardly radical for a novel published a full generation after the abolition of slavery to suggest, albeit with qualifications, that Black people are human beings. As Julius Lester says, "If the novel had been written before emancipation, Huck's dilemma and conflicting feelings would have been moving. But in 1884 slavery was legally over." Furthermore, it is difficult to read *Huckleberry Finn* as anti-racist without ignoring the book's ending, during which, as Arnold Rampersad puts it, Jim again "becomes little more than a plaything, like a great stuffed bear, for the white boys over whom he once stood morally." Indeed, as Fritz Oehlschlaeger points out, by the end of the novel, "We are asked to forget Huck's process of moral education, his growing awareness of Jim's value as a human being." Likewise, "we are asked to forget Jim's nobility, revealed to us repeatedly in the escape down the river. Instead, Jim becomes again the stereotyped, minstrel-show 'nigger' of the novel's first section, a figure to be manipulated, tricked, and ridiculed by the boys." Though Huck does recognize Jim's humanity during the first half of the story, Jim begins and ends *Huckleberry Finn* as a "nigger."[14]

Beyond demonstrating the absurd lengths to which people will go to defend a novel from itself, Gribben's decision to replace the n-word with "slave" naturalizes the racism in Huck's caricature of Jim. Though Huck is less racist than other characters in the book (such as his Pap), his liberal use of the n-word makes his prejudice more palpable. Yet Gribben downplays the profound significance of removing this word: "Although the text loses some of the caustic sting that the n-word carries, that price seems small compared to the revolting effect that the more offensive word has on contemporary readers." The problem with Gribben's reasoning is that *the caustic sting* is the point now and was the point at the time of the book's publication. As Hosea Easton writes in *A Treatise on the Intellectual Character and Civil and Political Condition of the Colored People of the United States: and the Prejudice Exercised Towards Them* (1837), the n-word "is an opprobrious term, employed to impose contempt upon [blacks] as an inferior race. . . . The term in itself would be perfectly harmless were it used only to distinguish one class of society from another; but it is not used with that intent. . . . [I]t flows from the fountain of purpose to injure." In Harriet Beecher Stowe's *Uncle Tom's Cabin* (1852), when George Shelby threatens to charge Simon Legree with the murder of Tom, Legree challenges him to try and prove it (since Blacks could not testify against Whites in the South), and adds, "After all, what a fuss, for a dead nigger!" Stowe's narrator adds, "The word was as a spark to a powder magazine": George, "with one indignant blow, knocked Legree flat upon his face." As Arac reminds us, "a major point of *Uncle Tom's Cabin* has been to bring good-hearted white folks to realize that 'nigger' is a fighting word." A decade later, following the Emancipation Proclamation, Abraham Lincoln's Democratic opponents wrote a sarcastic "Black Republican Prayer," extolling "bands of fraternal love, union and equality with the Almighty Nigger." Throughout the nineteenth century, the n-word was offensive. Enduring the repeated offensiveness of the n-word is and has always been a core experience of reading *Huckleberry Finn*. Twain's views on race were those of a moderately progressive nineteenth-century White man: if *Huckleberry Finn* and

Tom Sawyer fail to offend contemporary readers, then we're not reading them closely enough.[15]

COLOR-BLIND RACISM

The frankness of the un-bowdlerized versions makes visible the ways in which these novels' defenders traffic in what Eduardo Bonilla-Silva calls "color-blind racism," a more subtle racism that masks structural prejudice via non-racial justifications for racial inequality. As Bonilla-Silva notes, "it aids in the maintenance of white privilege without fanfare, without naming those who it subjects and those who it rewards." *Doctor Dolittle's* defenders deploy what Bonilla-Silva calls the yes-and-no language of color-blindness. For instance, Nancy Springer admits "Lofting's racism shows" in the "scene in which Doctor Dolittle turns Prince Bumpo's face white," but insists that only *Lofting* and not his character is "biased": "The condescending comments regarding Prince Bumpo issue mostly from the narrator (Lofting) and the animals, rather than from the good doctor," who, she argues, "retains his characteristic bemused benevolence towards all." So, yes, Lofting is racist but Dolittle is not because he's *usually* not condescending to the Africans. Jerry Griswold offers similar yes-and-no logic, saying he would not "suggest . . . that . . . the book is free of racism" but also insisting that the book is anti-racist: "The gospel of all the Doctor Dolittle books is tolerance and mutual respect for all God's creatures." The novel may traffic in caricature, but, Griswold argues, that is only because "in the 1920s," when the Dolittle novels appeared, "Africa was still the 'Dark Continent,'" and "Hollywood's notion of Africans in the early Tarzan films" was of "dusky cannibals in grass skirts." The assumptions embedded in these claims justify the book's racism as, you know, not *that* racist—not really. As Bonilla-Silva says, "the language of color blindness is slippery, apparently contradictory, and often subtle."[16]

Modeling this rhetorical slipperiness, P. L. Travers both acknowledges that her original work has "blacks in the South who speak a picaninny [*sic*] language," and in her very next sentence ignores this acknowledgment, claiming that "while my critics claim to have children's best interests in mind, children themselves have never objected to the book. In fact, they love it." She then mentions nameless children of color who (she alleges) love the book, their fondness on display when she spoke to "an affectionate crowd of children at a library in Port-of-Spain in Trinidad." When "a white teacher friend" mentioned feeling "uncomfortable reading the picaninny [*sic*] dialect to her young students," Travers asked, "are the black children affronted?" The White teacher responded, "Not at all. It appeared they loved it." In addition to selectively citing unnamed children of color (who can hardly be considered a representative sample), Travers completely ignores the power dynamic in which these "affectionate" children fail to call out her book's racism. How likely is it that a young child would challenge the teacher or the author? Doing so would violate all that he or she has been taught about politeness and deference to one's elders; indeed, doing so may even result in punishment. Travers's claim that " 'Minorities' is not a word in my vocabulary" is her way of saying that she doesn't "see" race at all. In Travers's mind, her inability to see race means that she cannot harbor racist beliefs. More likely, it means that she is unconscious of her own racism and prefers denial to self-examination.[17]

Though his language is more nuanced than Travers's, Gribben's logic is just as tortured. He states that his goal is to create a *Huck Finn* that "can be enjoyed just as deeply and authentically if readers are not obliged to confront the n-word on so many pages."

That sentence merrily skates past the fact that it is impossible to create an "authentic" version of the novel *without* the n-word. *The Adventures of Huckleberry Finn* is a classic American novel and a racist American novel. Its racism cannot be separated from its genius. As a result, Gribben's "color-blind" *Huck Finn* bears only a superficial relation to Twain's *Huck Finn*. Even when Twain's novel tries to assert Jim's humanity, such as the scene in which he remembers his deaf daughter Elizabeth, it still calls him "nigger" and represents him as one. Just paragraphs prior to the Elizabeth scene, Huck hears Jim talking in his sleep about "his wife and his children," feeling "low and homesick." He then observes, "I do believe he cared just as much for his people as white folks does for their'n. It don't seem natural, but I reckon it's so. . . . He was a mighty good nigger, Jim was." Changing that line to "He was a mighty good slave, Jim was" not only softens Huck's racist condescension toward Jim, but conflates racist slur ("nigger") with job description ("slave")—and there are moments (in Twain's novel) when Huck distinguishes between *slave* and *nigger*. For example, at the beginning of Huck's crisis of conscience, he makes the distinction: "Once I said to myself it would be a thousand times better for Jim to be a slave at home where his family was, as long as he'd *got* to be a slave." When this passage appears in the NewSouth edition (as it does, unchanged), there is no way of knowing that Huck is distinguishing between the two terms because NewSouth replaces *all* instances of the n-word with "slave." Though Huck, Tom, the King, the Duke, and Uncle Silas all treat Jim as less than fully human *because of his race*, they never once—in the NewSouth edition—use the n-word when doing so. But changing the word does not change the stereotype. In the NewSouth edition, Jim may be called a *slave*, but the book still caricatures him as a *nigger*. Retaining the word is a necessary reminder of the novel's racism.[18]

RE-ENCODING RACISM

Though Gribben insists that this edition is "emphatically *not* intended for academic scholars," racism is *the* central theme of *Huck Finn*. Presenting the NewSouth text to young readers as Mark Twain's *Huckleberry Finn*, Gribben perpetuates structural racism, hiding the bigotry of "nigger" behind the job, "slave." In the original novel, even when Huck praises Jim's intelligence, he uses the n-word: "Well, he was right; he was most always right; he had an uncommon level head, for a nigger." Changing that word to *slave* suggests that perhaps his type of employment has merely afforded Jim few opportunities to develop his mind: "Well, he was right; he was most always right; he had an uncommon level head, for a slave." However, the novel caricatures Jim *as a nigger* throughout the book. For instance, it mocks Jim and other African Americans for being superstitious "niggers," not superstitious "slaves" (see chapters 2, 4, 8, 10, 24, and 36). It also presents Tom Sawyer's Uncle Silas as a kindly "old gentleman," despite the fact that he *owns* people. Huck calls Silas "the innocentest, best old soul I ever see," and praises him for having a "one-horse log church down back of the plantation, which he built it himself at his own expense," neglecting to mention that slaves' unpaid labor must have kept costs down considerably. Changing the word *nigger* to *slave* makes the novel's White supremacism more polite—though not quite as polite as Gribben seems to think. As Jonathan Arac points out, *slave* is not itself a neutral term: "Slavery is understood to be a shameful situation; to call someone a *slave* is to offer an insult." If Gribben sought to substitute a historically accurate polite term, then *servant* would be the correct choice: "*servant* was the usual genteel and polite term. In using it, slave owners dignified their own position as well as euphemizing that of their chattel, for it is honorable to be served by retainers, but degrading to be surrounded, like a tyrant, by slaves." Though *slave* carries its own derogatory connotation, it none-theless lacks the visceral, oppressive force of *nigger*. Replacing the n-word with *slave* masks *Huckleberry Finn*'s overt racism while retaining the novel's underlying assumption that Blacks are more gullible, fool-ish, and childlike than Whites.[19]

Comparably, removing the word "black" and changing "the Land of the White Men" to "the Land of the Europeans" more sub-tly encodes the same racial and colonial messages of the original *Doctor Dolittle*. Though hailing from "the Land of the Europeans" (in the current edition) instead of "the Land of the White Men" (in the original), Doctor Dolittle is an enlightened White European who goes to civilize the natives. The King of the Jolliginki may now be colorless, but he still lives in a palace "made of mud" in the jun-gle, and is foolish enough to be duped by a bird (Polynesia). Both he and his men are prone to childlike tantrums, which (even *sans* color) invoke the stereotype of Africans as childlike. The monkeys still stand in for indigenous people. They are sick because they lack proper sanitation (flies infect their food supply), and theirs is an oral culture: "the monkeys had no history books of their own before Doctor Dolittle came to write them for them, they remem-ber everything that happens by telling stories to their children." Removing skin color from the text and illustrations does not con-sequently remove colonialism. As Suhl wrote of the Doctor Dolittle series back in 1968, "These attitudes permeate the books . . . and are reflected in the plots and actions of the stories, in the characteriza-tions of both animals and people as well as in the language that the characters use. Editing out a few racial epithets will not, in my view, make the books less chauvinistic."[20]

Likewise, in the revised *Charlie and the Chocolate Factory*, the Oompa-Loompas continue to live in "thick jungles infested by the most dangerous beasts in the entire world" and are still a "tribe" who do not learn English until they come to Britain. Even though the animals are now nonsensical ("hornswogglers and snozzwangers and those terrible wicked whangdoodles"), it is not unreasonable for a child to infer that a "tribe" living in "thick jungles" are Africans living in Africa. The Oompa-Loompas still happily acquiesce to being shipped to England "in large packing cases with holes in them," and find life in a factory preferable to life in their native land (fig. 2.3). Though Eleanor Cameron's palpable dislike of Dahl sometimes derails her 1972 critique, the 1973 revision of *Charlie and the Chocolate Factory* does nothing to contradict her concerns about "Willy Wonka's unfeeling attitude toward the Oompa-Loompas, their role as conveniences and devices to be used for Wonka's purposes, their being brought over from Africa for enforced servitude, and the fact that their situation is all a part of the fun and games." As Clare Bradford more sharply notes, "Willy Wonka's Oompa-Loompas are effectively enslaved, but through the mediating figure of Willy Wonka, Dahl positions children to read their enslavement as reward and privilege."[21]

Figure 2.3. Joseph Schindelman, illustration of Oompa-Loompas, from chapter 16 of Roald Dahl's *Charlie and the Chocolate Factory*, 1973. Illustrations by Joseph Schindelman, copyright © 1964, renewed 1992 by Joseph Schindelman; from *Charlie and the Chocolate Factory* by Roald Dahl. Used by permission of Alfred A. Knopf, an imprint of Random House Children's Books, a division of Penguin Random House LLC. All rights reserved.

Although the revisions of Travers's *Mary Poppins* more successfully excise the overt racism from within one particular chapter ("Bad Tuesday"), they do not alter the novel's fundamental assumptions about non-White people. In the original trip to the South point on the compass (fig. 2.4), Poppins and the children arrive at a "grove of palm trees," where, on "the knee of the negro lady sat a tiny black piccaninny with nothing on at all." The "negro lady" speaks in the stereotyped dialect of Joel Chandler Harris's Uncle Remus: "Ah bin 'specting you a long time, Mar' Poppins. . . . You bring dem chillum here into ma li'l house for a slice of water-melon now. My but dem's very white babies. You wan' use a li'l bit black boot polish on dem." In 1967, the scene changes slightly: "on the knee of the dark

The compass

Figure 2.4. Mary Shepard, illustration from "Bad Tuesday" chapter in P. L. Travers' *Mary Poppins*, 1934. Repr. 1962.

lady sat a tiny plum-black baby with nothing on at all!" In addition to the new exclamation point, "negro" becomes "dark," and "black piccaninny" becomes "plum-black baby." The dialect also vanishes, along with references to watermelon and boot polish: "We've been anticipating your visit, Mary Poppins. . . . Goodness, those are very pale children! Where did you find them? On the moon?" Curiously, the 1967 version does not remove Mary Shepard's illustration of the compass with Poppins and the children in the center, and an ethnic stereotype at each of the four points. The 1981 version changes the compass, placing animals instead of people at each of those points (fig. 2.5). The "negro lady" is now "a large Hyacinth Macaw," who asks Poppins to "take a turn" sitting on the eggs, currently his assignment while his "wife's off gadding."[22]

In replacing people with animals, Travers presents the exotic appeal of the foreign in a different guise. Though she eliminates stereotypes of humans, travel functions in a parallel way, other countries serving as exciting places for White tourists to visit. The cultural assumptions remain the same, but are instead displaced onto animals. The erasure of all non-European humans creates other problems, too: without people there, foreign lands seem even more ripe for colonization. Whether animal or human, each representative from the four compass points offers Poppins and the children food, as if native abundance exists solely for their consumption.

The revisions to all four books make them potentially more harmful for child readers because they render the original works' racism more subtle and insidious. Prince Bumpo being hypnotized by a bird is, as the 1988 edition's editor Lori Mack says, not "blatantly offensive"—as is the comparable moment in the original version, where Polynesia and Doctor Dolittle use the prince's desire to be White to trick him. But the egregiousness of the

The compass

Figure 2.5. Mary Shepard, illustration from "Bad Tuesday" chapter in P. L. Travers' *Mary Poppins*, 1981.

original's White supremacy may also serve as a warning flag. Blunt offensiveness can be less dangerous than this newer, subtler delivery of prejudices because the reader is more likely to reject the former.[23]

CRITICAL READING SKILLS

On the other hand, to claim that readers will be more likely to view skeptically a book with obviously racist imagery assumes that they have critical reading skills that children may not yet have developed.

So the intervention of a teacher or parent will be necessary here. I should further qualify this claim by noting that some narratives invite critical thinking more than others do. As Herb Kohl writes of *Babar*, "The reader is swept along without questioning any of the premises of the story. . . . [T]here is no time for reflection or examination. . . . [I]t is easy to accept the whole of it unquestioned and even to internalize some of the attitudes and ideas it presents." Unlike *Babar*, the original texts of *Doctor Dolittle* and *Huckleberry Finn* do at times provide opportunities for contemplation. In these moments, the unvarnished racism of the un-bowdlerized versions may be more effective in nudging a reader toward the critical examination that Kohl describes.[24]

Providing an occasion for reflection, Doctor Dolittle, Dab-Dab, and Jip debate whether they did the right thing in tricking Prince Bumpo. The doctor reflects, "It was the King, his [Bumpo's] father, who locked us up—I wonder if I ought to go back and apologize." The parrot's and the dog's arguments carry the day, and Dolittle does nothing. But their conversation *does* offer time for the reader to consider. *Huckleberry Finn* has many more such moments, as when, feeling ashamed for having tricked Jim into thinking that he was dreaming, Huck says, "It was fifteen minutes before I could work myself up to go and humble myself to a nigger—but I done it, and I warn't ever sorry about it, neither. I didn't do him no more mean tricks, and I wouldn't done that one if I'd a knowed it would make him feel that way." In addition to neatly displaying the conflict between Huck's conscience and what he has learned about people of color, his use of the n-word here displays the instability of his racial assumptions: he "warn't ever sorry about" humbling himself because he's momentarily able to empathize with Jim. Gribben's revision still provides that space for critical consideration, but substituting "slave" for the n-word displaces race onto class. However, for the characters in Twain's actual novel, these are interdependent phenomena—racial status underwrites class status.[25]

In its original and its revised versions, Travers's *Mary Poppins* also provides room for reflection—indeed, it frequently solicits the reader's response. Jane and Michael often ask variations on the question "Could we have imagined it?" When Mary Poppins alleges that Mr. Wigg does not float (despite the children just having seen him do so), a "look... passed between them [that] said: 'Is it true or isn't it? About Mr. Wigg. Is Mary Poppins right or are we?'" After Mrs. Corry and Mary Poppins hang the stars, Jane asks, "Are the stars gold paper or is the gold paper stars?"[26]

However, the "Bad Tuesday" chapter concludes not with such a moment of questioning, but with a sense of "other" as menace. It amplifies the earlier stereotypes, as Michael finds "the Eskimo with a spear, the Negro Lady with her husband's huge club, the Mandarin with a great curved sword, and the Red Indian with a tomahawk" all "bearing down towards him," with "huge, terrible, angry faces" looking "threatening and full of revenge," "their hot breath on his face." Inasmuch as pernicious racial ideologies do not otherwise permeate *Mary Poppins* to the same degree that they permeate the three other books discussed in this chapter, the 1981 revision to "the bear with his fangs showing, the Macaw fiercely flapping wings, the Panda with fur on end, the Dolphin thrusting out her snout" is relatively successful at excising the original's racism and keeping the focus on the narrative nonsense. As Travers herself said of this version, "I think the re-writing is an improvement—perhaps more Poppinish!" That may be so, but the rewriting also makes less visible the racialized language retained in the 1981 revision, such as Mrs. Banks's directive "You will *not* behave like a Red Indian, Michael" and Miss Lark's "Andrew, Andrew, come in, my darling! Come away from those dreadful street arabs!" Despite Travers's remark that the revision may be "more Poppinish," she also did not fully understand why the original was racist.[27]

Of the many possible consequences produced by "politically corrected" texts, the most troubling one is removing the occasion for a conversation about what Sianne Ngai calls the "politically ambiguous work" of "negative emotions." Reading Twain, Lofting, Dahl, and Travers in their original versions allows us to explore how ugly feelings can—to borrow Ngai's words again—"be used to expand the project of criticism and theory." Negative emotions can be mobilized for critically productive ends. Books containing stereotypes invite children to participate in that way of thinking, but children do not have to accept the invitation. As Karen E. Fields and Barbara J. Fields write, to succeed, "a racist caricature must have the viewer's assent to its point of view." Readers and viewers need not assent. Instead, words and images that offend can help us understand and reject offensiveness. There is a case for allowing Jim to remain a "nigger," the Oompa-Loompas to stay African pygmies, Prince Bumpo to continue being "black," Dr. Dolittle to retain his "white" color, and for Travers to keep her Eskimos, "Negro family," Mandarin Chinese man, and the Indian Chief. That case is: Affective relations can be critically effective ones.[28]

AFFECTIVE RESPONSES TO RACISM

Teaching racist literature can help direct the anger of those readers who are racism's targets. Finding the appropriate target for one's anger is a vital survival skill. As Martha Nussbaum points out, "submerged anger" can emerge as depression. However, expressed anger can be "a valuable effort to seize control and to assert the integrity of damaged selfhood." Giving voice to one's anger is "adaptively valuable, teaching the child the importance of its boundaries, and rescuing it from a sense of helpless passivity before the world." As Nico Frijda notes, "Anger implies nonacceptance of the present event as necessary or inevitable, and implies that the event is amenable to being changed. . . . Anger implies hope. Further, anger implies that fighting is meaningful; one is not reduced to mere passivity." Stereotype-laden children's classics offer an occasion to learn how to express that anger, showing the child how that emotion might be used in the fight against prejudice. Importantly, while we think of emotions as innate, both emotions themselves and the ways we express them are also learned. As Nussbaum says, "We teach children what and whom to fear, what occasions for anger are reasonable, what behavior is shameful." Furthermore, anger is "often taught differently to different social actors. Many studies show that angry and aggressive behavior by boys is subtly encouraged . . . , where similar behavior by girls is sharply discouraged."[29]

So Dahl's vision of happily enslaved Oompa-Loompas is upsetting, but young readers may need to learn (a) why the book should trouble them, (b) that it's OK to be angry at a book, and (c) how they might productively direct that anger. Since Dahl attempts "to persuade his readers that the Oompa-Loompas love the chains that bind them" (as Clare Bradford aptly says), children might first need to be alerted to *why* the treatment of the Oompa-Loompas could give a person pause. In the original 1964 edition, Wonka cheerfully explains that these "tiny miniature pigmies" have been "Imported direct from Africa!"—as if treating people as things were perfectly acceptable. He then justifies his behavior by presenting enslavement as benevolent rescue. The "Poor little Oompa-Loompas" were "practically starving to death" because they had to live on a diet of "green caterpillars, and the caterpillars tasted revolting." Wonka learns that the Oompa-Loompas "were crazy for" the cacao bean: "You only had to *mention* the word 'cacao' to an Oompa-Loompa and he would start dribbling at the mouth." So, he tells "the leader of the tribe":

> look here, if you and all your people will come back to my coun-
> try and live in my factory, you can have *all* the cacao beans you
> want! I've got mountains of them in my storehouses! You can
> have cacao beans for every meal! You can gorge yourselves silly
> on them! I'll even pay your wages in cacao beans if you wish!

Despite the condescending tone and unfavorable terms (live in a factory, be paid beans), the Oompa-Loompa leader gives "a great whoop of joy" and says, "It's a deal! Come on! Let's go!" After reading these paragraphs, one might ask younger readers: What would happen to your body if you *only* ate chocolate? What would it be like to be paid *only* in cacao beans? Do you know any stores that accept cacao beans for payment? Where will the Oompa-Loompas be able to spend theirs? Has Mr. Wonka offered the Oompa-Loompas a good deal or a bad one?[30]

If these questions prove unproductive, subsequent passages display the book's White supremacism even more openly, such as when Wonka enthusiastically describes the "middle passage" por-tion of the Oompa-Loompas' journey: "So I shipped them all over here, every man, woman, and child in the Oompa-Loompa tribe. It was easy. I smuggled them over in large packing cases with holes in them, and they all got here safely." To emphasize the notion that Black people *like* being cargo, artist Joseph Schindelman depicts comical crates of Oompa-Loompas, their legs and arms sticking out as they amble about during their voyage (fig. 2.6). (Questions to ask young readers include: How long would it take to travel from Africa to England? What would it be like to sit for all of that time packed in a crate? Would *you* enjoy traveling that way?) Then Dahl tops it

Figure 2.6. Joseph Schindelman, illustration of Oompa-Loompas, from chapter 16 of Roald Dahl's *Charlie and the Chocolate Factory*, 1964. Illustrations by Joseph Schindelman, copyright © 1964, renewed 1992 by Joseph Schindelman; from *Charlie and the Chocolate Factory* by Roald Dahl. Used by permission of Alfred A. Knopf, an imprint of Random House Children's Books, a division of Penguin Random House LLC. All rights reserved.

all off by describing the Oompa-Loompas as a version of the "happy darky" stereotype:

> They love dancing and music. They are always making up songs. I expect you will hear a good deal of singing today from time to time. I must warn you, though, that they are rather mischievous. They like jokes. They still wear the same kind of clothes they wore in the jungle. They insist upon that. The men, as you can see for yourselves across the river, wear only deerskins. The women wear leaves, and the children wear nothing at all.

Wonka sees the Oompa-Loompas as primitive, not-quite-human beings, and Dahl's novel does not contradict him.[31]

Of course, interpretations of any book will differ. Furthermore, the fact that these novels also entertain and amuse might direct attention away from their infuriating parts. There may be those so intoxicated by the fantasy of living in a candy factory that they are unable to perceive why Dahl's novel is at the very least ethically troubling. There may be readers so amused by Twain's satire that they are inclined to overlook his equally powerful racism. The comedy of Lofting's nonsensical menagerie might divert the focus away from his colonialism.

We need to foster critical reading strategies that acknowledge mixed feelings. A key emotional experience of *Huck Finn* is the collision between anger and humor—mocking the King and the Duke's con-artistry or Emmeline Grangerford's turgid verse elicits a smile, but mocking the gullibility of "niggers" like Jim and Nat does not. Or, in *Charlie and the Chocolate Factory*, Dahl's (sometimes cruel) jokes and inventive candy-making technology bump uncomfortably into Wonka's mistreatment of the Oompa-Loompas. As Catherine Keyser noted in a comment on a draft of this chapter, the delights of Wonka's factory "make the subaltern labor seem an inevitable part of that system," as if these sugary pleasures justify the exploitation of human beings.

Beyond listening to these unsettling juxtapositions, students need, first, to know that it's OK to be upset or angry, and, second, to be given a venue in which to express that anger. As Audre Lorde has said, "Anger is an appropriate reaction to racist attitudes, as is fury when the actions arising from those attitudes do not change." For members of the group caricatured, being able to direct this anger can help establish the boundaries of the self, and provide a source of insight. As Lorde notes in that same speech, "My anger has meant pain to me but it has also meant survival."[32]

If, when facing racist art, children do not learn how to express anger, they may be left only with pain. In her memoir, *Men We*

Reaped (2013), Jesmyn Ward recalls her uncomfortable response to reading one of America's most famous and beloved racist books:

> In seventh grade I read *Gone with the Wind*; while Scarlett's and Rhett's relationship spoke to the teenage romantic in me, the defeated Confederates' vilification of the freed slaves did not. And the fact that the book and movie were so beloved in America, across regions, horrified me. *Do they really think of Black people like this?* I wondered.

Reading this on her own (instead of guided by a teacher or parent), Ward was unable to summon any anger or to otherwise assert herself against the novel's White supremacist propaganda. Indeed, throughout her memoir, encounters with racism leave young Ward feeling depressed, worthless, full of self-loathing. Only much later is she able to place events like these in perspective, make sense of her experience, and establish a stronger sense of self. A healthy anger, directed outward, might have helped her better navigate through the prejudice she suffered. Unfortunately lacking any guidance in how to cope with offensive art, she instead struggled on her own.[33]

Children need to learn healthy expressions of anger because there are types of anger that can damage the self. As Maya Angelou has noted, we need to prevent anger from turning into bitterness because "Bitterness is like cancer. It eats upon the host. It doesn't do anything to the object of its displeasure." Instead, she argues, "So, you use that anger, yes. You write it, you paint it, you dance it, you march it, you vote it. You do everything about it. You talk it. Never stop talking it." And, I would add, never stop trying to understand it. In pursuing that understanding, learning how (for instance) Dahl draws upon colonialist narratives and caricatures of Africans, other emotions will certainly emerge, including sadness, grief, anxiety, and fear. These emotions have much to teach us as well. Left unmanaged, anger, shame, and fear can otherize difference, and mutate into hate. However, sadness and grief can provide a counterbalance, expand the boundaries of the self, and create opportunities for compassion and sympathy.[34]

I am *not* arguing for "tough love." Suffering is *not* ennobling. Rather, I am arguing that children understand more than they can articulate, and without the ability to name or diagnose what they have experienced, they may—in the words of Mari J. Matsuda et al.—"internalize the injury done them and are rendered silent in the face of continuing injury." Or, as Meg Rosoff more plainly says, "If you don't talk to kids about the difficult stuff, they worry alone." Teaching racist classics is one way to prepare children, so that they do not suffer alone, or internalize the injuries of racism.[35]

As Michelle Martin has said of books like Tom Feelings's *Middle Passage*, "exposing young readers to the many faces of racism . . . gives them a greater appreciation for the way that oppressed people create alternative ideological apparatuses to help them survive the dominant ideological systems that restrict their freedoms." Describing her experience of reading Doreen Rappaport and Bryan Collier's *Martin's Big Words* with children, Martin notes: "Sharing this picture book with them has taught me many lessons, the first of which is that I should never assume what children can or can't handle. . . . From this book, they are also learning the hard lesson that fame and goodness don't necessarily protect people from danger."[36]

That said, books offering a critical examination of racism's cruelty are (obviously) quite different from those that passively perpetuate racism. The intervention of a thoughtful adult will be vital in reading the latter type of book. Un-bowdlerized versions of these books require guidance, critical questions, and emotional support for the strong feelings that they may elicit. They must also be read in the context of other books that (a) offer affirmative images of racial group members, and (b) supply some of the necessary history that will help young readers make sense of the structures of racism.

To expose the illusion of kindly White slave-owner Uncle Silas and the kind-but-gullible Jim, readers might turn to realistic novels like Christopher Paul Curtis's *Elijah of Buxton* (2007), where slavers are murderers and torturers, and Canada—not America—is "the land of the free." Set in 1859 in Buxton, a community of ex-slaves and free people of African descent in what is now Ontario, Curtis's novel also offers, via the character of ex-slave Mr. Leroy, a lesson in why people should not casually sling about the n-word, "a word them slavers done chained us with," and that is "keeping [slavers'] hate alive." Readers might also dip into *To Be a Slave* (1968), a powerful collection of ex-slaves' narratives edited by Julius Lester and illustrated by Tom Feelings. There, they will learn of living quarters "more fit for animals than human beings," mothers who killed their own children rather than allow them to be sold, and ways that slaves resisted their White masters. Though set about fifty years prior to Twain's novel, M. T. Anderson's *The Astonishing Life of Octavian Nothing, Traitor to the Nation* (two volumes, 2006 and 2008) takes readers to the founding of the United States, where the son of an African princess learns of his unwitting role in a "scientific" experiment designed to measure whether Blacks are as intelligent as Whites, and confronts American revolutionaries fighting for slavery. Speculative fiction also offers antidotes to Twain's patronizing view of Blacks and tolerance of White supremacy. Zetta Elliott's *A Wish after Midnight* (2010) and Octavia Butler's *Kindred* (1979), both time-travel narratives, represent the past in a sharply realist mode, rendering enslavement with

painful clarity and inviting contemporary readers to imagine themselves enduring the psychic and physical traumas of slavery.[37]

To counter Dahl's implication that the middle passage was fun,
students might read Tom Feelings's wordless and often harrowing
picture book *The Middle Passage* (1995), in which cruel Whites cram
enslaved Africans into the ship's hold, beat the men, rape the women,
and hang or shoot those who resist. Or they might read Marilyn
Nelson's verse novel, *The Freedom Business* (2008), which interprets
and reprints Venture Smith's *A Narrative of the Life and Adventures of
Venture, a Native of Africa: But resident above sixty years in the United
States of America* (1798). Nelson emphasizes that other Africans on
Venture's "ordinary passage" died, typically the only way that the
enslaved gained their freedom: "smallpox/amok in the hold set sixty
people free./The sea gulped them down in a boil of grins and fins,/
men and women tossed like offal to the sharks." Those who survived
the eleven-month journey managed to do so amidst "*Discharge excre-
tion diarrhea spew/oozing pustular nausea vomit snot.*"[38]

For a more playful rebuttal of the colonialist ideologies of Dahl,
Travers, and Lofting, Thomas King and William Kent Monkman's
A Coyote Columbus Story (1992) counters typical presentations of
a benevolent European savior and helpless natives. In this narrative, Columbus is a clownish, greedy invader with—as the trickster
Coyote remarks—the "bad idea full of bad manners" to enslave people. As Clare Bradford notes, this picture book "shows Columbus
simultaneously as a comic and a sinister figure, to be both laughed at
and feared," and challenges "the ways in which dominant discourses
produce normative versions of the past, namely the treatment of
Columbus as a heroic figure and his 'discovery' of the New World
a triumph for European civilization." As *A Coyote Columbus Story*
does, John Marsden and Shaun Tan's *The Rabbits* (1998) locates
the narrative power with the colonized, an indigenous civilization

of what Tan describes as "numbat-like creatures," who tell the story of invading "rabbits." Located in a science-fictionalized Australian landscape, these "rabbits"—imperial in bearing, wearing high-collared coats that conceal their faces and their intentions—speak a different language, exploit nature, "and stole our children" (an allusion to the treatment of both Native Americans and aboriginal Australians). Instead of the merry goodwill of the colonizer meeting a warm welcome from the colonized, these books by Marsden, Tan, King, and Monkman display the pain inflicted by invading cultures, countering the tendency of Dahl, Lofting, and Travers to depict colonization as a form of benign human progress.[39]

Just as the preceding narratives that challenge racist assumptions do not constitute an exhaustive list, so the four books examined in this chapter are not the sole bowdlerized works for children. Many other racist and colonialist children's books remain in print. To face racism in other classic books for young people, students might read Hergé's *Tintin in the Congo* (1931) and *Tintin in America* (1932, rev. 1945); Laura Ingalls Wilder's *Little House in the Big Woods* (1932), *Little House on the Prairie* (1935), and *The Long Winter* (1940); and Lynne Reid Banks's *Indian in the Cupboard* series (1980–1998). To challenge passive endorsements of colonialism, students might examine critically Arthur Ransome's *Swallows and Amazons* (1930), Jean de Brunhoff's *The Story of Babar* (1934), or H. A. Rey's *Curious George* (1941). Teachers may find useful the title essay of Herbert Kohl's *Should We Burn Babar?* (1995) for de Brunhoff, and June Cummins's essay, "The Resisting Monkey: 'Curious George,' Slave Captivity Narratives, and the Postcolonial Condition" (1997) for Rey. There are plenty of opportunities to teach against racist and imperialist children's literature.

Indeed, for this very reason I view skeptically arguments that publishers should continue publishing racist children's literature, so that it can be used as an educational tool. When the National Coalition Against Censorship criticized Scholastic's decision to withdraw Ramin Ganeshram and Vanessa Brantley-Newton's *A Birthday Cake for George Washington* (2016), the group lamented the educational opportunity that will now be missed. The book, NCAC writes, "generated important discussions about how our nation creates, perceives, and perpetuates narratives about slavery and slave ownership." It is true that children will not be able to use this book to explore the ways in which it promotes the myth of the happy slave. But it's unclear why the NCAC believes we might need *more* such books. Young readers can simply draw from the vast body of work that romanticizes antebellum plantations, presents enslaved people as cheerful comic storytellers, or otherwise minimizes the Founding Fathers' participation in denying people of African descent the same rights to "life, liberty, and the pursuit of happiness." In any case, as Farah Mendlesohn wrote in response to claims that Scholastic was stifling freedom of speech, "Censorship is when a government or authority prevents someone from speaking or writing. When a business stops producing something because it is faulty, that is product recall." Children can learn much from confronting racism, but they do not require this particular book to do it.[40]

I realize that teaching against racist books requires students and teachers to be uncomfortable. However, and I paraphrase Geffrey Davis here, as teachers, we should make our classrooms safe spaces for people to be uncomfortable. As Davis argues, we should let students know that some of what we are reading will make them uncomfortable, and that it's OK to be uncomfortable. One way I do this is to acknowledge my own discomfort, and specifically the ways in which my racially embodied self makes me uncomfortable. For instance, because I am White, I cannot deploy the word "nigger" with irony, or use it to wryly signify upon its history. When I read

Huckleberry Finn or Countee Cullen's "Incident" aloud, I read the n-word because it is part of the text. But doing so makes me feel a little sick to my stomach because I am highly conscious of the way the word has been used by Whites to subjugate and terrorize African Americans. As Charles Lawrence has said of "nigger," the word is "a form of violence by speech" that, as Randall Kennedy notes, "causes a target to feel as though he or she had been slapped in the face." As I tell my class, when I speak the word aloud, I feel queasy, sad, diseased. But reckoning with the discomfort is part of the point. When I show myself to be publicly vulnerable, my students are more ready to grapple with their own discomfort. It's a delicate balance, being (on the one hand) the authority figure in the room and (on the other) a flawed, confused, open-hearted fellow student, seeking understanding. But as Davis says, if students and their teachers commit to discomfort, we will not just learn. We will grow.[41]

A critical examination of these books while readers are still children may prevent youthful affection from curdling into adult nostalgia. Grown-ups' affective relationship with the works of their childhood often clouds their perception; fondness can deflect critical questions. In contrast, asking children questions about these books can foster a different, more critically engaged, more uncomfortable affective relationship. Children's emotional relationships with these books are still developing and open-ended, but many adults' emotional relationships with these books have closed, their feelings codified into facts. Their judgment now hardened by the passage of time and the book swathed in half-remembered affection, these older readers are now more apt to deploy that term—"classic"—as a defense against those who would criticize or bowdlerize.

To invoke a book's "classic" status as an argument against its bowdlerization—that, as Sharon Bell argues in the piece quoted in this chapter's third paragraph, excising the n-word from

Twain's novel would "instantly remove much of what makes the novel so great"—evades the core issue. Jonathan Arac's critique of the hypercanonization of *Huckleberry Finn* wisely notes that defenders like Bell participate in an idolatry of the novel that prevents them from considering it carefully: "idolatry means selective memory." As Julius Lester writes, when the slave owner called a slave "nigger," this "was a brutal, violent word that stung the soul of the slave more than the whip did his back." Or, as Farai Chideya has memorably observed, the n-word is "the nuclear bomb of racial epithets." *Huckleberry Finn*'s exuberant use of the n-word does *not* make the book great; it confirms the racism of the novel and its protagonist.[42]

Finally, I am aware that this chapter's argument takes issue not just with defenders of racist classics but also with the common wisdom of multicultural instruction. Proposing that we teach racist classics challenges the assumption that multicultural education requires young readers to see *only* the mirrors and windows that celebrate. Of course, *all* young readers (but especially those from underrepresented groups) *do* need books that offer such mirrors and windows, but we should also help children face those distorted mirrors and windows that may cause anger, confusion, or sadness.

The need to read and to teach un-bowdlerized books is an argument I make with reluctance and sadness. All children should be granted a childhood free from the injuries of prejudice. However, since encounters with hate are sadly inevitable, literature can offer a safer space for young people to explore the complex, difficult, painful emotions that racism elicits. Both shielding children from and exposing children to racist texts are poor choices, but failing to confront racism is far more dangerous than ignoring it.

These confrontations can even take place where racism does not seem a core issue of the work—where, at first glance, racial politics and race itself seem wholly absent. However, the stories in which race seems to disappear are also often those where racism is embedded more subtly, and more dangerously. Though William Joyce's works are hardly unique in their racial erasures, they do offer an excellent case study in how Whiteness makes itself invisible and appears to make race and racism vanish.

Chapter 3

Whiteness, Nostalgia, and Fantastic Flying Books

William Joyce's Racial Erasures vs. Hurricane Katrina

William Joyce's *The Fantastic Flying Books of Mr. Morris Lessmore*—an Oscar-winning animated short (2011) that became an electronic book app (2011) and a picture book (2012)—is an aesthetic marvel. Thanks to careful adaptations that recognize the possibilities and limitations of each medium, it may be the only children's story that works equally brilliantly as book, app, and film. *The New York Times* called the app "visually stunning." The London *Times* thought it would be "regarded as one of the most influential titles of the early 21st century." The film won fourteen awards, including an Academy Award for Best Animated Short Film. This praise is wholly justified. Visually, all three versions are beautiful, artistically effective, and emotionally affective.[1]

A moving tribute to both reading and mortality, the film begins with a red book titled *The Fantastic Flying Books of Mr. Morris Lessmore*, opening its front cover to reveal the title character, sitting on the balcony of a hotel in New Orleans's French Quarter, writing in and illustrating his own red book. Suddenly, strong winds transform the scene, objects and people fly past, words get lifted off his book's pages, and he finds himself whisked up into a tornado's vortex, chasing his book around and around on a spinning house. The house lands, upside-down, on a landscape turned black-and-white by the storm. Lessmore tumbles out its front door, as his hat, cane, and book fall from the sky to join him. Carrying his now blank-paged book, he walks through the ruins (which include many pages from other books). Overhead, a young woman in a white dress—borne aloft by a flock of books and rendered in full color—sends a Humpty Dumpty book down to Lessmore. It guides him across a pastoral landscape to a library, where other books have just alighted. This library becomes his new home and he the books' caretaker. In one scene resembling a nineteenth-century operating theatre, he repairs a damaged old book, wonders why it doesn't hop to its feet, and then—following a hint from the Humpty Dumpty book—starts reading it. It revives. (To live, books must be read!) Lessmore lends books to patrons. He reads. He writes in his red book. Years pass. Now an old man, Lessmore finishes writing his book. Walking into the bright light of the library's open doorway, he smiles gently, as a flock of books encircles him, and carries him up out of the building and into the sky. Just before they fly away with him, they pause and he releases his own red book, which flies back down to the library. Lessmore is gone, but his life story (in the book) survives. A little girl arrives and begins to read it. With that, the film ends. It is, as one reviewer noted, an "homage to a bygone era when elegantly printed books inhabited our world."[2]

However, this deserved acclaim overlooks *Morris Lessmore*'s erasure of race. Hurricane Katrina, a main inspiration for the story, killed nearly two thousand people, most of them African Americans. In Orleans Parish, the location of 73 percent of hurricane victims, the mortality rate among Blacks was 1.7 to 4 times higher than that of Whites. Throughout New Orleans, "African American victims outnumbered white victims by more than double," comprising "66 percent of the storm deaths," while "whites made up 31 percent." The storm also displaced many more people. In Katrina's wake, New Orleans lost half of its population to other areas of the United States. As Joe L. Frost noted at the time, "In recent memory, only the Holocaust and the ongoing African uprisings and concurrent AIDS epidemic have subjected children to as much pain, misery, and loss on such an epic scale." In this disaster, most of those children were Black. However, with the exception of a portrait of Duke Ellington hanging on the wall and glimpsed briefly near the end of both app and film, there are otherwise no characters of color in app, film, or book.[3]

Inspired by the intersection of Louisiana native William Joyce and Hurricane Katrina, this chapter explores one of the most common but unnoticed examples of structural racism in children's literature: the absence of characters of color from locations where we might expect to see them. A case study in racial erasures, Joyce exemplifies the tendency of mainstream children's culture to treat Whiteness as the "neutral" color of all humankind. *Morris Lessmore* also represents technological innovation's propensity for distracting us from the unexamined racial assumptions that underwrite its success. When new storytelling media emerge, the focus on digital or aesthetic achievement neglects the work's engagement (or lack thereof) with other social facts—notably race. Unacknowledged Whiteness is the midwife to all ostensibly transcendent, timeless stories: culturally unmarked White characters read as "universal" characters. The acclaim of *Morris Lessmore* as both film and app depends, in part, upon the way that they make race disappear beneath Whiteness's invisibility cloak. To remove that cloak, this chapter situates *Morris Lessmore* in the contexts of Joyce's larger body of work and children's culture about Hurricane Katrina. Other books and films register the fact that Katrina's destruction was not distributed randomly throughout the population, but centered in communities of color. Though many Katrina works are realist, the ones that veer toward the fantastic (as *Morris Lessmore* also does) offer the most incisive look at the systemic inequalities the storm exposed (which *Morris Lessmore* does not). Mapping Joyce's racial representations, this chapter considers his work as an example of how aesthetic pleasures can lead critics to ignore an artist's tendency to normalize Whiteness, even when (as is the case with Joyce) that artist often exoticizes, demonizes, or erases non-White characters.

INFLUENCES ON *MORRIS LESSMORE*

Given that Hurricane Katrina is one of several influences, it is tempting to explain away *Morris Lessmore*'s Whiteness as deriving from its many other sources. It alludes to MGM's *Wizard of Oz* (1939) with its flying bicyclist, flying house, substitution of a tornado for the hurricane, and transition from black-and-white to color. The protagonist wears Buster Keaton's porkpie hat, carries Charlie Chaplin's cane, and borrows movement and gestures from them both. The character's name comes from the publisher William Morris (c. 1929–2003), Joyce's late mentor. As Joyce said, while on a flight to visit Morris, "I wrote this little story about a guy who gives his life to books . . . and I got to read it to him when I went to see him. He died just a few days after that." The young woman carried overhead by a flock of flying books—she who sends the book that leads Morris Lessmore to the library of flying books—resembles Joyce's own daughter, Mary Katherine Joyce, who died of a brain tumor in 2010 at the age of 18.[4]

However, Joyce cites Hurricane Katrina as a major influence on *Lessmore*. At the beginning of all three iterations of the tale, Morris Lessmore sits on a balcony in New Orleans's French Quarter. Just seconds into the animated film, Joyce shows a sketch of the building, bearing in the bottom right-hand corner the label "NOLA"— the abbreviation for New Orleans, Louisiana (fig. 3.1). Survivors' post-Katrina experience deeply shaped Joyce's sense of the transformative power of stories, which is *the* dominant theme of *Morris Lessmore*. After the hurricane, Joyce visited sports arenas and other unlikely emergency housing, where people, he says, "were completely dislocated, and they had no privacy. And no sense of any of the comforts of home that we take for granted." Many organizations donated picture books and children's novels to the refugees. "It was amazing," Joyce said, "to see in this room full of 20,000 people that a kid can be sitting with a book in their hands, and they were totally lost in that story, that they'd escaped from all that was wrong with their situation."[5]

Figure 3.1. William Joyce, screenshot from animated film, *The Fantastic Flying Books of Mr. Morris Lessmore*: "NOLA."

NOSTALGIC FOR WHAT?

While I share Joyce's faith in the transformative power of narrative, I wonder why his narrative appears to grant imaginative escape only to White survivors. In the film, the displaced people are all White. (Both app and book omit the displaced, focusing instead on Lessmore's journey.) The library patrons in all three iterations are all White. The authors of all the books are White. Despite Morris Lessmore's declaration in both app and picture book that "Everyone's story matters," Joyce's story emphatically disagrees (fig. 3.2). Although it insists that "the books agreed with" Lessmore's claim that everyone's story matters, the collection in Joyce's idyllic library offers only nostalgia for an anti-multicultural world where

And Morris would always share the books with others. Sometimes it was a favorite which everyone loved, and other times he found a lonely little volume whose tale was seldom shared. "Everyone's story matters," concluded Morris Lessmore, and the books agreed with him.

Figure 3.2. William Joyce, image from animated app, *The Fantastic Flying Books of Mr. Morris Lessmore*: "Everybody's story matters."

"classic" means "book by a dead White writer." The film reveals two Shakespeare plays (*Merchant of Venice, Romeo and Juliet*), *Pierre* (though whether Melville or Sendak it doesn't say), William Jennings Bryan's *The World's Famous Orations Volume II: Rome* and *Volume VII: Continental Europe* (1906), Rumer Godden's *Mouse Time* (1984), a Dutch edition of *The Bible*, and a few invented titles, such as *Tim Swift and Stone Planet*—a reference to the Stratemeyer Syndicate's *Tom Swift and His Planet Stone* (1935). From the film's six dead White men, one dead White woman, and one anonymous English author, the app provides a larger but no less conservative bibliography. When you enter the library, touching fourteen of the books near the bottom of the screen prompts each one to speak a line of its text:

- "To be or not to be" (from William Shakespeare's *Hamlet*)
- "Bah! Humbug!" (from Charles Dickens's *A Christmas Carol*)
- "It was the best of times. It was the worst of times" (from Dickens's *A Tale of Two Cities*)
- "Last night, I dreamt I went to Manderley again" (from Daphne du Maurier's *Rebecca*)
- "Come, Watson. Come! The game is afoot!" (from Arthur Conan Doyle's "The Adventure of the Abbey Grange")
- "Second star to the right, and straight on 'til morning" (from J. M. Barrie's *Peter and Wendy*)
- "I wish I could write as mysterious as a cat" (often attributed to Edgar Allen Poe, but these are not his words)
- "Quoth the raven, 'Nevermore'" (from Poe's "The Raven")
- "Now is the winter of our discontent" (from Shakespeare's *Richard III*)
- "O Romeo, Romeo! Wherefore art thou Romeo?" (from Shakespeare's *Romeo and Juliet*)

- "Men and women came and went like moths among the whisperings, the champagne and the stars" (from F. Scott Fitzgerald's *The Great Gatsby*)
- "I say, beware of all enterprises that require new clothes" (from Henry David Thoreau's *Walden*)
- "Denial ain't just a river in Egypt" (read in a voice that resembles Mark Twain's, but he never wrote this)
- "To be awake is to be alive" (the actual quote is "To be awake is to be completely alive" and it is from Thoreau's *Walden*)

Later, in the scene where people line up to check out books from Lessmore's library, the app offers four nineteenth-century novels from the United Kingdom: Dickens's *A Christmas Carol*, Robert Louis Stevenson's *Treasure Island*, Mary Shelley's *Frankenstein*, and Carroll's *Alice in Wonderland*. In subsequent scenes, Godden's *Mouse Time*, a dictionary, and Jules Verne's *De la Terre à la Lune* (*From the Earth to the Moon*) all make an appearance. Film and app combined offer seventeen books by dead White men, three by dead White women, two by fake dead White men, and one by an anonymous English writer.

In and of itself, this literary canon may be unremarkable, but African Americans' absence from *Morris Lessmore*'s library fits a pattern in Joyce's larger body of work, which either omits people of color or uses them only as exotic secondary characters. *A Day with Wilbur Robinson* (1990) shows Duke Ellington twice, Louis Armstrong once, and an unidentified Black man once. But they are merely part of the eccentric menagerie at the Robinsons' house; and, unlike some of the other unusual characters, they do not even speak. In *Dinosaur Bob and the Family Lazardo* (1988), "Jumbu, their bodyguard, said nothing" is a running gag, recurring three times: Jumbu's only "speech" in the book is a smile on the final two-page spread (fig. 3.3). Named for a fruit native to India, Pakistan, Nepal, and the Philippines, the fair-skinned character Jumbu wears a turban, along with several "Indian" costumes, including a bright red military jacket, and a yellow sash (in some pictures) or robes (in others). His clothes and name align him with people from India, but his role as a silent servant to a White American family makes him an exotic "other." More troubling is Joyce's tendency to shade his villains in a dark color, such as the "attacking army of Dark Elves" in *Santa Calls* (1993)—which, as Daniel Hade has noted, traffics in Orientalism. Joyce even embeds darkness in the name of the character Pitch Black, who appears in his *The Man in the Moon* picture book (2011) and animated film *The Rise of the Guardians* (2012, fig. 3.4). In images that resemble 1930s magazine illustrations, Joyce's nostalgic vision subtly reinscribes early twentieth-century ideologies of race, while effacing a history underwritten by those same ideologies.[6]

That such nostalgia might inspire Joyce's *Fantastic Flying Books of Mr. Morris Lessmore* is disappointing, but not unusual. After the storm moved the New Orleans that Joyce knew from contemporary time into the receding tide of memory, it is not surprising that

Figure 3.3. William Joyce, Jumbu in *Dinosaur Bob and His Adventures with the Family Lazardo* (1988).

Figure 3.4. Pitch Black in *Rise of the Guardians* (story by William Joyce, screenplay by David Lindsay-Abaire, directed by Peter Ramsey, 2013).

longing for the pre-Katrina city would find expression in nostalgic reconstruction. Located where today dreams of forgotten yesterdays, nostalgia is itself a crossroads, with paths leading to childhood, creativity, and sorrow—all central concerns of *Morris Lessmore* and its creator. As Linda Hutcheon suggests, ever since nostalgia shifted from a physical condition (it was originally a diagnosis for severe homesickness) to a psychological one, nostalgia has been yoked to childhood. In 1798, Kant noticed of nostalgia sufferers—Hutcheon writes—"that people who did return home were usually disappointed because, in fact, they did not want to return to a *place*, but to a *time*, a time of youth." That the author of a children's story might revive earlier aesthetic motifs, possibly images encountered in his own childhood, not only resonates with Kant's insight, but also recalls the connections between creativity and nostalgia. Laurence Lerner, for example, has claimed that "Longing is what makes art possible"; Michael Mason has also located inspiration in longing, observing that "Nostalgia is a kind of sorrow, but it may be creative sorrow." I suspect that creative sorrow inspired William Joyce, as he invented a story that drew some of its emotional energy from his recently deceased daughter, his late friend, and the haunted landscape of post-Katrina New Orleans. Indeed, nostalgia's affiliation with inspiration, childhood, and loss endows *The Fantastic Flying Books of Mr. Morris Lessmore* with its aura of melancholic beauty.[7]

While Joyce's nostalgia may be inevitable, its unreflective telos is not. To borrow Svetlana Boym's useful distinction between *restorative nostalgia* and *reflective nostalgia*, Joyce's aesthetic project cloaks the former in the latter. As Boym writes,

> Restorative nostalgia stresses *nostos* and attempts a transhistorical reconstruction of the lost home. Reflective nostalgia thrives on *algia*, the longing itself, and delays the homecoming—wistfully, ironically, desperately. Restorative nostalgia does not think of itself as nostalgia, but rather as truth and tradition. Reflective nostalgia dwells on the ambivalences of human longing and belonging and does not shy away from the contradictions of modernity. Restorative nostalgia protects the absolute truth, while reflective nostalgia calls it into doubt.

Joyce's *Morris Lessmore* visually resembles reflective nostalgia, lingering "on ruins, the patina of time and history, in the dreams of another place and another time." The books in the library that Lessmore oversees bear the marks of time; one of his jobs is to repair them. Over the course of the tale, Morris himself ages. Near the tale's end, the scene of his departure—flying away from the library, the books looking sadly on—is a scene of mourning. However, these affective visual motifs belie a deeper longing for a true, unified whole—a past that Boym would describe as "not a duration but a perfect snapshot." *Morris Lessmore* yearns for that "transhistorical reconstruction" characteristic of restorative nostalgia. It imagines a past where, in the midst of a pastoral idyll, a library's open door invites a White reader onto beautifully polished hardwood floors, where he can peruse stacks of books by White authors, and lend some of them to White readers (fig. 3.5).[8]

To be clear, *Morris Lessmore*'s longing for an all-White library with all-White patrons does not indicate that William Joyce himself is consciously nostalgic for White supremacy. Rather, it means that a memory steeped in a White supremacist culture cannot easily filter out the racist bits. It means that aesthetics are bound up in emotions, tightly woven together, in a sticky, blurry mixture. More troubling is that the affective structures that underwrite this type of restorative nostalgia cannot be easily repelled or refuted. When the imagination mingles racist imagery (as in much of Joyce's work) or racial erasures (as in *Morris Lessmore*) with a deep yearning for childhood or for a lost child, these strands become extremely difficult to disentangle. Because racially inflected aesthetics have deep affective

Figure 3.5. William Joyce, screenshot from animated film, *The Fantastic Flying Books of Mr. Morris Lessmore*: Lessmore hands a book to a patron.

roots, they resist uprooting, allowing racial and racist nostalgia to persist. In other words, the unconscious racism of restorative nostalgia tends to resist analysis: creators and audiences insist that because they are not personally racist, their affection for the work repudiates any allegation that it might contain even trace elements of racism. The absence of people of color, for example, is often interpreted as evidence that the artist simply does not see race, and thus his characters' Whiteness is merely a mark of his objectivity. Yet, as Richard Dyer notes, Whiteness's power derives from its ability to figure White people as ideologically neutral, as the human race, instead of as White. As Dyer puts it, "As long as race is something only applied to non-white peoples, as long as white people are not racially seen and named, they/we function as a human norm. Other people are raced, we are just people." Works that ask us to read their population of exclusively White characters as merely normal, universal people reinscribe White dominance via not just the erasure of Blacks but the denial of race itself. To borrow Robin Bernstein's words, *The Fantastic Flying Books of Mr. Morris Lessmore* invites us to participate in "the production of racial memory through the performance of forgetting."[9]

INVISIBILITY AS RACIAL INNOCENCE

African Americans' invisibility is a symptom of what Bernstein calls "racial innocence," in which racially charged images persist in the culture of childhood, their politics hidden by the apparent "innocence" of the form—a book, a doll, a toy. Joyce's Jumbu, Pitch Black, and the Dark Elves are typical examples of innocence's mystification of racist ideologies, and establish a pattern of unconscious stereotyping in his work. However, in writing people of color out of the narrative entirely, *The Fantastic Flying Books of Mr. Morris Lessmore* refigures racial innocence as racial absence. Via the invisibility of any non-White character, Joyce's work homogenizes childhood, inadvertently conveying the message that Black children are unworthy of representation.

There are many factors that may account for *Morris Lessmore's* erasure of Blackness, the first of which is that Joyce is a native of Shreveport, Louisiana. Like most US states, Louisiana is racially segregated, and, like most US cities, both Shreveport and New Orleans are racially segregated—the former more than the latter. According to the 2000 Census, in Shreveport, Whites lived in areas that were 75 percent White and Blacks in neighborhoods that were 78 percent Black. In New Orleans, Whites lived in neighborhoods that were 64 percent White and Blacks in areas that were 84 percent Black. In *The Fantastic Flying Books of Mr. Morris Lessmore*, Joyce is representing the world he sees. That is largely a White world. While I would not fault him for drawing from experience, I do wonder whether he realizes that his works are normalizing a segregated society for a new generation of readers and viewers.

In their inattention to non-White characters, his works perpetuate Larrick's "All-White World of Children's Books," and his racial absences remind us (via omission) that White authors have a responsibility, too. They do not all have to be Ezra Jack Keats, a White author who—starting with *The Snowy Day*—featured African American children in his picture books. But Joyce might consider joining those White picture book artists who do represent non-White characters in their work: Lane Smith features an African American girl in *The Big Pets* (1991) and *Abe Lincoln's Dream* (2012); Chris Van Allsburg's *Probuditi!* (2006) stars a Black family, as does Molly Bang's *Ten, Nine, Eight* (1983). If Joyce wishes to avoid racial segregation in his own work, he might follow their example and—at least occasionally—grant his readers a non-White protagonist. Of course, the occasional protagonist of color would not reverse the deficit of diverse books for young readers. Furthermore, white authors creating non-White characters must be especially vigilant against inadvertently perpetuating stereotypes. And, to increase diverse books, what we need most of all are more books *by* writers of color, not just more books featuring characters of color. We need a publishing industry that makes space for creators of color to write books reflecting their experiences. However, White artists granting characters of color prominent roles would acknowledge that they, too, share responsibility for our shortage of diverse books.[10]

The absence of sympathetic characters of color in the works of Joyce and other White creators perpetuates failures of the imagination. When children primarily consume culture that distorts or omits people like them, their psyches become damaged. The Nigerian-born contemporary novelist Chimamanda Ngozi Adichie has spoken eloquently of the effect that a childhood spent reading British and American children's books had on her. When she began writing her own stories, at the age of seven,

> All my characters were white and blue-eyed. They played in the snow. They ate apples. And they talked a lot about the weather—how lovely it was that the sun had come out. Now this despite the fact that I lived in Nigeria, I had never been outside Nigeria. We didn't have snow. We ate mangoes. And we didn't talk about the weather because there was no need to.

As she says, her young experience shows "how impressionable and vulnerable we are in the face of a story—particularly as children. Because all I had read were books in which characters were foreign, I had become convinced that books by their very nature had to have foreigners in them, and had to be about things with which I could not personally identify." Though she admires these books' power to stir her imagination, one "unintended consequence was that I did not know that people like me could exist in literature." Whether we call this process "the danger of a single story" (as Adichie does) or "colonizing the imagination" (as Zetta Elliot does), it demonstrates that racial invisibility is as harmful as racial stereotyping.[11]

Joyce's beautiful books and films illustrate both the need for and challenge of dismantling White supremacy. In fact, the vastness of the challenge underscores the urgency of the need. Structural racism's ability to replicate itself via unwitting participants (as I suspect Joyce is) reminds us that the work of anti-racism is both institutional and personal, and that creative decisions draw upon influences remembered and forgotten. Acknowledging the ways in which our choices (often unconsciously) perpetuate the problem can help us uncover the hidden biases that motivate those choices and, one hopes, make better choices in future.

HURRICANE KATRINA IN CHILDREN'S CULTURE

These biases come into sharper focus when we place *Morris Lessmore* in the context of other art inspired by a storm that, as Henry A. Giroux has argued, "broke through the visual blackout of poverty and the pernicious ideology of color-blindness to reveal the government's role in fostering the dire living conditions of largely poor African-Americans." Unlike *Morris Lessmore*, most children's culture inspired by Hurricane Katrina acknowledges that the storm visited far more misery and death on the poor and on people of color. Also unlike *Morris Lessmore*, most of these works—whether novel, picture book, graphic novel, or film—are realist. Seven of the eight Katrina novels I read are realist, as are three of four picture books, and both graphic novels. However, no single genre has a monopoly on depicting the real. Different genres offer alternate paths toward similar truths. Yet, while no genre is inherently more incisive than another, the fantastic, speculative, and richly figurative works inspired by Katrina do a more powerful job of exposing—to quote what Michael Eric Dyson has said of the storm—the United States' "callous disregard for poverty's colored face."[12]

To their credit, the realist Karina novels do show how this natural disaster exposed social inequalities that the American ruling class prefers to ignore. These books typically use a conversation between characters, sometimes amplifying their critique with specific, ordinary details. Jewell Parker Rhodes's *Ninth Ward* (2010), a Coretta Scott King Honor book, notes that class impedes mobility when Mama YaYa, the caretaker of the protagonist Lanesha, says in response to the "mandatory evacuation," "How can it be mandatory if I don't have a way to go?" In Julie T. Lamana's *Upside Down in the Middle of Nowhere* (2014), the protagonist's father explains that he can't evacuate his whole family because "I don't have room for Katherine and all the kids in my truck. And I've got [the protagonist's grandmother] Mama Jean to think about." Also registering the fact that one in four citizens of New Orleans lacked access to a car, and that the city's Black residents made up a far greater proportion of the carless, Brenda Woods's *Saint Louis Armstrong Beach* (2011) has the central character's father explain, "Some folks don't have cars, Saint." When Saint proposes that they "take a bus or a train or a plane," his dad says, "To where? Some folks got nowhere to go." Rodman Philbrick's *Zane and the Hurricane: A Story of Katrina* (2014) finds Zane and fellow refugees bullied by a wealthy neighborhood's racist private security force, and armed police threatening to shoot pedestrian refugees trying to cross a bridge into a different well-to-do neighborhood. Finally, Tamara Ellis Smith's *Another Kind of Hurricane* (2015) acknowledges structural inequalities when the police tell Zavion and his father that "they couldn't cross the bridge unless they were in a car, and he pointed a gun at them when he said it."[13]

As the novels do, the graphic novels and realist picture books also register that suffering was concentrated in communities of color. In Josh Neufeld's graphic novel *A.D.: New Orleans after the Deluge* (2009), a cast of racially and economically diverse characters illustrates (as you might expect) inequalities along racial and class lines. Insulated by his privilege, the wealthy white doctor who rides out the storm in his French Quarter home faces far less privation than any of the other six main characters—four of whom are people of color, and three of whom also stay in New Orleans for the duration. The narrator of Don Brown's nonfiction graphic novel *Drowned City: Hurricane Katrina and New Orleans* (2015) observes, "People who are fortunate enough to have a car jam the highways," and notes that "most who stay are without a means of escape." Brown's often harrowing pictures of people—hacking a hole in the attic, stranded on rooftops, boarding boats, wading chest-deep in brackish water, drowning beneath that water—all indicate that populations of color were hit hardest by the storm and the mismanaged aftermath. Renée Watson and Shadra Strickland's picture book *A Place Where Hurricanes Happen* (2010) follows four children of color, all of whom are separated by the storm: Michael rides it out in his attic, Keesha goes to the Superdome, Adrienne goes to stay with granny's friend in Baton Rouge, and Tommy takes refuge in Houston, after being stuck for hours on the highway. Denying the city's actual post-Katrina depopulation, the book has the improbable ending of all the children returning to New Orleans a year later. Though Myron Uhlberg and Colin Bootman's *A Storm Called*

Katrina (2011) also ends happily, chaos, danger, and uncertainty linger at the edges of this story, which addresses the experiences of Louis Daniel and his family as refugees in the Superdome (fig. 3.6). Even the most sentimental of the picture books, Kirby Larson and Mary Nethery's *Two Bobbies: A True Story of Hurricane Katrina, Friendship, and Survival* (2008, illus. Jean Cassels), registers one of the failures of the US government's rescue efforts: refusing to allow evacuees to take their pets with them. While it focuses on a blind white cat and a brown dog who look out for each other during the storm, it does include one named person of color—Rich, a construction worker and dog owner, who feeds the two animals. All of these works acknowledge the fact that Hurricane Katrina was not merely a natural disaster: it was a storm that revealed entrenched inequalities in American society.[14]

However, realist works so diligently cover the dominant tropes of the catastrophe that they risk reducing the Katrina experience to a checklist of clichés: lack of transport out of the city; the "boom"

Figure 3.6. Myron Uhlberg and Colin Bootman, two-page spread from *A Storm Called Katrina* (2011). First published in the United States under the title *A Storm Called Katrina* by Myron Uhlberg, illustrated by Colin Bootman. Text Copyright © 2011 by Myron Uhlberg. Illustrations Copyright © 2011 by Colin Bootman. Published by arrangement with Peachtree Publishers.

sound when the levee fails; as water rises, people fleeing to attic and then to rooftop; a dog that's saved, injured, or killed; the fetid, snake-filled flood water; the fetid, fecal Superdome; the absence of help from the government. The more courageous of these works find the protagonists reckoning with floating corpses, deaths of loved ones, and armed men (police, National Guard) preventing refugees from evacuating. Some—notably, Denise Patrick's *Finding Someplace*—extend the narrative timeline to months after the storm, exploring how survivors cope with trauma. The less imaginative insist on giving their protagonist a birthday on or near the date Katrina makes landfall, or on using the storm to engineer superficial interracial friendships that promise to transcend racism. As a result, many (though certainly not all) of these works have a familiar, paint-by-numbers quality. Indeed, from their very beginnings, most realist novels about Hurricane Katrina inevitably gesture toward a catastrophic future—referencing levees, weather reports, past hurricanes, inadequate transport, and so on. Suffering and death are present before the storm even begins. In contrast, the speculative and more richly figurative works acknowledge that trauma takes us by surprise, without warning or foreshadowing. The non-realistic landscapes and timescapes of the fantastic offer more opportunities for inflicting traumatic shocks upon readers and viewers. Trauma is not linear—it infects memories prior to the event, and colors experiences after the event. Those works willing to veer further toward the symbolic estrange the familiar in ways that help us understand more deeply.

The three most powerful works about Katrina—Jesmyn Ward's *Salvage the Bones* (2011), Kiese Laymon's *Long Division* (2013), and Benh Zeitlin and Lucy Alibar's film *Beasts of the Southern Wild* (2012)—succeed because they understand that veering toward the figurative or fantastic can be an even more powerful mode of social engagement. Though *Salvage the Bones* is a realist novel, its emotional intensity derives in no small part from Ward's ability to write like a poet, making her characters' pain legible via luminous imagery and taut metaphors. As the water rises up and surrounds the house, the book's fifteen-year-old narrator, Esch, likens the flood to a snake: "There is something long and dark blue between the trees." She at first thinks it is a boat come to save her and her family, but then realizes "It is Daddy's truck. The water has picked it up. . . . The snake has come to eat and play." At the moment she has to jump from her roof to a tree branch, Esch tells us, "My heart is a wounded bird, beating its wings against the cage of my ribs. I don't think I can breathe." After the storm, Esch says this of herself and her family: "We were a pile of wet, cold branches, human debris in the middle of all of the rest of it." When she comes upon the school where, just days ago, her brother played basketball, she thinks: "Suddenly there is a great split between now and then, and I wonder where the world where that day happened has gone, because we are not in it." Ward's surprising, striking images cut directly to the emotional and psychological core of her characters' experiences. They also resist easy assimilation. The floodwater did contain snakes, but figuring the water *itself* as a giant snake suddenly drops us into the terrifying transformations of Greek mythology (an obsession of Esch's). In so doing, it amplifies the characters' fear, making their trauma more vivid. The dissociative experience of feeling that "great split between now and then" makes her characters' dislocation palpable precisely because it evokes the science-fiction scenario of leaving one world ("the world where that day happened") for another. As Mark Jerng observes, "Realism uses speculative modes in order to be more realistic."[15]

Speculative modes can intensify the real. Kiese Laymon's *Long Division*—a metafictional novel narrated by a high-school student named City—refracts the history of Katrina through science fiction. In a contemporary Mississippi landscape haunted by the storm, City and his fictional/autobiographical counterpart (also named City, in a novel also named *Long Division*) move between three different historical moments: the present day (2013), 1985, and 1964. In addition to marking changing expressions of structural racism, the novel's time-traveling main character challenges the tendency to use time as an index of social progress. When present-day City describes visiting his grandmother in southern Mississippi as a form of time travel, he emphasizes how poverty teleports people vast distances away from modern opportunities: "I know Melahatchie was only a bus ride away, but it felt like a time warp. It always felt like it was behind whatever time we were up in Jackson, but after Hurricane Katrina, it's like time went fast in reverse instead of just slowing down." Figuring class difference as time travel makes vivid the barriers built by poverty.[16]

Fantasy and science fiction—as any casual reader of these genres knows—uses an alternate universe to reflect upon real-world concerns. A very different take on Hurricane Katrina, *Beasts of the Southern Wild*—which is not a children's film, though its protagonist, Hushpuppy, is a child—combines the fantastic and realistic in startling ways that reveal how race and class limit a person's choices. The impoverished but resilient residents of "The Bathtub," a fictional Louisiana island, face rising floodwaters, government incompetence, and prehistoric Aurochs released from melting ice caps (fig. 3.7). These are the people without the resources to flee a hurricane, the people abandoned by a society that blames the poor for their poverty, that tells the disadvantaged: *You're on your own.* Compounding these problems, Hushpuppy—who has already lost her mother—must now face the prospect of losing her father, Wink. As Michelle Martin puts it,

Figure 3.7. Quvenzhané Wallis as Hushpuppy, confronting an Auroch in *Beasts of the Southern Wild* (screenplay by Behn Zeitlin and Lucy Alibar, directed by Zeitlin, 2012).

Because Wink knows he is dying, his primary goal is to make Hushpuppy as self-sufficient as possible before he goes. This desire results in a brand of tough love rarely seen inflicted on a child by a parent in American cinema. Small as she is, though, Hushpuppy is no wimp; she confronts Wink with the same ferocity and determination that she meets the titular beasts, staring each challenge in the face, both figuratively and cinematically, to figure out how to manage.

If many critics embraced Hushpuppy's strength and heroism, bell hooks memorably criticized the film as perpetuating the myth of the "strong black female matriarch" in its six-year-old protagonist, who endures violence, privation, and mortal danger. hooks argues that the film espouses "the age old politics of domination" in which "only the strong survive, that disease weeds out the weak (i.e. the slaughter of Native Americans) that nature chooses excluding and including." If *Beasts of the Southern Wild*'s critical engagement sometimes falls short, it does recognize the direct correlation between race, class, and the severity of suffering inflicted by this "natural" disaster. Furthermore, having Hushpuppy face off against mythical, giant Aurochs powerfully dramatizes the gargantuan challenges faced by children of color.[17]

As these artistic responses indicate, Joyce could use his considerable gifts in fantastic narrative to reveal rather than efface Katrina's sharply unequal distribution of suffering. On the one hand, his works rarely use fantasy to examine real-world problems: so it is not surprising that the storm should, for Joyce, inspire a beautiful, moving work that "sees" neither class nor race. On the other hand, Joyce's elision of non-White people reinforces their political and social invisibility without acknowledging that it is doing so. Though Joyce's *Fantastic Flying Books of Mr. Morris Lessmore* draws inspiration from Katrina survivors finding books to be a welcome (if temporary) escape, his own book erases all survivors of color from its pages.

The legal scholar Jerome McCristal Culp Jr. calls this sort of invisibility "The Woody Allen Blues," by which he means the naïve belief that if artists do not represent Black characters, then their work cannot be racist. In a film titled *Manhattan* (1979), Woody Allen has no characters of color; in a film/app/book set in Louisiana, Joyce has no African American characters. The problem, Culp argues, is that ignoring the validity of other identity categories establishes White, male, heterosexual as universal, depriving all others of power. As he puts it, "This is, for gays, lesbians, and people of color, an erasure of their stories and their political existence. It is the 'Woody Allen Blues' sung nationally by a 'special' Amen chorus—majority rules." Joyce does not need to and may not even be able to tell a "Black" story. However, his erasure of

Black characters and literature colludes in *real* Black people's marginalization. The absence of non-White characters in *Morris Lessmore* is not merely benign neglect, in part because that term is itself an oxymoron, but mostly because social invisibility is a form of structural oppression.[18]

Morris Lessmore's refusal to represent people of color establishes White people as—to borrow Richard Dyer's words—"being without properties, unmarked, universal, just human." In creating a community that is always already White, Joyce's story not only rejects the diverse mix of people who live in Louisiana; it removes White from the category of race. Whiteness becomes objectivity, the non-color of all humankind. The story thus tells viewers and readers that indigenous Americans, African Americans, Latinos, Asians, and other peoples of color are *not* part of the human family. Invisibility subtly but clearly says that Black lives do not matter, nor do the experiences of any non-White group.[19]

Visibility is always about power. *Morris Lessmore* mystifies not just racial ideology, but ideologies of gender, sexuality, class, and even reading itself. As Erica Hateley writes of Joyce's technological marvel, "a spectacle about books is not the same as an invitation to consider the meaning and significance of reading." The *Morris Lessmore* texts (film, app, book), she says, "show that texts can be about books without also being about reading." Comparably, texts can be about race without also being about Blackness. The racial erasures are not only a symptom of *Morris Lessmore*'s mystification through technology, but a side effect of Joyce's unearned privilege of seeing himself and his characters as not-raced. His "unmarked" status as White man prevents him from recognizing his complicity in promoting a vision of a de facto White America.[20]

HOW (NOT) TO TALK
TO WHITE PEOPLE ABOUT RACISM

While writing this chapter, I have been wondering what William Joyce, his admirers, and other White creators of children's literature would think of it. As an educator, I frequently wonder: how do I speak directly, name racism when I see it, and yet minimize the chance of a White artist, writer, editor, agent, or reader rejecting my argument? While I have never met Mr. Joyce and cannot predict his response, it is certainly easy to imagine a White artist accusing a critic of "reading too much into" a work, or (as P. L. Travers does) pointing to young Black readers who allegedly did not perceive any stereotypes in the work, or even (in the case of a film or app) saying that x number of non-Whites worked on it. Confronted with the possibility that they may have perpetuated racist ways of seeing and thinking, many Whites respond with denial, deflection, or even anger.

White people frequently seem more concerned with being called "racist" than actually reflecting on why their behavior might sustain racist ideas. This is why "racist" often seems like the n-word for White people. To be clear, the two terms are *not* morally equivalent: The n-word carries with it a long history of oppression, functioning as (in Richard Delgado's words) "an attempt to injure through the use of words"; in contrast, "racist" names that oppression and opposes its violence. However, since Whites have little experience grappling with race, the word "racist" often yields a highly agitated response. Discussions of racism tend to trigger what Robin DiAngelo calls "White Fragility," prompting "defensive moves" motivated by "anger, fear, and guilt." As DiAngelo notes, "Whites have not had to build tolerance for racial discomfort and thus when racial discomfort arises, whites typically respond as if something is 'wrong,' and blame the person or event that triggered the discomfort (usually a person of color)."[21]

So, first, it may be helpful for Mr. Joyce, admirers of his work, and other White creators of children's literature to know that everyone is a little bit racist sometimes—and not in the facile if amusing sense portrayed in the satirical musical *Avenue Q* (2003). Rather, everyone is a little bit racist in the sense that, as a 2015 Pew Research Center Survey found, almost no adults are free of some subconscious racial bias. The survey arrived at these conclusions via an Implicit Association Test (IAT), a technique that "measures subconscious or 'hidden' bias by tracking how quickly individuals associate good and bad words with specific racial groups." In the Pew Survey, three-fourths of all respondents "demonstrated some degree of implicit racial bias"; only around one-fourth "were found to have little or no bias toward the races they were tested against." The IAT also confirmed that racial biases cut across *all* demographic categories: "Roughly equal levels of implicit racial bias were found among men and women, old and young, and college educated and those with a high school diploma or less formal schooling. Republicans and Democrats with the same racial background also had similar levels of underlying racial bias." If there are racial biases in your work, then you are statistically normal. So, what to do? Well, as the YA novelist Justina Ireland writes, "The challenge is for you to recognize your own inherent biases, and to move past them. You can't do that if you refuse to acknowledge it in the first place."[22]

Second, White creators of children's books should consider why they might be unaware of their own racial assumptions. While it is impossible to grow up in a racist culture and not absorb some of its messages, it is very easy to be unconscious of what you have absorbed. That is how dominant ideologies work: their messages seep in subtly, persistently, without your noticing. When I was preparing to teach the book in a college class, I picked up Helen Bannerman's *Little Black Sambo* for the first time. As I read it, I had the unsettling experience of realizing that I already knew the story. This was *not* the first time I had encountered *Little Black Sambo*. Had I read Bannerman's version? Or perhaps an edition with more grotesque racial caricature, such as John R. Neill's? What other half-remembered stories (suffused with racial caricature or otherwise) were lurking in my subconscious? As I mentioned in the introduction, only when I reflect upon the racist culture of my childhood—the Gollies, the Uncle Remus stories, *Little Black Sambo*, the near-absence of narratives featuring people of color—can I begin to contemplate how it shaped my own racial and, yes, racist assumptions about other people. A writer, artist, or critic may not intend to perpetuate stereotypes, but—especially when left unexamined—ideology trumps intention. Joyce may not mean to traffic in Orientalist imagery or to marginalize people of color. I doubt Dr. Seuss intended to either. But well-intentioned people can still act in ways that reinforce racism, unaware that they are doing so. Since the United States is such a segregated country, White people live in an environment structured to prevent our awareness of race and racism. These geographies and the culture itself make it easy for Whites to avoid reflecting upon our raced selves. All who work in the field of children's literature and culture need to reflect, and strive to do better.

Finally, even if a White person is one of the 25 percent who (in the Pew Survey) have little to no unconscious racial bias, he or she is still a beneficiary of structural racism. White people do not have to endorse institutional racism to benefit from it. I realize that it can be uncomfortable, even painful, to come to terms with the ways in which racism structures our lives and imaginations. But it has to be done. As the primary beneficiaries of structural racism,

White people have the strongest moral obligation to work toward dismantling it. As John Metta writes, "White people are in a position of power in this country *because of racism*. The question is: Are they brave enough to use that power to speak against the system that gave it to them?"[23]

If people who create children's culture fail to engage in such self-examination, they risk continuing to transmit the misery of racism to a new generation. *Morris Lessmore* is a lost opportunity here because fantasy affords creators greater possibilities for diversity. As Metta points out, "Racism is our acceptance of an all-white Lord of the Rings cast because of 'historical accuracy,' ignoring the fact that this is a world with an *entirely fictionalized history*." In Peter Jackson's adaptation of Tolkien, in Joyce's *Morris Lessmore*, and in so many works for children, the covert ideological work of White supremacy makes non-White identities invisible, leaving those young readers hidden and earthbound, as they watch other people's stories take flight.

Such erasures are not limited to works with all-White casts, either. Publishers can even perform racial vanishing acts on books featuring characters of color. Beneath a mask of Whiteness, dust jackets hide non-White protagonists and their experiences from the readers who would like to meet them.

Chapter 4

Don't Judge a Book by Its Color

The Destructive Fantasy of Whitewashing (and Vice-Versa)

The novel's protagonist is not White. But the girl in the cover photograph is White. Or she is racially ambiguous, and thus able to be read as White. Or she and her friends are in silhouette, or have their backs to the camera—preventing us from guessing their races. The name of this practice is whitewashing, and this is why it happens: Believing that books with a person of color on the cover will not sell, publishers put a White face (or a silhouette, or an ambiguously raced face) on the dust jacket of a book whose protagonist is not White.

Whitewashing may be better known in other visual media, via the long-standing cinematic practice of White actors playing non-White characters: Mickey Rooney as Mr. Yunioshi in *Breakfast at Tiffany's* (1961), John Wayne as Genghis Kahn in *The Conqueror* (1956), and most of the cast of the live-action *Avatar: The Last Airbender* (2010). However, whitewashing has a long history in print culture, too. Over a century before whitewashing began afflicting books for young readers, White faces introduced Black books in different but parallel ways. Nineteenth-century slave narratives typically begin with forewords by White abolitionists vouching for the veracity of the Black ex-slave's story. Lydia Maria Child wrote an introduction for Harriet Jacobs's *Incidents in the Life of a Slave Girl* (1861). William Lloyd Garrison and Wendell Phillips provided prefaces for Frederick Douglass's *Narrative of the Life of Frederick Douglass, American Slave* (1845). In the twentieth century, White authorization has continued to be a means for selling a Black book. For example, Dorothy Canfield Fisher—a White author and Book-of-the-Month Club judge—famously wrote the introduction for Richard Wright's *Native Son* (1940), a novel revised specifically to receive the endorsement of (and sales guaranteed by) the Book-of-the-Month Club. As Kenneth Kinnamon notes, Fisher's introduction is "a latter-day example of the process of white authentication," reminiscent of White editors' introductions to slave narratives. In each case, the White introduction does not replace the visage of the Black character within, but it does invest authority in Whiteness, letting the patron's statement stand between the reader and the African American author or characters. In its market-driven logic and address to White authority, the White introduction is a literary ancestor of the contemporary practice of whitewashing.[1]

Beyond upholding Whiteness as normative, putting a White face on a book about non-White characters is typically a form of structural racism that is simultaneously obvious and insidious. That said, visual appearance is not always a reliable index of racial identity. Just as the Cat in the Hat obscures the messiness of his literary ancestry, so the politics of whitewashing can be more complicated than they at first appear. However, in preventing readers of color from finding characters of color, whitewashing can directly harm members of diverse communities. They have fewer opportunities to see themselves in works of fiction. A scarcity of characters who look like them can deter them from reading, and literary invisibility compounds that injury by telling them they do not matter. Yet publishing's plainly injurious choices are frequently presented as objectively rational ones. That is, by cloaking this decision in the logic of the marketplace, advocates of whitewashing present a racist practice as a rational, sensible business decision. But allegedly economic choices are never morally neutral ones. Giving a book cover a "race lift" alters young readers' perception of the characters within, and of the way they see themselves.

A BRIEF, INCOMPLETE HISTORY OF THE ALL-WHITE WORLD OF YOUNG ADULT BOOK COVERS

Today, in literature for young readers, whitewashing happens primarily in fantasy, science fiction, and the speculative more generally. Although I am not sure when this current practice started in children's and young-adult publishing, it almost certainly began flourishing after authors and characters of color entered mainstream children's book publishing en masse in the late 1960s and the 1970s. The earliest modern example I know of is Ursula K. Le Guin's *A Wizard of Earthsea* (1968). Though Ruth Robbins's original Parnassus Press cover art (fig. 4.1) shades title character Ged in the "red-brown" hue the novel describes, most subsequent covers show him as White, omit his face, or use a different image. The 1971 Puffin paperback illustrates Ged as White (fig. 4.2). Pauline Ellison's wraparound art for the 1975 Bantam paperback shows a White Ged (on the back cover), sailing toward an island threatened by a dragon (on the front cover). Yvonne Gilbert's art on my 1984 Bantam paperback portrays him as White. The 2012 Houghton Mifflin paperback depicts a hawk (Ged's nickname is Sparrowhawk) instead. Covers to subsequent novels in the *Earthsea*

Figure 4.1. Ursula K. Le Guin, *A Wizard of Earthsea* (Parnassus Press, 1968): original cover by Ruth Robbins. Image courtesy of Special Collections and University Archives, University of Oregon Libraries, Eugene, Oregon.

series also Whiten Ged, or otherwise obscure his race. Though Le Guin gives a reddish-brown color to the protagonist of one of the most influential fantasy series ever published, almost all *Earthsea* covers whitewash him, reinforcing the impression that fantasy is a mostly White genre.[2]

Whether representations of Le Guin's Ged initiate this practice or are just a prominent early example, whitewashing has become more widespread in the last couple of decades, a period when children's publishing has grown more commercial and trade-oriented. The decline of the institutional market, the power of chain stores (like Barnes & Noble), the rise of Amazon, the decline of

Figure 4.2. Ursula K. Le Guin, *A Wizard of Earthsea* (Puffin, 1971): cover. Reproduced by permission of Penguin Books Ltd.

brick-and-mortar stores, and the increasing power of sales-and-marketing people within publishing houses have all led to a greater emphasis on Producing An Easily Assimilated Product. With few independent booksellers or librarians to intervene (by, say, telling a young White reader that, yes, she or he *will* like a book that features a Black protagonist), the cover has become the primary way to make the sale. Marketing departments assert that, statistically, people of color buy fewer books than White people, even though that claim is hard to verify. Couple that with the assumption that White readers will be more likely to read books about White characters . . . and, beneath the guise of the Good Business Model, whitewashing emerges as the dominant logic of YA publishing.[3]

It is unclear how much of that sales-and-marketing claim derives from data, and how much is simply a conventional wisdom that reinforces a set of "common sense" assumptions. However, the publisher's rationale certainly *seems* more accepted practice than data-driven business strategy: if the policy were data-driven, then publishing companies would soon recognize that whitewashed covers are depriving them of a large potential audience. As Zetta Elliott notes, in the twenty-first century "so-called 'minority babies' now make up the majority of births in the US, and yet 95% of books published for children annually are still written by whites, and these authors find their mirrors in the team of professionals who acquire, edit, publish, and market those books." So, *if* people of color *do* buy fewer books, one cause could be that publishers print fewer books written by or starring people of color. Fewer books featuring characters who resemble readers of color may lead to fewer purchases. Similarly, if whitewashed jacket art obscures the non-White characters between the covers, then it may further deter non-White readers and their parents from buying these books. The publishing business thus creates a circular, self-justifying logic: publishers print fewer books by writers of color, or, when they do print them, omit characters of color from the covers; in response, people of color buy fewer of these books; publishers then claim there is less of a market for such books, and so print fewer books by writers of color. As Elliott writes, the problem is "institutional and systemic."[4]

Depending on which survey we consult, American publishing is between 79 percent and 89 percent White. The publishing industry's Whiteness either prevents it from seeing or, when it does see, from correcting its institutional biases. The well-intentioned, good-hearted people in publishing are no match for the entrenched implicit policies and practices that govern the workplace. As the Asian American editor Alexander Chee observes, "Racism in

America is a part of structural white supremacy. We're all trained to put white people first and to act like that's just normal, whatever color we are." So, he says, "You can't just imagine dealing with racism is a one-time purge of the system—checking yourself for racism should be a regular thing." Whitewashed covers exist because people in marketing departments imagine White audiences who only buy books featuring White characters. However, as the Indian American novelist Mira Jacob puts it, "White Americans can care about more than just themselves. They really can. And the rest of us? We are DYING to see ourselves anywhere." Books featuring characters of color need covers that do not obscure the races of those characters.[5]

Thanks to the publishing industry's neglect of a large portion of the young reading public, in the realm of speculative fiction the "All-White World of Children's Books" has become "the All-White World of Young Adult Book Covers." Or *nearly* all-White, certainly. Examining over six hundred YA books published in 2011, author Kate Hart discovered that 90 percent featured a White character, 10 percent a character of ambiguous race or ethnicity, 1.4 percent a Latino/a character, 1.4 percent an Asian character, and 1.2 percent a Black character (fig. 4.3). That does not add up to 100 percent because Hart tallied by *cover*, rather than by *cover model*—and a cover can have more than one cover model. Of those with models of color, most African Americans are in the background, have their faces cropped out of the picture, or are turning away. Asian and Latino/a models do at least get to look at the camera—which is better, even if there are still far too few such covers. Whitewashing undermines the already insufficient diversity in children's and YA literature, creating even fewer books that (to judge by their covers) seem to be about people of color.

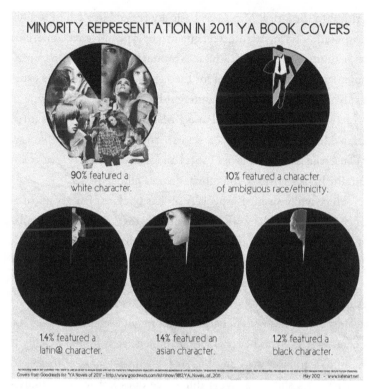

Figure 4.3. Kate Hart, Minority Representation in 2011 YA Book Covers.

It is quite pervasive. Though Sticky Washington has "light brown skin the very color of the tea that Miss Perumal made each morning," the cover for Trenton Lee Stewart's *The Mysterious Benedict Society* (2007) makes him White. In response to criticism, Little, Brown and Company later darkened him on that cover and subsequent books in the series. The covers for Kelley Armstrong's *Darkness Rising* trilogy (2011–2013) conceal the fact that Maya, the series's protagonist, is Native American. As Annie Schutte points out, "the fact that she is Native American isn't just a sidebar. It's critical to the story: Maya was basically created in a lab by an evil corporation trying to resurrect an ancient type of Native-American super humans who can morph into mountain lions." So using a conspicuously Caucasian model for the *Darkness Rising* covers is especially misleading. Offering a different but equally common type of whitewashing, Bil Wright's *Putting Makeup on the Fat Boy* (2011), Irfan Master's *A Beautiful Lie* (2011), and Meg Medina's *The Girl Who Could Silence the Wind* (2012) all focus on characters of color, but the books' covers depict them only in silhouette.[6]

Since whitewashing especially afflicts books of fantasy and science fiction, this chapter's central literary texts are recent speculative novels for young readers—Justine Larbalestier's *Liar* (2009), Jaclyn Dolamore's *Magic under Glass* (2010), Cindy Pon's *Silver Phoenix* (2009), and Rae Carson's *The Girl of Fire and Thorns* (2011). All have endured whitewashed covers. Examining their jacket art against the stories within, I argue that though visually changing the character's race can occasionally be beneficial, it more typically is harmful, and is always complex. As the whitewashing of these and other novels shows, denying difference does not increase understanding. Instead, it enforces Whiteness as normative, via racism masquerading as reason.

CAPITALISM: AN ECONOMIC SYSTEM, NOT A MORAL PHILOSOPHY

Whitewashing shows how putatively economic arguments sustain systemic inequalities. Noting marketing departments' tendency to whitewash her book covers, Ursula Le Guin has pointed out that " 'what sells' or 'doesn't sell' can be a self-fulfilling prophecy. If black kids, Hispanics, Indians both Eastern and Western, don't buy fantasy—which they mostly don't—could it be because they never see themselves on the cover?" In other words, if a whitewashed cover hides characters of color from readers of color, then we should not be surprised that fewer readers of color buy the book.[7]

Or read the book. The lower rates of reading proficiency among children of color amplify the importance of having a face on the cover that a non-White child sees as "like me." In 2003, the National Center for Education Statistics found 24 percent of Black adults at below basic literacy, along with 44 percent of Hispanic adults and 14 percent of Asian/Pacific Islanders. Only 7 percent of White adults were below basic literacy. The dominance of books that either are or appear to be about White characters, along with far fewer books that are about characters of color, creates an uneven playing field. White children can find lots of books about people who look "like them"; non-White children have fewer options. So, citing marketing to justify giving the cover a "race-lift" exemplifies the ways in which "purely" economic arguments discriminate against children of color. As Ari, the teen blogger behind *Reading in Color*, writes, "The message a whitewashed cover sends is that POC [People Of Color] are worthless, that we mean so little that even if a book is written about us, we can't be on the cover because the image of a POC won't sell."[8]

As Ari's comment indicates, economic rhetoric often justifies indifference to oppression, and presents inaction as benign. Disguising White supremacy as an objectively rational decision— a form of color-blind racism—has a long history. Sixty-five years ago, Zora Neale Hurston's "What White Publishers Won't Print" (1950) laid bare the moral bankruptcy of publishers' marketplace logic: "publishers and producers take the stand that they are not in business to educate, but to make money. Sympathetic as they might be, they cannot afford to be crusaders." When publishing houses today argue that sales justify the whitewashing of a Black author's novel, they are again using profitability to excuse themselves for their failure to act morally. The idea that any publisher imagines that "it won't sell" is a defensible justification for whitewashing indicates how deeply our culture has been infiltrated by the idea that free markets are an index of freedom, and that capitalist success also confers moral worth. Yes, publishing companies are businesses and not charities; they need to worry about their bottom line. But one would hope that the human beings who make decisions within these companies have also developed the capacity to consider the social impact of their choices. As Clémentine Beauvais points out,

> No one's asking publishing to be non-profit, but it's not true that it's simply enslaved to the market and condemned to producing "what sells." It can create its own readerly niches. It can foreground its values. It can pave the way for difference. Children's publishing needs to stop hiding behind the claim that it's "not a charity." It needs to accept the fact that it has social and a literary responsibility beyond money-making.

Exactly. Deciding to whitewash a book cover on the unproven assumption that White people buy more books may seem a sound business decision, but it is a morally suspicious one. What children see on the covers of their books tells them who matters, and who does not.[9]

THE BANALITY OF WHITENESS: CASUAL ERASURES, LASTING EFFECTS

A whitewashed cover naturalizes Whiteness as "normal," and promotes the idea that to be White is to be raceless, falsely suggesting that characters somehow exist outside of race. But they do not. In Jacyln Dolamore's *Magic under Glass*, racial difference underwrites hierarchies of power. Nimira, the novel's protagonist and narrator, is conscious and critical of being treated as an exoticized "other" in the country of Lorinar, where she lives and works. A native of Tiansher (which the Lorinarians incorrectly call "Tassim"), she has brown skin that marks her as different. Smollings, the villain, offers a condescending smile to Nimira, "as if a mere smile would soothe my shallow foreign feelings." Knowing that she has performed as a "trouser girl" in a music hall, he says, "Trousers are good liars." Nimira explains, "He dropped the 'girl,' as Lorinarians did when they insulted women of my race in general." Though Nimira has "brown skin" with a "golden glow" and encounters racial prejudice, the initial cover of *Magic under Glass* used a White model to depict her (fig. 4.4). Only after readers protested did Bloomsbury (the publisher) apologize and issue an edition in a new cover featuring a darker-skinned model (fig. 4.5). Their change is welcome because the whitewashed cover obscures themes central to the novel by altering the way that readers see the character.[10]

Because images leave deep impressions on our visual imaginations, Whitening a character on the novel's cover can permanently alter the way we see that character. As Peter Mendelsund observes, "One should watch a film adaptation of a favorite book only after considering, *very carefully*, the fact that the casting of the film may very well become the permanent casting of the book in one's mind. This is a *very real hazard*." While a cover's pictorial interpretation is not the same as a filmic interpretation, both have real and lasting effects on the way we see the characters. When I think of Jeff Brown's Flat Stanley, I can only see him in Tomi Ungerer's original illustrations (1964)—not the later renderings by Steve Björkman (1996), Scott Nash (2003), or Macky Pamintuan (2009)—because

Figure 4.4. Jaclyn Dolamore, *Magic under Glass* (2010): original cover.

I first met Stanley via Ungerer's artwork. That childhood impression (I read the book in first grade) overrides all subsequent ones. If, via the cover art, a young reader encounters Jacyln Dolamore's Nimira as White, then Nimira would on a very deep level *always be White* for that reader. Comparably, if readers first met Justine Larbalestier's Micah (from *Liar*) via a cover that announced her Whiteness, it would be very hard to re-see her as the mixed-race character that the novel itself describes. Visual images—especially the photographic ones that dominate YA book covers today—confer the sense of a verifiable reality upon fictional characters. They define those characters' visual appearances in readers' minds.[11]

Like books with an all-White cast of characters (*The Fantastic Flying Books of Mr. Morris Lessmore*), whitewashed covers make

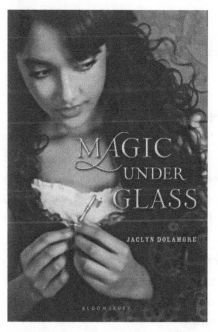

Figure 4.5. Jaclyn Dolamore, *Magic under Glass* (2010): new cover.

Whiteness invisible by affirming it as the normal, race-neutral setting for all people. The prominence of race in *Magic under Glass* might prevent the novel's cover from obscuring the subject for too long, but a novel like *The Hunger Games* more easily hides racial diversity. It has a multiracial cast, but its critical engagement is almost entirely focused on class and gender, rather than on race. Further turning attention away from its racially embodied characters, *The Hunger Games*' iconic cover omits humans altogether. The text's explicit ideological interests and its faceless jacket may have been the reason that some White moviegoers expressed surprise when Rue, who has "satiny brown skin" in the novel, also had brown skin in the film. They should have been more surprised that Katniss, who has "straight black hair" and "olive skin" in the novel, was played by the light-skinned Jennifer Lawrence (who died her blonde hair black). Instead, however, they Tweeted "why does rue have to be black not gonna lie kind of ruined the movie" or "call me racist but when I found out rue was black her death wasn't as sad" or comments worse than these. Their responses affirm Robin Bernstein's thesis that childhood innocence is "raced white" and "characterized by the ability to retain racial meanings, but hide them under claims of holy obliviousness." Or, as one of the *Hunger Games* Tweeters put it, "Did anyone picture Rue being black? No offense or anything but I just didn't see her like it." Such oblivious responses also remind us that race can be invisible to those readers—White readers—who have become accustomed to not seeing themselves as raced. In this sense, whitewashing offers another example of how, as George Lipsitz has observed, Whiteness "never has to speak its name, never has to acknowledge its role as an organizing principle in social and cultural relations."[12]

NO NEED FOR TRICKS: WE CANNOT INCREASE UNDERSTANDING BY DENYING DIFFERENCE

Surprisingly, some have alleged that a kind of literary whitewashing might actually increase understanding between people of different races. However, and contrary to what Laura Miller has argued, whitewashed covers are unlikely to "trick" White readers "into identifying with" non-White characters. They are much more likely to cause White readers to miss the ethnicity of the characters altogether. Miller cites a study by Lisa Libby and Geoff Kaufman, in which straight males read a story featuring a gay protagonist and White males read a story featuring a Black protagonist. According to the study's authors, the later the story revealed the fact of the character's race or sexuality, the higher the likelihood that the White or straight reader would identify with that character. "If we subscribe to the idea that literature ought to improve people's characters," Miller writes, "then perhaps authors and publishers should be encouraged to conceal a main character's race or sexual orientation from readers until they become invested in him or her." She concludes by coming out in favor of "a little judicious whitewashing" because it "has literally been demonstrated to change hearts and minds, at least for a while."[13]

Though a laudable sentiment, this is a dubious claim. The argument promoted by Miller, Libby, and Kaufman treats race and sexuality as hats that can be worn or discarded, and not as something central to a person's identity. In their study, Libby and Kaufman refer to both race and sexuality as "outgroup status," and the phrase's use in their description of their experiment is telling: "We predicted that delaying the revelation of a character's outgroup status in a narrative that otherwise encouraged experience-taking would allow readers to experientially merge with an outgroup member. To test this hypothesis we manipulated the sexual orientation (Study 5) and race (Study 6) of the main character—as well as the timing of that revelation." In identifying sexual orientation and race as something that can easily be withheld or revealed, the authors of the study do not treat sexual orientation or racial identity as complex social phenomena, but rather as inconsequential markers of difference. The motives of the study—and of whitewashing, were it used in this way—are excellent. But their treatment of difference as merely cosmetic risks propagating a deeper misunderstanding. A society that embraces diversity does not agree merely to overlook dissimilarity; it does not say that we can only respect one another if we ignore our differences. Instead, it tries to understand these dissimilarities and encourages us to learn from what we lack in common (as well as what we share). The notion that difference can only be bridged by trickery—the subterfuge of a misleading cover or ambiguous textual description—makes human variance into an obstacle, instead of recognizing it as an opportunity to learn about someone different from you.[14]

Whitewashing and Kaufman and Libby's argument both rest on the assumption that a White reader is incapable of identifying with a non-White character. Proponents of whitewashing reinforce racism by suggesting that identification can only occur between readers and characters of the same race. However, we do not need to be of the same race—or gender, or sexual orientation, or religion—to invest ourselves in the experiences of a fictional character. When, as a small White boy, I read Ezra Jack Keats's *The Snowy Day*, I identified with Peter, the book's small Black protagonist: we were both shy, creative children. When I read L. M. Montgomery's *Anne of Green Gables*, I identified with Anne Shirley, even though I was (and am) neither Canadian nor female: I well knew how the imagination could lead a person astray. We need to grant White children the opportunity to find themselves in a character whose race is different from their own, just as surely as we need straight children to read about gay children, or boys to read about girls. We cannot increase understanding by denying difference. Non-White readers manage to identify with White characters. If we provide them the opportunity to do so, White readers can identify with non-White characters, too.

For non-White readers, however, the problem is different. Children of color can identify with White characters, but that should not be their primary option. Whether via whitewashed covers or the relative scarcity of diverse books, denying non-White children the option of identifying with characters of color teaches them that they are invisible, and that their stories do not matter. In other words, Miller's argument conspicuously neglects the effects that whitewashed covers have on the psyches of readers of color. But librarian Allie Jane Bruce has looked more closely. In 2013, she and her sixth-grade class—who, to judge by the accompanying photos, are a racially diverse group—discussed book covers. The students noticed that, though the hardcover of Jacqueline Woodson's *Locomotion* (2002) featured a child who (like the book's protagonist) is African American, the 2010 paperback cover instead shows a flock of birds. As one child responded, "Do illustrators think that if a person of color is fully shown, it won't sell as many copies?" After further discussions on "how book covers and content can marginalize groups," Bruce took the students to a Barnes & Noble, where they looked at the book displays. As one of the students said afterward, "In the chapter book section, I saw that most of the books that had non-Caucasian characters didn't have that character on the cover." Another student observed, "Society is almost afraid of putting a dark-skinned or Asian character on the cover of a book. I feel like these are minor forms of segregation." True, these students entered the bookstore with the benefit of Bruce's curriculum. However, even children who have not formally studied whitewashing understand when they are being excluded. They may lack the language to express it, but the dominance of Whiteness in book covers, comics, and throughout popular culture lets them know, on a fundamental level, that their aspirations and histories are just not as important. As the physician and author Sayantani DasGupta has said of whitewashing, "Images matter. They tell us who counts."[15]

CHANGING COLORS, MANGLING MEANING

Beyond telling us who matters and who doesn't, whitewashing can profoundly alter a text's racial meanings. Justine Larbalestier's *Liar*

(2009) is a case in point. The novel is an exploration of race, identity, and the stories we tell about both. As the protagonist Micah says, "No one is exactly what they think they are. We all have every kind of DNA floating in us: black, white, Asian, Native American, human, monkey, reptile, junk DNA, all sorts of genes that do not express." A mixed-race, tomboyish teenage girl who might be part werewolf, Micah is a compulsive liar who is trying to stop lying. The challenges in distinguishing Micah's truths from her fictions mirror the ways in which binaries (black/white, masculine/feminine, human/animal) impede the construction of a unified self. *Liar* is an intriguing narrative experiment that depends upon a balance between plausibility and implausibility. Bloomsbury's decision to feature a very clearly White model on the book's cover tips the balance toward the implausible (fig. 4.6). As Larbalestier writes, "One of the most upsetting impacts of the cover is that it's led readers to question everything about Micah: If she doesn't look anything like the girl on the cover maybe nothing she says is true. At which point the entire book, and all my hard work, crumbles."[16]

After Larbalestier posted a critique and the whitewashed cover on her blog, her fans rallied in support and Bloomsbury backed down. The White model appears only on the US advance reader copies. A model of color adorns the US hardcover and paperback editions (fig. 4.7). Larbalestier herself prefers the model-less cover created by Bruno Herfst, a designer at Allen & Unwin, her Australian publisher (fig. 4.8). As she says, "I never wanted a girl's face on the cover. Micah's identity is unstable. She spends the book telling different versions of herself. I wanted readers to be free to imagine her as they wanted." Herfst's substitution of typeface for a human face may deprive us of a person of color on the jacket, but it at least does not mislead us into thinking that Micah is Caucasian.[17]

Both covers of Rae Carson's *The Girl of Fire and Thorns* (2011) misrepresent that novel's main character, changing the way that race

Figure 4.6. Justine Larbalestier, *Liar* (Bloomsbury, 2009): US advance review copy cover.

signifies in the story. The advance reading copy depicts Elisa as a slender White girl with dark hair (fig. 4.9). However, the Elisa in the novel is overweight and her skin has a "dark cast." The final version of the cover uses the same photo but shows only the face, refracted through the Godstone that Elisa bears (fig. 4.10). Though slightly more ambiguous than the ARC, the published cover nonetheless still suggests that Elisa is White. Within the novel, however, not only is Elisa dark, but her enemies all have "the same pale skin," and their leader—whose face "is pale and slick"—says of Elisa and her comrades, "You barbarians are all filthy." Carson's book reverses the ways in which color typically signifies: in *The Girl of Fire and Thorns*, the malevolent characters have light skin, and the heroes have a darker physical appearance.[18]

Figure 4.7. Justine Larbalestier, *Liar* (Bloomsbury, 2009): final US cover.

Beyond muddling Carson's rejection of stereotypical associations between color and morality (dark intentions, bright disposition, etc.), the White cover model also messes with the book's rewriting of imperialist adventure narratives. In *The Girl of Fire and Thorns*, the invading army's superior technology represents brutality, not ingenuity; their White leader's disdain for his non-White opponents displays his barbarism, not the virtues of his superior civilization. When Elisa is captured by the enemy, one soldier demands, "Where are your companions?" Though she does speak his language, she decides to maintain her cover by speaking the language of the hill folk, saying (in that tongue) "I don't understand you!" The soldier hits her, accusing her of being "filthy" and "speaking such a filthy language." Later, when the leader interrogates her, he speaks the hill folk's language, but says, "It is distasteful for me to speak your language. It is

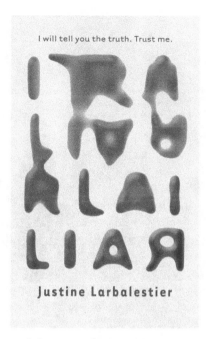

I will tell you the truth. Trust me.

LIAR

Justine Larbalestier

Figure 4.8. Justine Larbalestier, *Liar* (Sydney: Allen & Unwin, 2009): Australian cover.

like dirt in my mouth." He insists that Elisa answer "Quickly, so I do not have to sully myself with too many barbarian words." Since we already know her to be fluent in three languages, and are sympathetic toward her, his behavior indicates that *he* is the barbarian here, a fact underscored by his lack of manners. When he eats, the man gobbles like a wild beast: "He scoops a chunk of meat toward his mouth. His teeth clamp down on it so that bits of grizzle and stringy flesh dangle from his thick lips. He shakes his round head, flinging meat across his cheek, before jutting out his chin and gulping it down." The "stringy flesh" dangling from his mouth, the shake of his head, and his "gulping" all make him seem more animal than human. Later, when the army attacks her city, its leaders perform human sacrifices in order to activate their Godstone-based weaponry. In making the invading

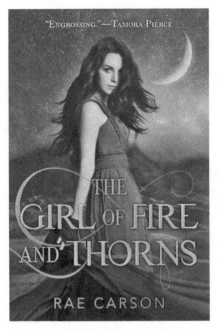

Figure 4.9. Rae Carson, *The Girl of Fire and Thorns* (2011): prepublication US cover.

White man the savage, Carson's fantasy endorses the perspective of the colonized, and rejects that of the colonizer. Choosing a pale cover model completely misrepresents the novel's racial politics.[19]

MIXED MESSAGES; OR, IT'S COMPLICATED

That said, beyond altering a book's racial meanings in troubling ways, on rare occasions a whitewashed cover may actually mitigate against stereotypes, rather than perpetuating them. In the case of Taiwanese-American novelist Cindy Pon's *Silver Phoenix* (2009), the Asian girl on the hardcover matches the race of the protagonist, but

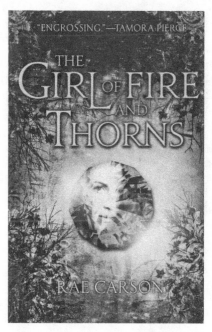

Figure 4.10. Rae Carson, *The Girl of Fire and Thorns* (2011): US cover.

the girl on the paperback is more racially ambiguous (figs. 4.11, 4.12).
However, the hardcover also presents the girl as a mystical, somewhat exotic figure. As the novelist Mitali Perkins notes, "Sometimes
books may be packaged with covers depicting a character as more
foreign than he or she is described in the story," likely in an effort "to
tap into a fascination with all things foreign, amping up the exotic
factor." That seems to be the case here: given that married women
(in the novel) have braided hair, the cover image seems to refer to
the arranged marriage of the protagonist Ai Ying, near the book's
end. However, its pink is not the "crimson-and-gold" gown with
"embroidered" phoenixes she is forced to wear. This heavy garment
makes her feel "boxed in, claustrophobic" and unable to breathe. She
is barely able to move in this dress, much less raise her arms above

Figure 4.11. Cindy Pon, *Silver Phoenix* (2009): hardback cover.

her head in the vaguely "martial arts" pose of the cover model. Yet, as she looks off into the distance, the model representing Ai Ying has her arms raised, while her jade pendant glows on her chest. If her "otherness" here is a feature of the fantasy genre (she *is* a chosen one, she *does* have special powers), it also veers toward Orientalism. The paperback cover largely avoids that problem: it omits the model's eyes, and her skin tone is lighter. Obscuring the model's ethnicity allows us to read her as "White" (which colludes in the erasure of people of color), but also diminishes the problems of the original hardback's cover. In this sense, the results of the change are mixed.[20]

Liar's whitewashed cover produces mixed readings, too—but for different reasons than *Silver Phoenix*. Whatever problems its original cover may introduce, Pon's novel does create a fantasy

Figure 4.12. Cindy Pon, *Silver Phoenix* (2009): paperback cover.

world that draws upon cultural traditions of Taiwan and China. Ai
Ling's nemesis, Zhong Ye, is morally suspect because his behavior
violates a Buddhist understanding of life and death. He keeps himself alive by "devouring others' spirits, keeping them bound to him,
so they are unable to truly die and reincarnate. Hundreds of spirits
have been sundered from the Life Cycle." One result is "babes . . .
born without spirit." As Ai Ling's ally Chen Yong asks, "Who knows
how he has skewed the Life Cycle by keeping those spirits trapped?"
In Buddhist terms, Zhong Ye has been interfering with samsara—
the cycle of death and rebirth that defines human existence. He is
upsetting the natural and spiritual order, so that people cannot be
reborn again. While the cover may veer toward the exotic, Pon's fantasy world is grounded in cultural specificity.[21]

In contrast, the Australian-born Larbalestier creates a mixed-race American character whose cultural life is curiously muted. *Liar* addresses race, but says little about the social components of racial identity. To put this another way, the novel seems less invested in the lived experience of its mixed-race protagonist and more interested in theorizing race, insisting on its lack of scientific standing and its dubiousness as a marker of identity. As Micah says, "Biologically speaking, the so-called races have more similarities than they have differences. There is only one race: the human race." Refuting the notion that race tells us useful information about a person, she observes, "No one is exactly what they think they are" because "we all have every kind of DNA floating in us." In other words, for Micah, conventional understandings of race are lies. Like these statements, *both* photographic covers accentuate the mutability of Micah's identity—though the whitewashed one does so more radically than the final US version. If (as I argued earlier), the whitewashed cover robs Micah of too much credibility by suggesting that she is lying about her race, it also very usefully challenges the assumption that all people who "look" White identify as White. In this sense, the whitewashed cover is the more provocative one. Though the final US cover (which features a model of a darker complexion) does less of this sort of provocation, it too raises the question of whether Micah is lying. The cover model's face is mostly hidden by the hoodie she's pulling around it, but the long strands of her tightly curly hair, zigzagging down above her left eyebrow, do not match Micah's description of her own "cropped short" hair, which she describes as "nappy hair" worn "natural and short, cut close to [her] scalp." If we argue that this mixed-race cover confirms the narrator's racial identity, then we may make race more essential to Micah's character than Larbalestier's depiction does. In other words, in favoring the final US cover, we would be guilty of using the mixed-race model to confer a kind of authenticity upon Micah (if the narrator "looks like" the girl in the photograph, then that's "really" her). In contrast, the whitewashed cover resists race as a measure of authenticity: the model who seems White suggests that Micah is merely masquerading as mixed-race, or perhaps her race cannot easily be read, pictorially. The whitewashed cover, then, offers a tacit acknowledgment that the politics of racial representation are more complex than are commonly acknowledged.[22]

The practice of whitewashing usefully reminds us that, as the artist Susan Guevara has observed, "There is no either/or definition of cultural authenticity. There is no simplistic scale upon which either you or I can weigh the artist or his or her work. The question, the work, and the artist must be set in context. Context gives breadth and enhances meaning." A book's cover provides some of that context, as does the text within. But so do more elusive attributes, like individual experience. We could, for instance, argue (as Virginia Hamilton does) that there are key features of African American experience:

> The life of the people is and has always been different in a significant respect from the life of the majority. It has been made eccentric by slavery, escape, fear of capture; by discrimination, and constant despair. But it has held tight within it happiness, and subtle humor, a fierce pride in leadership and progress, love of life and family, and a longing for peace and freedom. Nevertheless, there is an uneasy, ideological difference with the American majority basic to black thought.

We could make similar claims about the collective identities of other marginalized groups. However, there would always be variance within those groups, variance that might not be legible via the apparent race of the cover model. As Guevara notes, she and her sister have the same parents, but she more closely resembles her

Anglo mother, while her sister more closely resembles her Mexican father. Neither of the sisters speak Spanish, but many people assume her sister does, simply because they read the sister's "jet black" hair, "dark olive" skin, and "nearly black" eyes as Mexican. Race is not always as visible as people assume it is.[23]

For a novel that makes its protagonist's unreliability a core concern, a cover that does not seem to match the protagonist's race offers unique interpretive possibilities. *Liar*'s central theme invites an interpretation that at least finds subversive potential in its whitewashed cover. However, similar arguments cannot be made for the covers of *Magic under Glass*, *The Girl of Fire and Thorns*, and most other whitewashed dust jackets. For nearly all such books, whitewashed covers obscure clearly racialized characters, and so stand between readers of color and characters of color. Sure, if a reader picks up the book and reads it closely, she might well reflect on the vagaries of racial signification. However, it is sadly more likely that a White-faced jacket will prevent a book's non-White protagonist from meeting non-White readers. This is a big problem. As the novelist Daniel José Older writes, "Besides teaching us who we are, books are where we learn whose lives matter enough to read about." A whitewashed cover tells children of color: *Your kind doesn't read, and so doesn't need to be represented.* It says: *Your stories don't matter.* Equally harmfully, it says: *"Children" always refers only to "White children."* [24]

FIGHTING WHITEWASHING:
JOIN THE RESISTANCE

That is why readers need to continue to resist. Their resistance is one reason why whitewashing has emerged as a battlefront in the fight for diverse books. A blogger-led revolt has made whitewashing more visible, and galvanized people to agitate for cover images that better represent the characters. Another reason is that internet activism has developed concurrently with the same changes in children's publishing that have led to this proliferation of race-lifted book covers. On blogs and social media sites, advocates for diverse books have been quick to call out publishers on whitewashed covers. Protests have helped two of the four books I have focused on—*Magic under Glass* and *Liar*—gain new covers, each featuring a model whose racial makeup more closely matches that of the character.

The results of this activism are encouraging, but whitewashing persists, and book jackets featuring people of color remain scarce. Elisa, the protagonist of Rae Carson's *Girl of Fire and Thorns*, remains White on all three books in that series. Maya, the Native American protagonist of Kelley Armstrong's *Darkness Rising* trilogy, remains White on all of its book covers. Though it features a pale model on both dust jackets, Esther Friesner's *Sphinx's Princess* (2009) and *Sphinx's Queen* (2010) focus on Nefertiti's rise to Egyptian queen. The whitewashing of a famous African ruler emphasizes just how ordinary erasing people of color has become. While representations of a fourteenth-century-B.C.E. queen differ, images do exist. Though there are plenty of lighter-skinned contemporary Egyptians and (I would guess) ancient Egyptians, a conspicuously White Nefertiti endorses Whiteness as the de facto non-color of all humankind.

The practice of whitewashing is another reminder of the daily, subtle, entrenched racism that infects the publishing industry. Whitewashed covers are thus another index of the considerable gap between the children's and young adult books published each year and the diverse children who read them. Though the old adage cautions us not to, we do judge books by their covers: those that render people of color invisible tell them that their life experiences are not important enough to read about. Young readers notice. As one of Allie Jane Bruce's sixth-graders put it, the absence of people of color on book covers "are minor forms of segregation." Book covers matter—for marketing, and, more importantly, for young readers learning about the world and their place in it.[25]

Whitewashed covers illuminate how economic decisions passively perpetuate inequalities, naturalize Whiteness, and alter a text's racial politics. They highlight the power of the cover image, but also the power that readers and authors have when they resist the dictates of sales-and-marketing. When they see a whitewashed cover, readers need to keep pressuring the publisher. They might also join blogs like *Racebending.com*; Malinda Lo and Cindy Pon's *Diversity in YA*; Audrey Gonzalez, Crystal Brunelle, and K. Imani Tennyson's *Rich in Color*; Mitali Perkins's *Mitali's Fire Escape*; and Allie Jane Bruce's *Reading while White* in raising consciousness. A market-driven decision like whitewashing can be changed if enough members of that market get organized and speak out. After all, activism not only continues to be a vital way of changing what gets published, but it made diverse books possible in the first place. Without activism, the publishing business would be much more White than it is now—and it's already *very* White.

Chapter 5

Childhoods "Outside the Boundaries of Imagination"

Genre Is the New Jim Crow

In December 2015, the producers of the play *Harry Potter and the Cursed Child* announced that Noma Dumezweni, an acclaimed Black actress (born in Swaziland and raised in England), would play the role of Hermione Granger. Some fans immediately tweeted their disapproval. One asked, "Why has Hermione, a described white character, been cast as black? It makes no sense." Another asked, "Why would they make Hermione black?! So damn stupid." However, as other fans were quick to point out, Rowling's novels never specify Hermione's skin color. The first book describes her as having "lots of bushy brown hair"; the third book says she's "very brown." As Rowling herself tweeted in response to the critics, "Canon: brown eyes, frizzy hair and very clever. White skin was never specified. Rowling loves black Hermione."[1]

Given the Tweetstorm surrounding Rue's casting in *The Hunger Games* film, and cover artists' inability to imagine Le Guin's Ged as non-White, the opposition to Dumezweni as Hermione should not surprise us. As Chitra Ramaswamy put it, "I imagined Hermione as, well, Emma Watson. The default assumption of whiteness is so strong and unspoken, it's a hard habit to kick." In her mind, Hermione had always been White, even though Ramaswamy supported the casting decision, writing (as she said) "as your average Anglo-Indian girl starved of black and Asian characters in mainstream culture. Especially leading characters with proper storylines, personalities and love interests." Prior to the casting, some fans of color had already imagined Hermione as non-White, posting their own portraits of the character online. Search for Black Hermione on Tumblr, and you'll find art depicting Hermione in many shades of brown. It's wonderful that some have managed to push back against fantasy's default Whiteness. However, it's less wonderful that non-White fans have had to imagine themselves into fantasy narratives if they want to see themselves there at all.[2]

The Whiteness of children's publishing Whitens what kinds of stories get told, and consequently what kinds of stories we are inclined to imagine. According to *Publishers Weekly*'s 2015 survey, 89 percent of people employed in the industry identify as White or Caucasian. Only 5 percent identify as Asian, 3 percent as Hispanic, and 1 percent as African American. Lee & Low's 2015 survey yielded comparable results: 79 percent of those working in publishing identified as White or Caucasian, 7 percent as Asian/Native Hawaiian/Other Pacific Islander, 6 percent as Hispanic/Latino/Mexican, and 4 percent as African American. Those numbers do not represent the population at large, nor do the books published each year (fig. 5.1). In 2014, only 11 percent of children's books published that year were *about* people of color—and the number *by* people of color was only 8 percent. Furthermore, look more closely at the 11 percent or the 8 percent, and you'll notice something else: realism, historical novels, and nonfiction are, by far, the most frequent genre categories.[3]

Children's Books By and About People of Color and
First/Native Nations Received by the CCBC*
2002 -

See next chart for count of books from U.S publishers only

Last Updated: April 5, 2016

Year	Number of Books Received at CCBC	African / African Americans		American Indians / First Nations		Asian Pacifics/ Asian Pacific Americans		Latinos	
		By	About	By	About	By	About	By	About
2015	3,400	106	269	19	42	176	113	58	82
2014	3,500	84	180	20	38	129	112	59	66
2013	3,200	68	93	18	34	90	69	48	57
2012	3,600	68	119	6	22	83	76	59	54
2011	3,400	79	123	12	28	76	91	52	58
2010	3,400	102	156	9	22	60	64	55	66
2009	3,000	83	157	12	33	67	80	60	61
2008	3,000	83	172	9	40	77	98	48	79
2007	3,000	77	150	6	44	56	68	42	59
2006	3,000	87	153	14	41	72	74	42	63
2005	2,800	75	149	4	34	60	64	50	76
2004	2,800	99	143	7	33	61	65	37	61
2003	3,200	79	171	11	95	43	78	41	63
2002	3,150	69	166	6	64	46	91	48	94

Figure 5.1. Cooperative Children's Book Center, "Books by and about People of Color Published in the U.S. 2002–."

GENRE, COLOR-BLINDNESS, AND BIAS

As I argue in this chapter, one reason for these discrepancies is that, in children's and young-adult publishing, genre is the new Jim Crow—a "post-racial" way of regulating the literary experiences of people of color. In other words, the publishing industry's genre-based rationale is parallel to the logic that, as Michelle Alexander has shown, underwrites America's prison industrial complex. As her *The New Jim Crow* demonstrates, the criminal justice system has supplanted the old, explicitly race-based Jim Crow method, offering in its stead an apparently color-blind way of enforcing a racial caste system. Genre is the publishers' version of this system. Where fifty years ago people of color were almost entirely excluded from mainstream publishing, now they can publish—but mainly in a few select neighborhoods, the borders of which can be mapped by genre.

Every author of color has a story that illuminates the invisible barrier of genre. Christopher Myers remembers that his father, Walter Dean Myers,

> once wrote a story about Dr. Cosmos, a talking chimpanzee who wore a sequined turban, and some kids from Harlem who were matching pets to people by their astrological signs. I remember Pop coming home disappointed after he was told that the story would not be published, because astrology, the occult, witchcraft and the like would not sell—or so The Market had dictated.

In other words, under the guise of "The Market," editors told Walter Dean Myers that fantasy was off-limits to African American writers. As Zetta Elliott asked in her article on self-publishing as an alternative to mainstream publishers' indifference, "How many books show Black children using magic and/or technology to shape an alternative universe?" Fantasy and science fiction are only two of the genres that publishers tacitly treat as mainly for White writers. As the novelist Malinda Lo tweeted in response to Elliott's article, "There can be a zillion white authors who write [whatever kind of book] but if one marginalized author exists who does it, that's enough." Writing of her experience shopping a manuscript, I. W. Gregorio noted, "Three different editors from three different publishers said that it was too similar to another book with an Asian-American protagonist on their list." As she said, "What comments like this tell me is: 'We've filled our quota.' It tells me that publishers think: 'One

Asian American book is quite enough, thank you.'" There are count-less stories like these.[4]

Until recently, we have had to rely on only these sto-ries. However, in February 2015, the University of Wisconsin's Cooperative Children's Book Center—which does a fantastic job of tracking how many diverse books get published each year—for the first time posted a list of all of the titles in its annual "African/ African American" and "American Indian" categories for books pub-lished in 2014. It did not list titles in any other categories, and has not released titles for 2015 or any other year. Using the CCBC lists for 2014, I read reviews of each book (and, in some cases, the book itself), counting which books fit which genres. Nearly all books fit more than one genre, so my genre percentages do not add up to 100. Indeed, given that genre is itself a subjective assessment (on which more in a moment), another reader may arrive at slightly different percentages. For instance, I counted *Brown Girl Dreaming* under both poetry and autobiography, but I could have listed it with his-tory and realism, too—I stuck to the first two because those seemed the strongest "fit," generically. My metrics' imperfections may blur some precision from my numbers, but my data are sufficiently accu-rate to outline the trends for 2014. Here they are.[5]

Of the 193 books on the "African/African American" list, 66 (34%) are realism, 58 (30%) have a historical focus, 20 (10%) are biographies, 18 (9%) are poetry, 18 (9%) feature animals, and 16 (8%) are what Corinne Duyvis calls "incidental," recognizing that the char-acters are, as Michelle Martin puts it, "unextraordinarily black." For these books (of which Ezra Jack Keats's *The Snowy Day* is the classic example), race is not central to the story. Other genres have lower numbers: 13 adventure stories, 11 autobiographies, 10 mysteries, 10 devoted to sports, 9 early readers, 7 fantasies, 7 science fiction works, 7 concept books, 6 fairy tales/folk tales/fables/parables, 4 dystopian novels, and 1 horror. When fully *one-third* of the titles are nonfiction or realism, all other genres crowd together in a much smaller space. The "American Indian" list's numbers are similarly lopsided. Of the 40 titles, 14 (35%) are realism, 13 (33%) historical, and 9 (23%) fairy tales/folk tales/fables/parables. In the remaining categories, the list yields only 4 fantasy, 4 biography, 3 adventure, 2 poetry, 2 featuring animals, and 1 horror. No incidentals, science fiction, mystery, dystopia, autobiography, or early readers.[6]

In case that paragraph of numbers caused your attention to wander, the same information in graphs is on the next page (figs. 5.2 and 5.3).

Lisa Bartle's *Database of Award-Winning Children's Literature*—including 12,006 titles, 824 of which feature African Americans and 296 of which focus on Native Americans—corroborates these findings, with one caveat. My history category (in which I include historical fiction) overlaps with realism since history and historical fiction tend to be narrated via a realistic mode; she keeps realism separate from history, and restricts it to "gritty fiction dealing with serious issues for the older reader." So, leaving "realism" aside, her database—which covers 1921 to the present—otherwise produces results that affirm my own single-year survey from 2014. Of history titles (combining her numbers for historical fiction and history), her database finds that 35% of all African American titles are historical fiction or history, compared with 31% of all Native American titles, and 20% of all titles. (Bartle offers no "White" category. I am therefore using the "All Titles" category as a point of comparison.) The nonfiction percentages of African American and Native American books are closer to the percentage of all nonfiction titles, but still exceed them: 41% of all African American titles are nonfiction, compared with 34% of all Native American titles, and 31% of all titles. The lopsidedness of biography's numbers more closely resembles those of history's: 22% of all African American titles are biography, compared with 13% of all

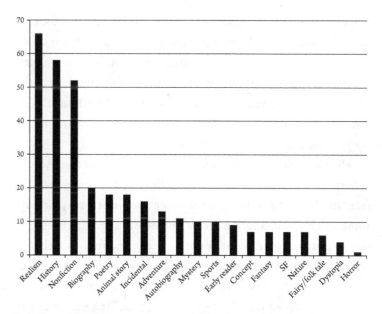

Figure 5.2. Chart: African American Children's Literature: Number of Books by Genre, 2014.

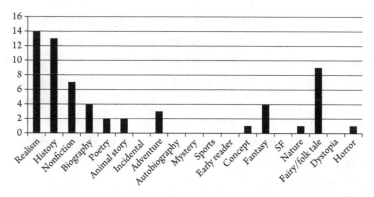

Figure 5.3. Chart: Native American Children's Literature: Number of Books by Genre, 2014.

Native American titles, and 8% of all titles. Bartle's database also confirms the significantly lower numbers of fantasy and science fiction novels. Only 2% of all African American titles are fantasy, as are 2% of all Native American titles. In contrast, 7% of all titles are fantasy. In the science fiction category, 0.4% of all African American titles are science fiction, and 0.7% of all Native American titles are science fiction, but 2% of all titles are science fiction.[7]

History, realism, and nonfiction dominate lists of African American and Native American children's literature, but the fact that books in other genres *do* get published may prompt some to challenge my Jim Crow metaphor: after all, if segregation meant separate water fountains (and bathrooms, schools, etc.), then wouldn't publishing's version of Jim Crow mean that some genres would be "Whites only"? No. It wouldn't. As Karen Fields has pointed out, the term "segregation" is a misnomer. In the Jim Crow South, segregation did not literally mean the separation of races—but rather identified a way of regulating the spaces in which the races interacted. Just as (to quote Fields) "Jim Crow was a historically specific set of arrangements for living separate lives together," so genre is publishers' specific set of arrangements for bringing the experiences of people of color into children's and YA books while also keeping those experiences separate. During Jim Crow, African Americans shared the same spaces with White Americans, but they shared them unequally. As Fields says, "Jim Crow on the railways offered an exemption for the Afro-American servant attending her mistress or the mistress's child." Comparably, African American authors and characters do find a place in genres outside of history and realism, but only in a tokenistic way, rather like the servant in the Jim Crow railway car or the sole Black friend on a TV sitcom. So, in 2014, the presence of four dystopian novels—one of which is Walter

Dean Myers's *On a Clear Day*—does not contradict the fact that dystopia is mostly closed to writers and characters of color. These exceptions both prove the rule and provide a color-blind alibi for structural racism within the publishing industry. The occasional African American fantasy "proves" that genre does not enable institutionalized discrimination (look—a fantasy novel by a Black author!), and perpetuates the myth that each genre is equally open to authors and artists of all races.[8]

This sort of structural racism is not unique to children's literature. As John K. Young notes, publishers of books for adults also impose "aesthetic limits" on African American writers:

> The predominantly white publishing industry reflects and often reinforces the racial divide that has always defined American society, representing "blackness" as a one-dimensional cultural experience. Minority texts are edited, produced, and advertised as representing that "particular" black experience to a "universal," implicitly white (although itself ethnically constructed) audience.

In children's literature, White publishers serve a parallel gatekeeping role, determining what kinds of "Blackness" get represented.[9]

I say "White publishers" not just because publishing is mostly run by White people (though it is) but because its ability to perpetuate its own Whiteness impedes diversifying the industry and the stories that it prints. Low salaries for starting-level jobs—assistant editors, publicists—discourage those without independent means. As an executive at Henry Holt & Company said in 1998, "The system of assistant editors is a self-recruiting system for the cultural establishment of this country. . . . You can only get a job if your parents subsidize you or pay your rent." Or, as a White editor at a mid-size press said in 2016, publishing is "self-selecting for people who don't necessarily need to live on a salary alone." Even getting the interview for the position requires the non-White applicant to overcome the subtle segregation built into the hiring process. The three major summer publishing institutes—Columbia Publishing Course, Denver Publishing Institute, New York University Summer Publishing Institute—all provide credentials for those who aspire to work in the industry, but all are prohibitively expensive (they cost between $6,000 and $8,000). CUNY's Publishing Certificate Program, founded in 1997 with the explicit goal of making publishing more diverse, has had some success in challenging the dominance of the major three: 50 percent of its graduates go on to work in publishing for at least one year, and 20 percent continue to stay employed in publishing. However, their success has been limited. David Unger, director of the program, said in 1998 that "it was hard to place interns because the business is so clubby. . . . The children of editors and writers get most of the internships." In 2016, Retha Powers—assistant director of the CUNY program—cited comparable obstacles. "I've heard the word *pedigree* used many times," she said. "There's this assumption that a student who comes from NYU—who is more likely white—is going to be better suited for the publishing industry than our students, who have incredibly diverse backgrounds, racially, culturally, and also in terms of class." She continued, "I think it's odd that a student who is the editor-in-chief of the newspaper, interned at ABC and MTV, and is Phi Beta Kappa doesn't even get a call back for an interview. [W]hat's missing is that the student has a very [racially] identifiable last name and goes to City College as opposed to NYU."[10]

Those non-Whites who do find positions in the industry then face structural obstacles at every turn, not only because beneficiaries of privilege do not yield their power, but also because passive acquiescence perpetuates the status quo. Even those well-intentioned White people who are vocal about making publishing more diverse do not necessarily follow through on their stated ideals. As an executive at one of the Big Five publishers said in 2016, "You can have someone say all day long that he's really committed to [making his company more diverse], and maybe he is, but when the real world creeps in, it's another story. . . . That person doesn't want to fight with a publisher who wants to hire his godson." When a non-White applicant does get the job, she soon discovers that advancement depends upon networking, and many employees of color lack access to the elite circles that influence the profession. These barriers extend to all areas of the business, from finding an agent to shaping the content of a book. As one publishing industry professional put it, "Minorities and agents live in segregated worlds." This same person said that the most frequently heard question from Latino/a writers was "How do I find an agent?" The most common query from agents was "How do I find Latino writers?" Should a writer of color get a White agent, the writer may receive comments like "loved your writing, but couldn't connect with the character" or suggestions to "delete moments when a character of color gets mean looks from white people because 'that doesn't happen any more.'" (White literary agents shared both of these observations with Daniel José Older. He sought and found a better agent.) And if the agent is fortunate enough to secure the book contract, the writer may well find White editors or marketing people who lack the experience to imagine stories different from their own. It is not uncommon for non-White writers to be asked to make changes in their manuscripts to make them more "believable." Even when authors of color get the book contract, they cannot always tell the stories they want to tell in the ways they want to tell them.[11]

Genre is the most visible manifestation of White regulation of non-White experience in books for young people, but subject matter is another. As my colleague Cameron Leader-Picone points out, the three central events for defining Blackness in the twenty-first century are: (1) Hurricane Katrina, (2) the election and presidency of Barack Obama, and (3) the Black Lives Matter movement ignited by the 2012 murder of Trayvon Martin and galvanized by the 2014 Ferguson protests. Though subject matter is not the primary focus of this chapter, another way to measure publishing's institutional racism would be to evaluate the representation of those three subjects. How many of the dozens of Barack Obama children's books address the virulent racism that he had to contend with as president, from racial caricatures in political cartoons, to bizarre allegations that he is a "secret Muslim," to so-called "Birthers" (including candidate and now President Trump) denying his citizenship? Of the African American children's books published each year, how many address the Black Lives Matter movement?[12]

I imagine that some—perhaps many—White editors and agents would either reject my claims or presume that, while my analysis may apply to *some* editors and agents, it certainly does not apply to them . . . because *they* are not racist and therefore do *not* discriminate against any author or artist. There are many good people in publishing, but to categorically reject the possibility of racism is to fail to account for how discrimination operates unconsciously, sneaking into our thought processes and influencing us in ways of which we're not aware. The vast majority of people do not think of themselves as racist, and do not want to be racist, but self-concept and wishful thinking have nothing to do with unconscious biases. As Michelle Alexander reminds us, "The fact that you may honestly believe that you are not biased against African Americans, and that you may even have black friends or relatives, does not mean that you are free from unconscious bias. Implicit bias tests may still show that you hold negative attitudes and stereotypes about blacks even though you do not believe you do and do not want to." Indeed, "there is often a weak correlation between degrees of explicit and implicit bias; many people who think they are not biased prove when tested to have relatively high levels of bias." I suspect that nearly all people reading this book do not want to be racist. However, irrespective of one's wishes or race, it is impossible to grow up in a deeply racist culture without absorbing some of those biases.[13]

At the 2014 National Book Awards, Daniel Handler did not intend to tell a racist joke, but we can behave in racist ways without meaning to do so. After presenting Jacqueline Woodson with the National Book Award in Young People's Literature for her verse memoir, *Brown Girl Dreaming*, Handler said,

> And I said that if she won, I would tell all of you something I learned this summer, which is that Jackie Woodson is allergic to watermelon. Just let that sink in your mind. And I said, "You have to put that in a book."
>
> And she said, "You put that in a book."
>
> And I said, "I am only writing a book about a black girl who is allergic to watermelon if I get a blurb from you, Cornell West, Toni Morrison, and Barack Obama saying, 'This guy's OK! This guy's fine!'"

He laughed, as did some of the audience. In the following days, Handler tweeted an apology for his "ill-conceived attempts at humor," acknowledging that his remarks "were monstrously inappropriate and yes, racist." He donated $10,000 to the We Need Diverse Books campaign and then matched donations for a twenty-four-hour period up to $100,000. But the point of this story is neither Handler's sincere apology and belated realization that his ironically racist joke was also unironically racist. The point is that *any* White author could easily make a mistake like Handler's. Because race begins shaping us so early in life, racial and racist assumptions lurk in the psyche's shadowy corners, out of sight but not out of mind.[14]

As Woodson wrote in response to the incident, by the time she was eleven years old, she "had seen the racist representations associated with African-Americans and watermelons, heard the terrifying stories of black men being lynched with watermelons hanging around them," and even wonders if her "allergy [to watermelons] was actually a deep physical revulsion that came from the psychological impression and weight of the association." Handler—like most Whites in America—did not grow up with that deeply painful association. As Woodson says, "His historical context, unlike my own, came from a place of ignorance." Ignorance, in turn, enables the amnesia of color-blindness.[15]

Any social arena that permits unconscious assumptions provides an opening for racism to emerge; if we listen closely to what is said in these places, then we can shake off the fog of color-blindness. Jokes are one such space. Genre is another. Both reveal more about the speaker's beliefs than he or she may be aware. As Amy J. Devitt has observed, "Defining genre as a kind of text becomes circular, since what we call a kind of text depends on what we think a genre is." Instead, Devitt suggests, genres might better be understood as "shorthand terms for situations." Since genres have such blurry borders, identifying a manuscript as one genre or another depends a great deal on the discretion of the person making the judgment. If we associate African American children's literature with history or with realism, then it's a very small step from there to deciding that African Americans' manuscripts that fail to neatly fit these categories are not publishable. Without any formal rules guiding an editor's or an agent's decision, works by authors of color easily get segregated into a few narrow categories.[16]

The unconscious, often invisible, nature of this type of racism makes the Cooperative Children's Book Center's annual count and Lisa Bartle's database so valuable. Patterns emerge through data; statistics make bias visible. When 11 percent of children's books published in 2014 were about people of color (and, remember, only 8 percent were by people of color), those numbers highlight the vast discrepancy between the Whiteness of what gets published and the children of color who make up 50 percent of school-age Americans today. When a third of all diverse children's books published are nonfiction, realism, or have a historical focus, these numbers highlight genre as an index of racism in the publishing industry. The numbers help make institutional prejudice legible. Genre helps us see structural racism.

AFRICAN AMERICAN CHILDREN'S LITERATURE AND THE PUBLISHING BUSINESS: A BRIEF HISTORY

We often fail to see structural racism because of the widespread belief that only actively racist behavior counts as truly racist. Nearly everyone recognizes that calling an African American the n-word is racist, but far fewer people will concede that an award-winning author who has to self-publish her stories about African American children also may be experiencing institutional racism.

It is not that publishing is easy for White authors. Michael Hoeye self-published the first of his Hermux Tantamoq series, *Time Stops for No Mouse* (1999), before Penguin Putnam picked it up and ultimately went on to publish all four Hermux books. Penguin,

TransWorld, and HarperCollins each turned down the manuscript for J. K. Rowling's *Harry Potter and the Philosopher's Stone* (1997), claiming that its 120,000-word length was far too long for a children's novel. There are many stories of White writers facing rejection. Yet, though publishing is challenging for everyone, writers of color face distinct obstacles that White writers are much less likely to encounter. When an editor or agent lacks the lived experience from which the manuscript grows, that editor or agent can find the work less compelling, less easy to relate to, and less publishable. As Mira Jacob puts it,

> Here is the thing about how discrimination works: No one ever comes right out and says, "We don't want you." In the publishing world, they don't say, "We just don't want your story." They say, "We're not sure you're relatable" and "You don't want to exclude anyone with your work." They say, "We're not sure who your audience is."

The overwhelming Whiteness of the mainstream publishing industry means that there are far more editors likely to find non-White writers' work not "relatable." This is one reason that many writers of color turn to self-publishing, founding their own presses, or seeking small independent presses.[17]

Lee & Low published Zetta Elliott's award-winning realist picture book *Bird* (2008), but traditional publishers otherwise turned down her manuscripts. So she put out her historical science-fiction novel *A Wish after Midnight* (2008) via print-on-demand, and later republished it via Amazon.com's Encore, which also published her fantasy *Ship of Souls* (2012). Like many authors of color before her, she has since embraced self-publishing, releasing over a dozen more books for young readers in a range of genres: historical fantasy, low

fantasy, realism, an allegorical animal story, and Christmas stories. Jerry Craft, award-winning creator of the weekly comic strip
Mama's Boyz (1987–), turned to self-publishing for similar reasons.
As he put it, "Publishers have so many arbitrary rules—no flash-
backs, too many characters. . . . If publishers want to portray kids
of color effectively, they need to go outside their conventional pool
of writers and artists." Though his comic strip has been syndicated
by King Features since 1995, he launched it as a self-published venture, and (not finding any interest from mainstream presses) has
self-published both *Mama's Boyz* collections, and his middle-grade
novel *The Offenders: Saving the World while Serving Detention* (2014).
Wendy Raven McNair decided to self-publish her science-fiction
trilogy *Asleep* (2009–) because of industry indifference and because,
as she says, her teenage daughter "loves fantasy stories, but my challenge was finding an age appropriate fantasy story with a lead character that reflected her, a teen and an African American girl." There
are many stories of non-White authors turning to self-publishing.
As Elliott puts it, "When publishing gatekeepers exclude so many
talented writers of color, self-publishing is often our only recourse.
If we wait for the industry to change, another generation of children
will grow up as I did—without the 'books-as-mirrors' they need
and deserve."[18]

Independent presses are another means of creating children's
literature that is as diverse as the children reading it. Founded by
Patsy Aldana in 1978 with a primary focus on Canadian children's
books, Groundwood Books has long championed (as its website
notes) "the stories of people whose voices are not always heard,"
including books by First Nations authors, people of Latino/a ori-
gin, and (to again quote the website) "others who through cir-
cumstance have been marginalized and whose contribution to our
society is not always visible." In 1985, Bobby Byrd and Lee Byrd

founded Cinco Puntos Press, which specializes in Latino/a stories and bilingual Spanish-English books. Frustrated by mainstream publishers rejecting her Afro-Bets books (concept books featuring Black children), Cheryl Hudson and Wade Hudson founded Just US Books in 1988. As Michelle Martin writes, the company "remains the only one dedicated solely to the publication of black children's literature" and has "enabled the Hudsons to circumvent the type of censorship that they encountered from mainstream publishers either rejecting or severely editing their work." In 1991, Philip Lee and Tom Low founded Lee & Low to "meet the need for stories that children of color can identify with and that all children can enjoy." Their independence also allows them to reject mainstream publishing's structural racism. As Jason Low (son of co-founder Tom and now director of the company) says, they can feature "people of color on the covers of our books" instead of using "whitewash[ed] covers because of the belief that books with people of color on the covers presumably do not sell."[19]

It is great that all four of these independent presses are publishing diverse books, but the fact that writers of color nevertheless have to seek independent presses or self-publish is a measure of the considerable distance between mainstream children's publishing and the multicultural society in which we live. That authors and artists of color need to seek indies or to self-publish illustrates both the persistence of Jim Crow in corporate publishing and the crucial role that non-mainstream publishers have played in supporting diverse voices in children's books. A century ago, self-publishing created African American children's literature. W. E. B. Du Bois and Augustus Granville Dill (business manager of *The Crisis*, edited by Du Bois) founded Du Bois and Dill Publishing, the "first black-owned publishing enterprise established to produce reading materials expressly for black children." Though it lasted for only two years, Du Bois and Dill published *The Brownies Book* (1920–1921), a monthly magazine that featured all genres of children's literature, and included many notable African American writers, including James Weldon Johnson, Jessie Fauset, Nella Larsen, an eighteen-year-old Langston Hughes, and Du Bois himself. In the first issue of *The Brownies Book* alone, Du Bois and Fauset (who served as literary editor and, in 1921, as managing editor) included poetry, photography, a lyrical leftist fable, didactic stories, realism, news, historical nonfiction, and biographies of contemporary children. A hundred years ago, each issue of *The Brownies Book* offered greater generic variety than mainstream children's publishing does today.[20]

The same year *The Brownies Book* ceased publication, the historian Carter G. Woodson founded Associated Publishers, which—as Rudine Sims Bishop notes—focused on "Black history and culture for school-aged readers," though it also published "folklore collections, biographies, and poetry." Associated published Woodson's own *The Negro in Our History* (1922, for high-school students), *Negro Makers of History* (1928, for younger readers), and *Plays and Pageants from the Life of the Negro* (1930, historical drama for schoolchildren); Effie Lee Newsome's *Gladiola Garden* (1940, poetry); Jane Dabney Shackelford's *My Happy Days* (1944, realism); and others. Associated's emphasis on history—with some realism, poetry, and other genres—may seem an echo of contemporary commercial publishing. However, at that time, commercial publishing all but ignored writers and young readers of color. When Woodson founded the press, exactly one major publisher had issued a book for and containing the work of African Americans: *The Upward Path: A Reader for Colored Children* (1920), published by Harcourt, Brace and Howe, and edited by Myron T. Pritchard and NAACP co-founder Mary White Ovington. The book included works by Phyllis Wheatley, Paul Laurence Dunbar, Booker T. Washington, W. E. B. Du Bois, Jessie Fauset, James Weldon Johnson, and others.[21]

In 1932, Langston Hughes and Arna Bontemps became the first two writers of color to have original work for children issued by a major publishing house. Knopf published Hughes's *The Dream-Keeper and Other Poems* (a few of which had appeared in *The Brownies Book*), and Macmillan published Hughes and Bontemps' *Popo and Fifina: Children of Haiti*. Working with these publishers granted their books a wider readership, but also required them to work within White notions of acceptable representations of Blackness. As Katharine Capshaw notes, Hughes and Bontemps "recognized that a national audience would reject direct depictions of ethnic injustices, preferring instead to encode social critique in ways that young readers would apprehend but that might not attract the attention of white adult mediators." While *Popo and Fifina*'s politics are more understated than Hughes's "Sharecroppers" (a 1937 poem in *New Pioneer*, a children's magazine published by the Communist Party), the novel does subtly address poverty and even obliquely nods toward Haiti's revolutionary past. As Rudine Sims Bishop notes, E. Simms Campbell's illustrations for *Popo and Fifina* offer "noteworthy alternatives to the comic pickaninny images that passed as portraits of Black children in many children's books of the day."[22]

In the first hundred years of its existence, African American children's literature repeats this pattern over and over again. First, small publishers issue the books, or the Black writers and artists self-publish. Next, mainstream presses publish books by Black creators—but never enough books, and always under the guidance of White editors who have the final say on what types of African American experiences are represented. The novelist (not the civil rights leader) Jesse Jackson's tales of a Black child seeking acceptance in a White community—*Call Me Charley* (1945), *Anchor Man* (1947), and *Charley Starts from Scratch* (1958)—seem designed to rouse the consciences of White readers, rather than to explore the lived experiences of Black children. Tellingly, Jackson later explained that these novels "reflected the perspectives of White authors writing for a White audience." At least he was able to get them published. It took Lorenz Graham twelve years to get his YA novel *South Town* (1958) published because its focus was not on integration, but on a strong Black family. As Bishop writes,

> the publisher who had originally contracted to issue it believed that the American public of the mid-1940s would not accept Black characters who did not fit the stereotype of the day. They thought the Williams family was too "American"—dignified, intelligent, just like everybody else—to be believed. Even in the late 1950s when the book was finally published, the editor sought expert verification that the social conditions in the South were as Graham described them.

That a White editor required an expert to verify Black experience of *racism in the American South in the late 1950s*—the period of the Montgomery Bus Boycott (1955–1956) and the integration of Little Rock Central High School (1957)—neatly illustrates how White privilege sustains White supremacy.[23]

It also shows how the US publishing industry manages narratives about race. During the ninety years that mainstream publishers have printed African American children's literature, two main genres—realism and historical fiction—have expressed two main ways of conceiving of race in America. From the 1930s to the 1960s, the ethnicity model is really the *only* way in which publishers' African American books for young people conceive of race.

This multicultural approach was radical in, to borrow Omi and Winant's description of this paradigm, "challenging the biologistic (and at least implicitly racist) view of race which was dominant" in the early twentieth century. As the ethnicity model became "the progressive/liberal 'common sense' approach to race," however, problems emerged, one of which was that assimilation is the ultimate goal of these books. It is immoral to expect people of color to strive to fit into a society that has—from its beginning—treated them as less human. This is, as Omi and Winant point out, a key flaw in the notion of ethnicity as a way of thinking about racial formation: a model that works well for talking about White immigrants works poorly for understanding descendants of slaves. Despite its flaws, the ascendancy of this model in mainstream children's publishing is a tribute to the independently published and self-published works that paved the way, and illustrates the limits of a marketplace dominated by Whites. In the 1930s, Macmillan could publish *Popo and Fifina*. But for a sharp look at 1930s racism in the United States, we would have to wait until the 1970s, when Dial published Mildred Taylor's *Roll of Thunder, Hear My Cry*. For a novel like Taylor's to be published, the civil rights movement had to first push a different idea of racial formation into mainstream publishing.[24]

From late 1960s to the present, the other model of racial formation that emerges in African American children's literature draws upon the ethnicity model, but resists its assimilationist goals. Inspired by Nancy Larrick, the Council on Interracial Books for Children, and the Black Arts Movement, children's books began to acknowledge that racism is structural. In some ways, the successful introduction of this perspective into mainstream African American children's literature has accounted for the institutionalization of history and realism as its dominant modes.[25]

Of the ninety-eight Coretta Scott King Award Winners from 1970 to 2014, 55 percent have a historical focus, 50 percent are realism, 18 percent are poetry, 12 percent are biographies, and 9 percent are fairy tales, folk tales, fables, or parables (fig. 5.4). Whether inspired by the rewards of awards or simply shaped by the dominant understanding of which genres are "African American," the two major publishers with an African American children's literature imprint also focus primarily on history and realism. Founded in 1998, Disney/Hyperion's Jump at the Sun imprint has published seven Coretta Scott King Award winners since then: Sharon Flake's *The Skin I'm In* (1998), Kim L. Siegelson's *In the Time of the Drums* (1999, won for Brian Pinkney's art), Julius Lester's *Day of Tears: A Novel in Dialogue* (2005), Jamie Adoff's *Jimi and Me* (2005), Carole Boston Weatherford's *Moses: When Harriet Tubman Led Her People to Freedom* (2006, won for Kadir Nelson's art), Kadir Nelson's *We Are the Ship: The Story of Negro League Baseball* (2008), and Andrea Davis Pinkney's *Hand in Hand: Ten Black Men Who Changed America* (2012). Launched as a HarperCollins imprint in 1999, Amistad (which began as an independent press in the early

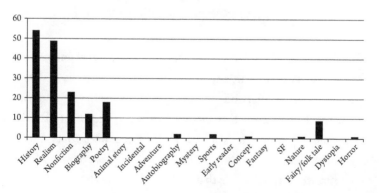

Figure 5.4. Chart: Coretta Scott King Award Winners: number of books by genre, 1970–2014.

1970s) has since published three Coretta Scott King Award winners: Joyce Carol Thomas's *The Blacker the Berry* (2008, for Floyd
Cooper's art), Rita Williams-Garcia's *One Crazy Summer* (2010),
and Williams-Garcia's *P.S. Be Eleven* (2013). All but one of these are
realism or historical: *The Blacker the Berry* is poetry.

While these publishers' imprints deserve praise in their advo-
cacy for African American children's literature, their choices reinforce the perception that not all genres are for Black writers or
readers. The Coretta Scott King Award is constrained by what is
published, but if it began to recognize other types of books more frequently, that might encourage mainstream presses to publish more
African American children's literature that is not history or realism.
Perhaps Christopher Myers's new Random House imprint will help
diversify genre. Launched in July 2016, Make Me a World aspires to
publish, in Myers's words, "children's literature of the future" today.
As Myers says, "I want this imprint to build worlds for young people
to grow up in. Each book is a world—and there are so many worlds
that have yet to be created."[26]

FOUR REASONS TO DIVERSIFY GENRE

Though we need to diversify genre, there are excellent reasons
for publishers and awards to promote historical novels and realism. Novels that focus on African American history offer a vital
corrective to narratives that marginalize, omit, or distort histories
of peoples of color. As Mildred Taylor's character Mary Logan
says, defending her decision to teach against Mississippi's White-
supremacist textbooks, "all that's in that book isn't true." Though
she gets fired for teaching "things some folks didn't want to hear,"
Roll of Thunder, Hear My Cry (1976) identifies accurate history as

necessary to the family's survival. From the earliest days of African American children's literature, history has been central and vital. Du Bois' advertisement for *The Brownies Book* (published in the October 1919 *Crisis*) lists second among his monthly magazine's goals "To make them [African American children] familiar with the history and achievements of the Negro race." Two generations later, Eloise Greenfield's 1975 *Horn Book* manifesto, "Something to Shout About," argues that African American children's literature should "give children a true knowledge of Black heritage . . . that they may develop a sense of direction for the future." We continue to need African American children's literature that reflects the realities of the past and the present. [27]

While historical and realist books are necessary, they should not dominate the field at the expense of other types of literature. Here are four reasons why we need not just diverse books, but genre diversity among those books. First, the institutional emphasis on history has the unintended consequence of implying that temporal progress necessarily correlates with progress toward justice. The disproportionally high number of historical fiction and nonfiction titles published each year subtly conveys the message that America's crimes happened in the past, that the present is better, and that the future will be better still. Individual historical narratives *do* resist this regressive tendency, with (for example) epilogues that gesture toward the troubled present. For example, Christopher Paul Curtis's *The Watsons Go to Birmingham—1963* ends with a historical note telling us that civil rights heroes "walk among us today. One of them may be sitting next to you as you read this, or standing in the next room making your dinner, or waiting for you to come outside and play." In a six-word concluding paragraph, he adds, "One of them may be you." While these gestures can be as important as the histories the books convey, the dominance of historical fiction nonetheless creates a cumulative understanding that racism is in the past. There are few novels or picture books about Ferguson and the Black Lives Matter movement. Likewise, there are few about the prison industrial complex, or racist profiling—the practice commonly referred to as "racial profiling." Part of diversifying genre requires a richer selection of contemporary realist and historical texts that address present crises. Or, to put this another way, we do not need fewer realist and historical texts; we need more of everything else.[28]

Second, a different genre offers a new perspective on the real. One risk of the dominance of realism and historical fiction is that readers can get jaded—*oh, another realistic novel about the civil rights movement.* But novels can explore history via fantasy, science fiction, dystopia, mystery, horror, or just about any other mode of storytelling. Historical fiction is not the only genre in which we encounter history; realism is not the only genre that strives to depict lived experience. Speculative fictions propose alternate histories that illuminate unexamined facets of our own. An African American dystopian novel shifts the narrative's center of gravity, examining structures of power from an angle that a Caucasian American dystopian novel (aka "dystopian novel") might neglect. Genre alters perspective, changing the way we understand, shaking us out of our habits of thought.

Placing African American voices at the center of a dystopian novel does not merely yield *The Hunger Games* from Rue's perspective; it fundamentally shapes the narrative's concerns and the focus of its critique. For example, Alaya Dawn Johnson's *Love Is the Drug* (2014)—a YA dystopian thriller (one of the four dystopian novels on the CCBC's 2014 African American list)—extrapolates its universe from that of contemporary teens of color in Washington, D.C. Their experiences supply the narrative's emotional and moral core. So, while the novel's central critique is America's post-9/11 surveillance state, its analytical energies also grapple with structural racism. The possibility of Coffee's imprisonment on drug charges looms over his character, and the novel makes a couple of allusions to Alexander's *The New Jim Crow*, as when Emily Bird (the protagonist) has "always understood that the drug laws were the latest incarnation of Jim Crow, a way to target minorities for incarceration (and free labor) without explicitly denying their rights." Beyond reminding readers of the racist nature of the "war on drugs," having characters of color critique abuses of citizens' rights illuminates how race underwrites power. That is, on the one hand, the Patriot Act violates the civil liberties of all Americans. On the other hand, African Americans also have specific reasons to be suspicious of a government that has historically denied their rights and humanity. *Love is the Drug* mentions in passing the Tuskegee syphilis experiment, in which—as Coffee says—the US government "watched four hundred Black men die slowly of syphilis for decades after they'd developed a treatment. For an experiment." The novel does not return to this specific point, but it does not need to; it and other parallel moments establish the ways in which racism motivates the US government's violations of people's lives and liberties.[29]

Beyond figuring time travel as a metaphor for the persistence of historical trauma, Kiese Laymon's *Long Division* also unsettles the assumption of temporally linear causality, enmeshing the reader in a version of the confusion experienced by those living under the subterfuge of racism. When City moves around in time, typical cause-and-effect unravels: Events from past, present, and future now all have the potential to influence one another. Comparably, when you're used to White people's motives not being what they seem, it's harder to calibrate your own reaction, because possible causes proliferate. So, for example, City's display of anger on the quiz show turns out not to be an overreaction. He and LaVander Peeler *were* both being used—the contest was rigged so that one of the winners could be touted as an exceptional minority. The novel's temporal slipperiness immerses us in a more complex, nuanced, and confusing system of social relations, which in turn replicates the intensity of the challenges that City faces in his daily interactions with others.

Each genre refracts reality in its own way. Shifting genre is the intellectual equivalent of what a fitness trainer would call muscle confusion. If you work the same muscles in the same way each time, they accommodate the stress and do not develop further. In the same way, if we apprehend similar information via the same genre each time, the mind becomes habituated to the mode, and does not think more deeply. Different genres can shake us out of our customary modes of thinking. Present the "same" fact in a different way and it suddenly resonates anew.

Third, diversifying genre helps liberate the imagination. When we publish, teach, or read Black dystopian novels, Black fantasy, and Black speculative fiction, we challenge the unspoken assumption that certain genres are mainly for White writers and readers. As I write a chapter on how genre functions as a new Jim Crow in children's and YA publishing, my own imagination reinforces the very ideological assumptions that I seek to oppose. When I think of fantasies, dystopias, or science fiction, the first books that come to mind are *not* written by or about people of color. When I see the word *dystopia*, I first think of George Orwell's *1984*, M. T. Anderson's *Feed*, and Suzanne Collins's *The Hunger Games*, not Alaya Dawn Johnson's *Love Is the Drug* or Walter Dean Myers's *On a Clear Day*. When the term *fantasy* emerges, the books that initially come to mind are C. S. Lewis's *Narnia* series, J. R. R. Tolkien's *Lord of the Rings* trilogy, and J. K. Rowling's *Harry Potter* novels, not N. K. Jemisin's *The Inheritance Trilogy* and David Anthony Durham's *Acacia Trilogy*.

If you mentioned a *modern interpretation of Greek mythology*, Rick Riordan's *Percy Jackson* series would be my first thought, and not Justina Ireland's *Promise of Shadows*. When I think of science fiction, my imagination does place Octavia Butler's *Kindred* next to novels by Arthur C. Clarke and Isaac Asimov, but fails to include works by Samuel R. Delaney and Tananarive Priscilla Due. I cite my own genre bias as an illustration of the subtle perniciousness of White supremacy—and why it is both difficult and necessary to fight it.

Even more troubling is that, as Ebony Elizabeth Thomas points out in her forthcoming book *The Dark Fantastic*, when non-White characters *do* appear in fantasy and speculative fiction, they tend to be figures of fear or otherwise aligned with malevolent forces. So strong is the fantastic tradition of denigrating Blackness that, as Thomas argues, "Narratives with liberated Dark Others are rare, and are rarely as popular as those that feature trapped dark subjectivities. This is because subverting the traditional positioning of the Dark Other in the fantastic requires radical rethinking of everything that we know." This deeply embedded, racialized mythos not only infects the imaginations of writers and artists; it creates a public resistant to rethinking tropes that marginalize or demonize people of color. As Thomas says, "The principles of the dark fantastic are so ingrained in our collective consciousness that when the expected pattern is subverted, most audiences cannot suspend disbelief. Readers and viewers complain that dark heroic protagonists are not likable." The Dark Other's typical role makes it hard to conceive of and to market fantasies in which a protagonist of color is the hero or heroine.[30]

White children should not be the only ones encouraged to see themselves on a quest in an imaginary world, grappling with technologies of the future, inhabiting mythological tales, or banding together to resist a dystopian regime. We need diversity among genres in order to decolonize the imagination—to paraphrase the title of Zetta Elliott's wise essay. As she writes, "If we do not create stories that expose the beauty and complexity of our varied realities, we will indeed remain trapped by the 'fictions' created by those outside of our cultures and communities." The books she read while growing up—Frances Hodgson Burnett, Jane Austen, the Brontës—were, she writes, not "a mirror for my young black female self." Her response to "being so completely excluded from the literary realm" was to decide "I had to develop the capacity *to dream myself into existence.*" It is a testament to the strength of her imagination that she was able to do precisely this in her life and her work. But children should not be obliged to rely on *only* their own imaginations to see themselves in the full variety of children's and YA literature. Young people should not be required to decolonize their imaginations without assistance. Some—like Zetta Elliott—may succeed. But most will not. Many will simply turn away from reading altogether.[31]

So, fourth, to foster literacy among *all* children (not just the White ones), we need greater diversity within and among genres. Though a voracious reader as a child, Walter Dean Myers recalled the moment—as a teen—when, noticing that "there was something missing" in his books, he began to turn away from reading. He writes, "As I discovered who I was, a black teenager in a white-dominated world, I saw that these characters, these lives, were not mine." As a result,

> Books did not become my enemies. They were more like friends with whom I no longer felt comfortable. I stopped reading. I stopped going to school. On my 17th birthday, I joined the Army. In retrospect I see that I had lost the potential person I would become—an odd idea that I could not have articulated at the time, but that seems so clear today.

Years later, James Baldwin's "Sonny's Blues" would bring Myers back to reading and, ultimately, lead him to an acclaimed and prolific career of writing books for young people. But Myers is exceptional. For many people, the moment they "lost the potential person [they] would become"—such a powerful and deeply sad idea—begins a slide toward a hopelessness from which they never fully recover. Indeed, that Myers *continued* to be such an avid reader well into his teens, *despite* not seeing himself in the books he read, underscores how remarkable and unusual a person he was. He did not immediately turn away from reading; most other children of color give up long before Myers did. As Ebony Elizabeth Thomas writes, "It's not that kids and teens of color and other marginalized and minoritized young people won't read. It's just that many adults haven't thought very much about the racialized mirrors, windows, and doors that are in the books we offer them to read."[32]

#WENEEDDIVERSEGENRES

Racism is resilient, wily, and adaptable. Combat it in one form, and it mutates, finding expression in a new one. This is why we are still asking where the books for children of color are—though we are asking this question in different ways than we were fifty years ago. Thanks to the activists who have come before us, there are now many more books for young people of African descent, Asian heritage, Latino/a backgrounds, and indigenous cultures. However, since the percentage of non-White school children is about four times the annual percentage of books featuring non-White characters, we ask for *more*—we need diverse books. Since the gaps in representation are unequally distributed across genre, asking for *more* is not enough.

This is one reason that focusing on genre diversity is a path toward increasing representation.

Focusing on genre is insufficient in and of itself, but, then, so is any single approach. Structural racism is a many-headed hydra. We need to battle it on as many fronts as possible, which is why each chapter of this book examines these structures from a different angle. It is also why I am thankful that there are many great scholars doing sharp anti-racist work on children's culture. Robin Bernstein's *Racial Innocence* examines the ways in which innocence is raced, granted to White children but denied to Black children. Ebony Thomas's forthcoming work theorizes the "dark fantastic," her "term for the role that racial difference plays at the frontiers and at the forefronts of our fantastically storied imaginations"—specifically, various types of speculative fiction. Histories of African American children's literature by Rudine Sims Bishop, Katharine Capshaw, and Michelle Martin not only chronicle past struggles over representation and inclusion, but suggest ways to move forward.[33]

Structural racism's remarkable ability to reproduce itself reminds us that victory will not be quick, easy, or total. In a perceptive and honest article about her own work in the publishing business, Laura Atkins sums up this problem succinctly:

> The question here is not about particular racist individuals who work in the publishing industry, rather, this is an institutional problem. The way in which the acquisition, development, distribution and marketing of children's books currently takes place is a system based on patterns that are so pervasive they seem to become natural, inevitable and justifiable. I would argue that most children's publishing houses currently exist in order to serve the interests and needs of the white majority culture.

By making visible and then questioning these "natural, inevitable, justifiable" patterns, we expose them and hope that people of good conscience within the industry will oppose them.[34]

Yet hope is not enough. Presumably motivated by a concern for their bottom line, publishers are reluctant to acknowledge the ways in which racism shapes the industry. Random House insists that any mention of Dr. Seuss's racist cartoons be excised from his official biography at Seussville.com. Dell republishes a bowdlerized edition of Hugh Lofting's *The Story of Doctor Dolittle* (1988), with an afterword that strives to excuse the original version's racism, dismissing it as "minor" and "not an integral or important part of the story." Though publishers no longer actively seek out books like *Doctor Dolittle* (1920), Annie Vaughan Weaver's *Frawg* (1930), or Inez Hogan's many *Epaminodas* stories (1930s–1950s), they do keep some of their racist back catalogue in print. On the one hand, these publishers are offering a valuable service for historians of children's literature, and for those willing to teach children about racism. On the other, I find it surprising that HarperCollins's current edition of Helen Bannerman's *Little Black Sambo* (which includes her original 1899 artwork) includes a blurb on its back cover, proclaiming:

I cannot imagine a childhood without it. For it has fun—hilarious, rollicking fun, and that is rare enough in books of any size for any-sized children. The gift of being funny for little children is one of the rarest to be bestowed upon authors or artists: Helen Bannerman is both at once, and her tiger in blue trousers, her tiger with shoes on his ears—how they touch off the bright spark of laughter!

—*May Lamberton Becker*
in FIRST ADVENTURES IN READING

This quotation is eighty years old, but HarperCollins does not mention that. While *Little Black Sambo*'s racial politics are complicated, its dust jacket should at least acknowledge the book's use of racist caricature. As Michelle Martin has argued, *Little Black Sambo* is implicitly anti-racist yet explicitly racist: in tricking the tigers, Sambo "displays wit, intelligence, and savvy," underscoring his humanity and making him an admirable character; yet Bannerman's illustration style caricatures Sambo, diminishing his humanity. HarperCollins's blurb offers no reason why anyone might seek guidance before teaching or reading the book to young people. *Little Black Sambo* is short enough that a responsible publisher could easily provide a brief afterword with some context and critical questions for readers and instructors. HarperCollins, however, prefers simply to recycle a quotation from a book published in 1936, lauding *Sambo*'s "rollicking fun" and "laughter."[35]

While major publishers do not always elect to remain complicit with White supremacy, we nonetheless need to prod them to change. We also need to support smaller, independent publishers committed to books that represent a range of experiences in a full array of genres: Groundwood Books, Cincos Puntos, Afro-Bets, Lee & Low, and others. We must also support those who choose to publish their works independently: Jerry Craft, Wendy Raven McNair, Zetta Elliott, and others.

Finally, it is the responsibility of everyone—not just authors, writers, educators, and parents of color, but *everyone*—to support these efforts. As Roxane Gay writes, "Discussing diversity in publishing is the worst kind of Groundhog Day," not just because it is depressing that we still need to have these conversations but because it invariably falls to writers of color to start the conversations. Gay explains:

The problem is and has always been the exclusion of writers of color and other marginalized writers who have to push aside their own work and fight for inclusion, over and over and over again. We beg for scraps from a table we're not invited to sit at. We are forced to defend our excellence because no one else will.

In the meantime, we're still here, writing our fingers to the bone, hoping against hope that we can finally step off this hamster wheel of a conversation, and reroute that energy into the reading and writing that our own work requires.

It's up to all of us to change the status quo, allowing children of all races to see themselves in a panorama of literary experiences. If we all work toward such a change, then that takes some of the pressure off writers and artists of color. Instead of having to spend so much time as activists, they can devote more time to being artists. Instead of having to find the space to publish, market, and sell their own books, they can rely upon a publisher to help get their books out into the world. If we create this change, then instead of having to forcibly integrate themselves into narratives that exclude them, non-White children will learn that they are welcome in all genres. They will take for granted that they can defeat the evil wizard, invent the technology that saves the planet, or lead the rebellion against the dystopian regime. Because of course they can do these things— their stories will have been telling them so for all of their lives. This is the world of children's literature that we must create.[36]

Conclusion

A Manifesto for Anti-Racist Children's Literature

To dismantle our children's literature apartheid, we must change the ways we produce, promote, read, and teach literature for young people. As Ralph Ellison once observed, "while fiction is but a form of symbolic action, a mere game of 'as if,' therein lies its true function and its potential for effecting change. For at its most serious, just as true of politics at its best, it is a thrust toward a human ideal." To move closer to that ideal, we must recognize that We Need Diverse Books and Black Lives Matter are not just slogans. They are directives. Buy Diverse Books. Teach Diverse Books. Fight White supremacy in all forms, but especially in children's literature. What we read when we are young shapes us deeply because, when we are children, we are still very much in the process of becoming. That is why children's literature is one of the most important arenas in which to combat prejudice.[1]

About one-third of the suggestions that follow are explicitly directed toward Whites. There are two reasons for this. First, as the major beneficiaries of White supremacy, Whites have the strongest moral obligation to end it. Too many Whites leave the job of fighting racial inequality to non-White people. Whites cannot both benefit from an unjust system and deny any responsibility for that system: We may not have personally created racism, but if we reap rewards from it, then we are implicated in it. The second reason is power: a White-dominated children's book-publishing industry will be harder to change if people within that industry fail to address its systemic racism. However, in following these explicitly "White people" suggestions, Whites must never speak *for* people of color, nor assume that we know all the answers. We do not. We must listen to people and communities of color, and do our part in opposing racism.

1. **Recognize that personal racism is often unconscious, and that systemic racism is typically invisible.** In 1942, Dr. Seuss drew a cartoon that he called "What This Country Needs Is a Good Mental Insecticide" (fig. C.1). In it, a line of men stretches from the vanishing point up to the front of the frame, where the man in front is getting inoculated. At his left stands Uncle Sam, holding what looks like a giant Flit gun (Seuss was then famous for ads promoting Flit bug spray). Its spray goes in the one ear, while out of the other ear a "racial prejudice bug" emerges in a cloud of insecticide. The cartoon suggests that, with his head fumigated, racism will no longer afflict this man. While I admire the optimism of Seuss's metaphor and his activist aims, racism is more like cancer than an easily removable pest. Indeed, at the very time that Seuss drew this cartoon, he was creating other cartoons that stereotyped people of Japanese descent—inadvertently revealing his own confusion about how racism actually works. It is difficult to exterminate because it is systemic. Racism is what Raymond Williams would have called "a structure of feeling."[2]

In *Marxism and Literature* (1977), Williams describes structures of feeling as "meanings and values as they are actively lived and felt" and suggests that an "alternative definition would be structures of experience":

We are talking about characteristic elements of impulse, restraint, and tone; specifically affective elements of consciousness and

What This Country Needs Is a Good Mental Insecticide

Figure C.1. Dr. Seuss, "What This Country Needs Is a Good Mental Insecticide." *PM*, June 10, 1942.

relationships: not feeling against thought, but thought as felt and feeling as thought: practical consciousness of a present kind, in a living and interrelating continuity. We are then defining these elements as a "structure": as a set, with specific, internal relations, at once interlocking and in tension.

He is not specifically talking about racism here, but his idea illuminates how unconscious but deeply held beliefs structure consciousness, emotional responses, and our daily interactions with other people. There is a "lived and felt" component to racialized thought, which affectively interweaves racism throughout a person's experience of the world.[3]

In any area of life where emotions inform behavior, racial structures of feeling play a role. When evaluating books for young readers, these areas include judgments of whether a character is sympathetic (or not), a novel is believable (or not), a book has aesthetic merit (or not), a manuscript is marketable (or not). If you are a creative writer or teacher of creative writing, read Junot Díaz's "MFA vs. POC," in which he describes the challenges and deep unhappiness of being "a person of color in a workshop whose theory of reality did not include my most fundamental experiences as a person of color—that did not in other words include *me*." Irrespective of your role or your race, be aware of how racial and racist structures may guide your decision-making process. Ask yourself: how much of this judgment is purely *felt*? If you are White, how do your non-White friends or colleagues respond to the same work? Note: I am not suggesting that you *ask* your non-White friends and colleagues. Becoming less racist is *your* responsibility, not theirs. Instead, I am suggesting that you listen.[4]

2. Listen. Trust others' experiences. Too often, people regard with skepticism or simply reject claims that their own lives cannot verify. If you are a White editor, agent, or reviewer, and you find a book by a writer or artist of color to be "unrealistic," then pause and ask yourself *why*. Is it because the work omits a key piece of information, or does the perceived omission tell you more about your own different experience?

3. Diversify your media. In our fragmented age of social media, websites, and TV channels, it is easy to see primarily those sources that affirm your experience of the world. Read some of the ones that either refuse this affirmation, or that simply do not imagine you as their target audience. And remember that learning requires listening. While writing this book (and since then), I have spent a lot of time on Black Twitter. Though I did (and do) interact with some people, I devoted (and devote) most of my time to listening—reading others' tweets, following links, compiling read-ing lists, and taking notes.

4. Do not just "teach tolerance"; actually respect differ-ence. As Karen Fields and Barbara Fields write, the word *tolerance* is a well-meaning misnomer. The "curricular fad for 'teaching toler-ance,'" they write, underscores the word's

> anti-democratic implications. A teacher identifies for the chil-dren's benefit characteristics (ancestry, appearance, sexual ori-entation, and the like) that count as disqualifications from full and equal membership in human society. These, the children learn, they may overlook, in an act of generous condescension—or refuse to overlook, in an act of ungenerous condescension. Tolerance thus bases equal rights on benevolent patronization rather than democratic first principles.

The widespread acceptance of "tolerance" rhetoric exemplifies the harmful effects of good intentions. As the Fieldses write, tolerance's "shallowness as a moral or ethical precept is plain ('Tolerate thy neighbor as thyself' is not quite what Jesus said . . .)." Instead of "tolerating" difference, we must respect difference by, first, acknowledging that it is real. As Christopher Myers says, "The narrative 'we are all the same underneath' is a fear of differ-ence." Second, rather than insisting on narratives of similarity that obscure significantly different life experiences, we should instead recognize that we have difference in common. Our differences are interesting: we can learn from each other, if we listen to and respect different experiences.[5]

5. Be aware of the limits of empathy. As Leslie Jamison asks, "How do I inhabit someone's pain without inhabiting their particu-lar understanding of that pain?" The answer to this great question is that it is frequently impossible. For example, White people's well-meaning attempts to feel non-White people's pain not only often falls short, but can actually be harmful. As Naomi Murakawa says, "wanting to imagine that you can feel Black pain . . . is itself almost always an exercise in violence and privilege." Since she is addressing the US prison system, she instead invites people to consider how it feels to live in a country "that has built an elaborate system of cages . . . [for] Black people. . . . What does it feel like to be on the side of that where I pay taxes for that, and the defense happens mostly in my name?" She suggests that if you can feel

> yourself as someone who is inflicting massive pain, then that can become your barometer for where we are. My barometer for where I am is not how I imagine black criminality. My barometer for where we are is: How complicitous am I for this massive amount of systemized, enforced extraction of pain and death?

Comparably, in the field of children's literature, educators, publishers, and consumers must do more than just sympathize with historically and currently underrepresented groups. Instead, people need to ask: How is *my* action or inaction creating pain? How am *I* responsible? What can *I* do? If you are a teacher, do you have just a token Latino/a novel on your syllabus, or many Latino/a novels? If you are a publisher, are all of your African American children's books realism, historical fiction, nonfiction, memoir, and poetry? Or do you also publish Black dystopian novels, science fiction, and fantasy?[6]

6. Listen for racecraft, Karen Fields and Barbara Fields' term for a linguistic sleight of hand that conceals racial assumptions. For instance, "racial profiling" should more accurately be called "racist profiling" because, in the former term, the "victim's intangible race, rather than the perpetrator's tangible racism, becomes the center of attention." In other words, the act of suspecting, investigating, or harassing another person based on his or her race is not merely racial; it is racist. "Racial" conceals the racism inherent in this practice. If you listen for it, common phrases often hide racial ideologies. For instance, in this very book, I have used "people of color," "authors of color," "children of color," and similar phrases because these are currently accepted terms for non-White people. But notice the magic trick that these words perform: they efface race from White people (suggesting that, somehow, White is not a color). Though I intend these phrases to be racially inclusive, they locate White people outside of race. Similarly, "diverse books" offers a useful shorthand for an underrepresented literary constituency, but it also functions in a parallel way to "people of color." As Anna Holmes points out, the word "diversity" positions "one group (white, male Americans) as the default, and everyone else as the Other." In identifying only texts by non-Whites as "diverse books," the term inadvertently equates "books" with "books by Whites." Racecraft permeates the language so thoroughly that it is hard to avoid; this is why we need to listen for it, examine it, and question it.[7]

7. **Mark Whiteness.** Part of what gives Whiteness its ideological power is that it is unmarked. If, while reading, we encounter a character whose race is not named, *Whiteness* is automatically assumed. However, we can take away Whiteness's unmarked power by naming it. If you are a writer who only assigns race and ethnicity to non-White characters, then change that. If you are willing to identify a Native American third-grader or a Black teacher, then you should also identify the White football coach, bus driver, and guidance counselor.

In 2015, *Kirkus Reviews* began adopting this approach. Explaining the decision to name Whiteness, *Kirkus* editor Vicky Smith wrote that failing to do so makes all non-White readers "others": "Readers who are not of a book's default identity are at least temporarily forced into what W. E. B. Du Bois called double-consciousness: 'this sense of always looking at one's self through the eyes of others.'" So, Smith concluded, "to reflect the fact that large swathes of the audience of the books that we are reviewing are not white—and that not all of our own readers are white—in the fall of 2015, we started naming white characters as well as characters of color when describing humans." More reviewers should commit to making Whiteness visible. Rather than assuming that a non-raced character is White, readers must learn to withhold that assumption until they encounter evidence. Removing the ideological invisibility cloak from Whiteness offers a direct challenge to one of the more subtle forms of White supremacy.[8]

8. **Recognize that White supremacy infects all minds, not just White people's.** In White people, White supremacy produces prejudice. In non-White people, it produces self-hatred, self-doubt, and pain. It is impossible to grow up in a racist culture and not have these ideas infiltrate your thinking. This is why people are often not aware of the racist assumptions that have found refuge in their thought processes, and why they often bristle at the suggestion that they or their work somehow reinforces racist ideas. So, if someone suggests that your work reinforces racial stereotypes, open your mind to the possibility that such a critique may have merit. Of course, the claim may also lack merit, but many of us unconsciously harbor beliefs and assumptions of which we are not fully aware.

9. **Be aware of White fragility, but not deferential to it.** When confronted with what Robin DiAngelo calls White fragility, people of all races will likely find their patience taxed. In discussions about race and racism, White fragility tends to produce

(in White people) defensiveness, claims of victimization, and allegations of unfair treatment. Laying out the facts calmly and in as straightforward a fashion as you can will not convince all fragile White people. It is worth the attempt, but it is also worth remembering that it is not *your* job to correct others' false assumptions. If you want to try, keep in mind that these people are frightened, unaccustomed not only to being challenged on their own privilege, but also to thinking about race *at all*. This is one reason why White people are reluctant to face the possibility that their beloved childhood books, films, and toys propagate racist fantasies. Lacking experience in thinking about race, they bristle at the suggestion that their cherished memories, or works from which they derive personal meaning, may reinforce structural racism.

In case this is not obvious, White people—especially those afflicted with White fragility—should get over themselves. Listen to people whose experiences differ from your own. Listen with humility and thoughtfulness. Remember that, in America, people of color face racism nearly every day. So, White people, if you think someone is overly sensitive about race or weighing race too heavily in her analysis, then ask yourself: how would I feel if I faced racism daily?

10. **Know that being nice and being racist are not mutually exclusive.** This fact baffles people who assume that only mean people are racist, or that only evil people harbor White supremacist intentions. The kindest, most well-intentioned agents, authors, artists, editors, reviewers, and critics—of any race or ethnicity—may yet act in ways that uphold racist structures of power. My awareness of this fact has been one of the biggest challenges of writing this book. As a White scholar (who, via the unearned privileges conferred by Whiteness, has never had racism directed at me), I have been acutely aware of and concerned about the potential for my

analyses to reinforce what they seek to challenge. Indeed, I would not be surprised if reviews of this book discovered flaws that my racialized experience prevented me from seeing. That said, I also hope reviewers will call me out on these issues or other ones.

11. **Don't just be an ally. Be an accomplice.** I borrow this distinction from the anonymously authored essay, "Accomplices Not Allies: Abolishing the Ally Industrial Complex," which points out that "the risks of an ally who provides support or solidarity (usually on a temporary basis) in a fight are much different than that of an accomplice. When we fight back or forward, together, becoming complicit in a struggle towards liberation, we are accomplices." So, to promote the production of diverse books for young people, teachers need to do more than just assign the occasional book by a non-White author, and publishers need to do more than simply sustain the status quo of publishing multicultural literatures in a few select genres. They need to join the movement. They need to be willing to embrace discomfort. As the essay notes, "Accomplices aren't afraid to engage in uncomfortable/unsettling/challenging debates or discussions."[9]

The essay also advises, "Be suspect of anyone and any organization who professes allyship, decolonization work, and/or wears their relationships with Indigenous Peoples as a badge." I would expand this warning to *any* person who is not a member of the group for which she or he purports to advocate. I aspire to be an ally, but I would never call myself an ally. A member of a dominant group cannot confer allyhood on himself or herself. Nor, of course, does the power to designate allyhood reside in any one member of a group facing institutional oppression. However, that individual has a better ability to evaluate allyhood than I do. As Robin DiAngelo aptly puts it, "I don't call myself an 'anti-racist white' because I believe that it is for people of color to decide if, in any given moment, I am behaving in anti-racist ways." Exactly. A straight, White man like me does not get to call himself an ally. But all of us can and should try to be allies. How? Be an advocate. Speak up. Amplify the voices of the marginalized. In other words, being an ally all comes down to the work itself.[10]

12. **White people: recognize your complicity in White supremacy and use your privilege to fight it.** To quote DiAngelo again, "White racism is ultimately a white problem and the burden for interrupting it belongs to white people." Precisely. All White people need to acknowledge that you do not have to actively support White supremacy in order to be a beneficiary of White supremacy. *All* White people are beneficiaries of White supremacy, whether we want to be or not. As beneficiaries, we are also unwitting accomplices. Fortunately (though unfairly), our unearned privilege grants us a more receptive audience with those Whites who remain unconvinced. Therefore, we have a moral obligation to use White privilege to undermine White supremacy. As James Baldwin wrote in *The Fire Next Time* (1963), White people "are, in effect, still trapped in a history which they do not understand; and until they understand it, they cannot be released from it." Help them understand.[11]

13. **Do not use history as an alibi: instead, ask who is "they"?** When someone defends a racist book or movie or TV show by explaining to you, "That's how they thought back then," ask them: Who is this *they*? Is *they* all people everywhere? All White people? What about non-White people? At all times in all places, all people did *not* think alike. Claiming that they did offers an apparently benign excuse for past crimes against humanity. The "they thought" line naturalizes racism as inevitable. But racism is not inevitable. As Robin Bernstein notes, "in the United States, the range of racial beliefs has changed relatively little from the nineteenth century to the present." The "array of thinkable thoughts" has not changed, but

the proportion of people who think these thoughts has. In the past and in the present, both extraordinary and perfectly ordinary people have opposed White supremacy; similarly, both remarkable and unremarkable people have supported White supremacy.[12]

Yes, it is certainly much *harder* to find your way toward egalitarian beliefs in a White supremacist police state. But it is not impossible. Implying its impossibility (as Bernstein persuasively argues) posits that progressive change is inevitable. But it is not inevitable. Social change is not an endless march of progress toward a more enlightened present. It moves in fits and starts, makes gains and suffers setbacks, advances unevenly and sometimes retreats. The fight for equal rights, equal access, and equal representation always requires committed people fighting to make a positive difference.

14. Be a resistant, skeptical reader—and encourage others to read critically, too. Nathalie Wooldridge offers this useful set of eight questions to ask of any text:

- What (or whose) view of the world, or kinds of behaviors, are presented as normal by the text?
- Why is the text written that way? How else could it have been written?
- What assumptions does the text make about age, gender, [class, race, sexuality,] and culture (including the age, gender, [class, race, sexuality,] and culture of its readers)?
- Who is silenced/heard here?
- Whose interests might best be served by the text?
- What ideological positions can you identify?
- What are the possible readings of this situation/event/character? How did you get to that reading?
- What moral or political position does a reading support? How do particular cultural and social contexts make particular

readings available (e.g., who could you not say that to)? How might it be challenged?

These questions can easily be adapted for different genres and media, substituting (for instance) "images" for "text," asking about the relationship between words and images in a picture book or graphic novel, considering the camera angle in a film, and so on.[13]

15. Buy diverse books. Make the commitment to *buy* works by authors of color. Give diverse books to the young people in your life. To make it easier for you, Zetta Elliott created *The Birthday Party Pledge* <http://birthdaypartypledge.com/>, with suggestions of books to give. Remember: children of *all* races need books featuring characters of color. All children also need books that address the daily injustices that racism imposes upon young people of color. If your children, nephews, nieces, or young friends are White, give them diverse books, too.

16. Teach diverse books. I do not know any teacher of children's or young adult literature who assembles an all-White syllabus or an all-White classroom library. However, I do know that many of us (and I include myself here) could do better. Recall (in chapter 3) Chimamanda Ngozi Adichie's warning against the "danger of a single story." When we teach just *one* story by an African American author (or Nigerian author, in the case of Adichie), we risk making it "the definitive story" of that group. When only *one* of the required texts on the syllabus was written by a Latina or Latino author, it becomes the token Latino/a book. So we need to diversify what we teach *within* any given group, too.

Check your classroom and school libraries (if you teach younger students); check your syllabus (if you teach older students). Who is represented in the books, on the covers, and in the illustrations? How do these books represent non-White people? How many books represent non-White people? In your libraries, which racial groups have the widest array of representations? For example, are people of color restricted to only certain genres? How might you diversify your collection?[14]

17. **Publish diverse books.** As I noted at the start of this book, the modern movement to change the "All-White World of Children's Literature" started a half century ago. While we have made progress since then, progress is not the same as justice. The annual percentage of books featuring non-White characters is still only around 15 percent, even though 50 percent of school-age children in the United States are non-White. This gap measures both how far we have come, and how far we have yet to go (fig. C.2). Fifty years ago, Larrick concluded her article with these words: "White supremacy in children's literature will be abolished when authors, editors, publishers, and booksellers decide that they need not submit to bigots." Today, that bigotry persists in more subtle forms—disguised as color-blindness, or as genre, or as marketability.[15]

Consciousness-raising among editors, agents, and others in the publishing industry is a start. But it is not enough. The publishing industry is between 79 percent and 89 percent White. To create systemic change, the industry needs to commit to hiring non-White editors, commissioning editors, marketing people, designers, publicity people, distributors. As Ken Chen, poet and director of the Asian American Writers Workshop, observes,

> Your ability to imagine that there is a market has to do with your ability to imagine that those people exist. And if [you] can't imagine that people of color actually exist and can buy books, then you can't imagine selling books to them. That's not just about a company corporate diversity policy; it's about actually knowing what's going on in communities of color.

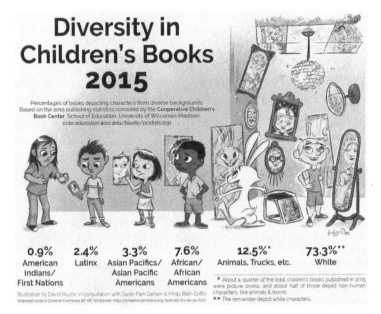

Figure C.2. David Huyck, in consultation with Sarah Park Dahlen and Molly Beth Griffin, "Diversity in Children's Books 2015."

Journals that review literature for young people also need to recruit reviewers of color—not just to read books by or about non-White people, but to read *all* types of literature.[16]

To address this systemic problem, Jason Low (of Lee & Low Books) suggests that publishers establish internship programs that specifically recruit candidates of color. They should be fully *paid* internships because unpaid ones discriminate against qualified candidates who cannot afford to work for free. As Low says, the reason for establishing such programs is that many people who work in publishing did internships there first. The failure to establish these internships leads to what Low calls "the pipeline problem": not enough diverse applicants seeking jobs in publishing. In other words, to change the system, we need to approach it systematically—with policies designed to increase diversity. Otherwise, little will change.[17]

The three major summer publishing institutes—Columbia Publishing Course, Denver Publishing Institute, New York University Summer Publishing Institute—need to be more accessible to applicants of color. Though these are main routes for people to enter the publishing industry, all three programs are very expensive (ranging from $6,000 to $8,000), and cannot be covered by federal loans. They should be eligible for federal loans, or, better, the programs should underwrite the costs for applicants of color. Making these cheaper would also help address the pipeline problem. So would publishers' willingness to hire people from other publishing institutes—such as CUNY's.[18]

While a more diverse workforce is an excellent start, publishers also need to recognize the ways in which White supremacy might impair non-Whites' judgment as well. Everyone in the business needs to undergo education in how racism works, what racist tropes are, and how they can stop promoting them in the books they publish. As the poet and editor Camille Rankine observes,

> I've found that if you want to work toward creating an inclusive literary culture, it's not enough to just be a person of color and let the rest fall into place. I grew up in a society that values white lives, white work, white ideas, and white stories above all others—a culture in which white is the norm and everything else is an aberration. So I'm not immune to the kind of biases that produces. But I've done the work it takes to recognize that, to acknowledge that I read through that lens, and to question the values I've internalized. It's not magic. And it's not a given, just because I'm a person of color.

A case in point: In January 2016, Scholastic published *A Birthday Cake for George Washington*, which perpetuates the myth of the happy slave via its portrayal of Hercules, Washington's enslaved head chef—who in actuality escaped *on* Washington's birthday. The book, which (in response to widespread criticism) Scholastic withdrew, is a symptom of racism's resilience, and not of any conscious malice from its creators. The cheerful slave is a durable trope in children's literature in particular, and in American culture more generally. The book's author, artist, and editor strove to include people who have been erased from American history's narratives: we know much about the first US president, but little about the human beings he owned. Its editor, Andrea Davis Pinkney, defended the book for precisely this reason: "the role African Americans played in celebrating the president's birthday is often not acknowledged, due to the fact that Hercules and his cake are not well known by many." Explaining her choice to portray the enslaved kitchen workers as joyful, Vanessa Brantley-Newton, the book's artist, says in an Artist's Note: "While slavery in America was a vast injustice, my research indicates that Hercules and the other servants in George Washington's kitchen took great pride in their ability to cook for a man of such stature. That is why I depicted them as happy people." That the book's African American artist and editor are both creators of picture books *about the civil rights movement* signals—to me—both a lack of racist intent and the normalization of White supremacy in American culture. For this reason, publishers of children's books need to go beyond diversifying their workforce and enroll their employees (new and old) in a Brief History of Racism in Children's Publishing.[19]

Publishers need to respond to the needs of a population that is growing more racially diverse, not just because this is the right thing to do, but because failing to respond risks engineering their own irrelevance. If statisticians are correct, by 2043 the US population will be majority non-White. While this claim masks the fact that non-Whiteness encompasses a wide range of identity categories and that race itself is hardly a stable category, the demographic trend does highlight the declining White population and the importance of reaching the increasing percentages of multiracial Americans, Asian Americans, and Latino/as. If, deterred by books that ignore or stereotype them, these children learn to read in lesser numbers or come to understand that reading is not for them, then they are less likely to grow into adults who read and buy books. Rather than discover, in twenty-six years' time, that a more racially diverse adult population is less interested in reading, book publishers need, right now, to create the diverse children's books that nurture the reading habits of future adults.

18. Support a US Anti-Racist Education Act because racism is a national emergency that threatens our democracy. As Donald Trump's 2016 presidential election has made plain, pandering to racists can propel a sociopathic con artist to the presidency. His openly bigoted speeches and the 46 percent of voters who supported him have made racist ideas mainstream again, and have led other countries to worry about the stability of the United States. Since his election, hate crimes have been on the rise. Trump's White House has included White supremacist Steve Bannon (former chairman of *Breitbart News*, a racist, misogynist, xenophobic "news" outlet) as senior advisor; White supremacist Jeff Sessions as Attorney General, and Islamophobe Michael Flynn as National Security Advisor. Trump's admiration for Vladimir Putin and disinterest in maintaining the NATO alliance could destabilize Europe, itself facing the rise of comparably dangerous nativist figures—from the forces behind Brexit (Nigel Farage, Boris Johnson), to Marine Le Pen in France, Geert Wilders in the Netherlands, Timo Soini in Finland, and Viktor Orban in Hungary. The spread of racist political parties, to say nothing of the many other dangers humanity faces, amplifies the danger of elevating to power a thin-skinned demagogue who flirts openly with using America's nuclear arsenal, and who sought to expand access to nuclear weapons abroad. Within the United States, President Trump will be able to loosen restrictions on gun purchases, and appoint justices to the Supreme Court who would overturn *Roe v. Wade*, revoke gays' recently won right to marry, and roll back civil rights for people of color. He can ban Muslims from entering the country, and advise the Justice Department to harass those groups and organizations he deems threatening.[20]

Trump's presidency, his supporters, and the racist violence they enable all demand a response—an Anti-Racist Education Act. While this is obviously not something a Trump administration would consent to, it is something his successor could pursue. There is a precedent for such an initiative. Following the Soviet Union's successful launch of the first space satellite (Sputnik) in 1957, the US government responded with the National Defense Education Act (1958), intended to improve postsecondary education so that America could compete with Soviet technology. A federal program along the lines of the National Defense Education Act, but devoted to fighting racism at all levels of education, would strengthen our democracy and provide an example to others working to stop the international racist right. By underwriting the purchase of diverse children's books and anti-racism education, a national anti-racist program would be patriotic, affirming America's commitment to its ideals, helping children resist the Trump Effect, and decreasing the likelihood that the next generation will need to cope with its revival. As Paula Young Lee puts it, "Even as far-right populism continues its global rise, the written word has become vibrant with danger precisely because it has the potential to challenge the mono-think tendencies of hyper-partisanship and authoritarianism."[21]

19. Get organized. Fifty years ago, the Council on Interracial Books for Children, co-founded by Nancy Larrick, led the fight for diverse books. In 2014, Ellen Oh, Malinda Lo, and Aisha Saeed launched the We Need Diverse Books campaign. Join them, and the others fighting for more inclusive reading for young people.

Here are eleven resources to get you started:

- **Black Lives Matter** <http://blacklivesmatter.com/>. To better understand what is at stake in the fight for diverse books, take a look at the work of the most prominent force in the new civil rights movement. Co-founded by Alicia Garza, Patrisse Cullors, and Opal Tometi, the loosely structured group seeks "Freedom and justice for all black lives." On Twitter, follow activists DeRay Mckesson <https://twitter.com/deray> and Netta Elzie <https://twitter.com/Nettaaaaaaaa>, co-editors of *This Is the Movement* and leaders in the Black Lives Matter movement.

- **Diversity in YA** <http://www.diversityinya.com/>, edited by Malinda Lo and Cindy Pon. Instead of writing reviews, contributors to *Diversity in YA* compile diverse books lists, offer "guest posts from authors about their books and writing process," analyze "data about diversity in YA literature," and interview "authors and those in the business of publishing diverse books."

- **EMIERT** <http://www.ala.org/emiert/>, the Ethnic and Multicultural Information Exchange Round Table of the American Library Association. Founded in the early 1980s, EMIERT recommends "ethnic collections, services, and programs," educates librarians about meeting the needs of ethnically diverse communities, and sponsors awards.

- **Lee & Low Books** have many diversity initiatives, including the Diversity Baseline Survey <https://www.leeandlow.com/about-us/the-diversity-baseline-survey> for publishers, its Diversity Gap Studies <https://www.leeandlow.com/educators/diversity-gap-studies>, and many blog posts <http://blog.leeandlow.com/> on diversity, race, and representation.

- **NAME** <http://nameorg.org/>, the National Association for Multicultural Education. Founded in 1990, NAME is a non-profit organization, some 1500 members strong, that "advances and advocates for equity and social justice through multicultural education." To get started, take a look at its page of Resources.

- **Racebending** <http://www.racebending.com/> is "an international grassroots organization of media consumers that advocates for underrepresented groups in entertainment media." It focuses more on film adaptations, but its efforts and analysis are applicable to print culture, especially to the practice of whitewashing book covers.

- **Reading while White** <http://readingwhilewhite.blogspot.com/>: "Allies for Racial Diversity & Inclusion in Books for Children and Teens," this group of White librarians pledges to "hold ourselves responsible for understanding how our whiteness impacts our perspectives and our behavior." They publish thoughtful essays and book reviews, and offer useful resources. As they say, "As White people, we have the responsibility to change the balance of White privilege."

- **Rich in Color** <http://richincolor.com/>—edited by Audrey Gonzalez, Crystal Brunelle, K. Imani Tennyson, and Jessica Yang—is "dedicated to reading, reviewing, talking about, and otherwise promoting young adult fiction starring people of color or written by people of color." Its primary areas of focus are reviews and announcements of new releases (via the blog and via a "Release Calendar"), but it also offers discussions about select titles, and interviews with authors.

- **Teaching for Change** <http://www.teachingforchange.org/>, founded in 1990, is dedicated to using education to promote social justice. As its website explains, it "provides teachers and parents with the tools to create schools where students learn to read, write and change the world." The organization offers an anti-bias curriculum, resources for teaching about the US civil rights movement, recommended books, and ways for parents to get involved.

- **We Need Diverse Books** <http://weneeddiversebooks.org/> is Oh, Lo, and Saeed's "grassroots organization of children's book lovers that advocates essential changes in the publishing industry to produce and promote literature that reflects and honors the lives of all young people." It includes resources for writers (including advice, awards, and grants) and readers (on where to find diverse books), and opportunities for you to get involved. So. Get involved!

- **Zinn Education Project** <https://zinnedproject.org/>, named for the educator Howard Zinn, offers a "people's history," a counter-narrative to dominant understandings of American history. If you're a teacher, and your textbook elides or effaces (for example) the Tulsa Race Riot of 1921 or the Black Panther Party's fight for social justice, you can fill in those omissions via the Zinn Education Project's resources. The site includes teaching materials on a range of subjects, helping students of all ages think critically about US history.

As we enter a period of backlash against equal rights, I still believe that children's literature and culture are among the best places to imagine a better future. Books tell children they belong (or don't belong) not only to a broader community of readers, but also in their neighborhoods, their schools, and their country. Apps and eBooks also tell children who matters enough to be represented, and who does not. Popular films, too, challenge stereotypes, or reinforce them, or do a bit of both. All culture tells us who is deserving of our care, and who is not. Via diverse books and their advocates, we can—and must—nurture a new generation that is less susceptible to bigotry and the many wounds it inflicts.

Afterword

*Why Adults Refuse to Admit Racist Content
in the Children's Books They Love*

I wrote this book in the hope that a close look at the insidious, sometimes subtle way that racism permeates children's literature might be useful to educators, parents, and creators of books for young people. I also hoped the book might help persuade the heretofore unpersuaded—those adults who think that the problem of racism in children's literature has been solved, or who believe that what we read in childhood has little influence on our adult responses to race and racism. In the year since the book's initial publication, many reviews, comments, and personal communications indicate that the book is at least partly achieving this goal.

However, I'm more interested in those who remain resistant or even hostile to the ideas presented here. Examining their responses helps develop a more nuanced taxonomy of "white fragility"—Robin DiAngelo's useful term for Whites' tendency, in conversations about race, to display "anger, fear, ... guilt," and defensiveness. An emotionally resonant site of racial formation, children's literature is the ideal site for developing a more detailed map of why Whites resist reflecting on racism's cultural legacy. By improving our understanding of that resistance, such a map can help us better educate others. So, I'm devoting this afterword to sketching that map of (mostly)

White hostility to authentic racial engagement, drawing on some of the thousands of reviews and critiques of the hardcover edition of this book. Those responses come from social media, personal email, reviews on Amazon, comments on my "Talks at Google" YouTube video, and on media stories of three kinds: (1) the book itself; (2) Cambridge Massachusetts school librarian Liz Phipps Soeiro, who cited the book in her rejection of a gift of Dr. Seuss books from Melania Trump (Soeiro was protesting the Trump administration's education policies); and (3) the decision of children's-book creators Lisa Yee, Mike Curato, and Mo Willems *not* to appear at the Seuss Museum in protest of its reproduction (in the museum entrance) of the racist "Chinaman" caricature from Seuss's *And to Think That I Saw It on Mulberry Street*. (Though this book has five other chapters, the title chapter—its sole chapter devoted to Seuss—received the most attention.)[1]

In considering these responses, I draw inspiration and parallels from the fifth chapter of Gloria Wekker's *White Innocence: Paradoxes of Colonialism and Race* (2016), which reads the 1,500 emails protesting a 2008 Van Abbemuseum of Modern Art exhibit that "critically interrogated the phenomenon of Zwarte Piet"—Black Pete, the racist caricature in Dutch lore who assists Sinterklaas (a.k.a. Santa Claus). Here, then, I've outlined eight strategies of mostly White denial and deflection—many of which intersect with the ten themes identified by Wekker—followed by suggestions on how we might respond to those who resist the reflection and introspection that successful anti-racist education requires.[2]

1. Defending (White) Children's Innocence. The possibility of racism in the work of a beloved children's author is perceived as an attack on innocence itself—which is always inextricably linked to Whiteness. Mirroring defenders of Zwarte Piet, defenders of Seuss's work mobilize (White) children's purported innocence, aligning it with a kind of "natural" anti-racism based in children's alleged inability to see color. According to this logic, children don't see race or racism in the work of Seuss or Dahl because, being children, they simply cannot be aware of racism—ignoring the fact that children as young as three already know what skin color they have and which advantages being White confers. In these defenses, both "innocence" and "children" are imagined as *White*, though never identified as such: the invisibility of Whiteness (to White people) is, as Wekker says, "a white delusion."[3]

2. Speaking About Race Means You Are the Racist. To borrow the words of one commenter, "The only people who are rasist [*sic*] are the only ones using it. Everytime you open your mouths and accuse someone of being rasist [*sic*] ... YOU are the ones who are rasists [*sic*] ... NOT the other way around. You think about that." This claim rests on a belief in "color-blindness"—a well-intentioned lie, propagated in public schools, that is the source of such nonsensical claims as "I don't see race." Though the laudable notion is not to *judge* someone based on her or his race, the effect is the denial of both race and racism.[4]

3. Imagining Racism in Everything. To quote a comment on a *USA Today* article, "Dr. Seuss books and many other innocuous things are only racist in the eyes of those who wear the beer goggles of racism and see racisim [*sic*] in everything." This claim conveys an obliviousness to the fact that racism is structural and so, yes, racism permeates the society in which we live. Whites often make this claim because White supremacy is not only less visible to its beneficiaries, but also uncomfortable to acknowledge because it upsets Whites' belief in meritocracy, confronting us with the fact that we benefit from the oppression of others. Joseph Barndt's apt term for this phenomenon is "the addictive wall of white privilege."[5]

4. Questioning Expertise About Children's Literature. Many assert that I do not know what I am talking about. Though I have written widely on Seuss, one commenter asked, "Has this dolt of a professor read *The Sneetches* by Dr. Seuss. He should before he made his comments." This response echoes those emails received by Wekker that claimed her genealogy of Zwarte Piet was wrong. (It wasn't.) A corollary is the *A Cat Is a Cat* argument, which rests in the belief that children's literature cannot be studied or children's books are to be taken literally. To claim that "the Cat in the Hat is a cat" is absurd. How many cats walk upright, are of adult human height, wear top hats, carry umbrellas, can juggle, and speak in anapestic verse?[6]

5. Proximity to Blackness, which is a variant on the "my Black friend likes Zwarte Piet" argument catalogued by Wekker. This is the belief that real or imagined proximity to Blackness cleanses a cultural artefact of any racist content. Many commenters cite the fact that, in participating in the National Education Association's Read Across America Day (which uses the Cat in the Hat as its mascot), Barack and Michelle Obama read Dr. Seuss books. Therefore, they conclude, Seuss books consequently could not possibly harbor even the residue of racism. As one "RM" commented, "If Dr. Seuss is tired and racist then why did Obama say 'pretty much everything you need to know is in Dr. Seuss.'"[7]

6. Angry Displays of Racism, Sexism, Transphobia, Etc. Rather than quote hate speech here, let me instead express doubt that this subset of commenters can be persuaded by reasoned argument.

7. The *Othering* of the Critic. The need to other the critic emerges as another strategy of denial, but not in the same way it does for Gloria Wekker. As an Afro-Surinamese Dutch scholar, she faced xenophobia, racism, and sexism directed at her personhood.

It is impossible to mobilize such dehumanization against a straight, cisgendered, White, American-born male. So, commenters found milder ways to *other* me. There were variants on the notion of the out-of-touch academic, performing useless labor. Other critics decided I must be motivated by a desire for publicity, or for financial gain. Some diagnosed me as mentally ill. Several claimed that I clearly had no sense of humor.

Wekker described the experience of reading the Van Abbemuseum emails as "like taking an undiluted dose of poison." Reading my hate mail was not fun, but it was not an attack on my basic humanity in the same way that the Zwarte Piet emails were an attack on Wekker's. The armor of White male, straight, cisgendered privilege shielded me from the worst of it. This armor is a key reason why Whites need to do anti-racist work.[8]

8. Blaming the Left/Political Correctness/Liberals/Democrats for All Social Ills was by far the most popular resistant response. As a comment at *Education Week* said, "This hit piece on The Cat in The Hat appears to have emerged from the dark cult of the radical left." A commenter on an *Atlantic* article asserted that this sort of "Lunatic liberal overreach" led to the election of Donald Trump. Those who cite opposing racism in children's literature as aiding Trump's "election" confuse symptom with cause, but inadvertently highlight the very real connection between childhood nostalgia and racism.[9]

So, how can we respond persuasively? Here are a few strategies.

A. Transform Nostalgia. What Svetlana Boym calls "restorative nostalgia" motivates both supporters of Mr. Trump and those who ask that we not look too closely at beloved children's books like *The Cat in the Hat* or *Charlie and the Chocolate Factory*. As explored in more detail in Chapter 3, restorative nostalgia wishes to revive a true tradition, takes itself seriously, and seeks to construct a vision of a unified, uncomplicated past. It expresses a longing for "an enchanted world with clear borders and values," but, as Boym warns, "Only false memories can be totally recalled."[10]

Restorative nostalgia emerges as a response to feelings of fear or uncertainty. In times of social upheaval, such nostalgic outbreaks become more frequent. Anxiety about perceived disorder or social change can be redirected toward the imaginary balm of this mode of nostalgia.

This is dangerous. Restorative nostalgia—whether for an imaginary era when America was "great" or when childhood was "innocent"—fuels totalitarian thinking.[11]

So, we need to transform restorative nostalgia into reflective nostalgia, which dwells in memory's imperfections, exploring the ambivalence and complexity that restorative nostalgia strives to erase. Children's books and children's culture are the ideal location for this work because nostalgia is *not* a longing for a place, as the term's creator—seventeenth-century Swiss medical student Johaness Hofer—thought it was. Instead, nostalgia is a longing for childhood. In the case of restorative nostalgia, it is a longing for an idealized version of childhood, one that forgets trauma, sadness, and pain. Via this selective amnesia, restorative nostalgia—in Boym's words—projects "personal affective memories onto the larger historical picture" in an attempt to "make sense of the chaotic present."[12]

How to move restorative nostalgia toward reflective nostalgia? To redirect this longing, we must show the damage done by restorative nostalgia. Restorative nostalgia merely relocates the psychic wounds; it does not heal them (because it cannot). As Boym warns us, restorative nostalgia is dangerous because, in confusing the real home with an imagined home, "it can create a phantom homeland, for the sake of which one is ready to die or kill. Unreflective nostalgia can breed monsters." We must show people that deeply felt memories do not authorize indifference toward others, and nor do they remove the need for reflection. We must ask, What would it mean to acknowledge ambivalent emotions? What would it mean to admit that what we loved as children could hurt someone today? What would it mean to acknowledge pain?[13]

B. Listen to the Pain. As James Baldwin wisely observed, "I imagine one of the reasons people cling to their hates so stubbornly is because they sense, once hate is gone, they will be forced to deal with pain." Pain is the key. The force with which commenters blame me, or liberals, or academics, or people of color, or women is a way of locating responsibility for their own pain in other people and avoiding looking inward.[14]

While reading the comments, I was frequently struck by the intensely affective—often angry—nature of people's responses. These are people who *feel* threatened. Considering racist content in beloved works of our youth can be triggering because it *feels* like a personal attack. Why? First, children's books are signposts not just to our childhoods but to the formation of our selves. Examining them closely can feel akin to a violation, because they reside deep at the core of the "me" that each of us have within us. Second, children's books evoke what is both cherished and lost, a combination that, as Walter Benjamin noted in 1929, has the potential to be make us reactionary:

> Whatever one reads or plays during one's childhood is remembered not only as the most beautiful and the best, but often, and quite incorrectly, as unique. And it is completely commonplace to hear adults bemoan the vanishing of toys that they could actually buy in the nearest store. In thinking about *these* objects, everyone becomes a *laudator temporis acti*, a reactionary. (251)

Marinated in affect, the memories evoked by childhood books and toys are more likely to arouse fierce protectiveness than they are to inspire reflection.[15]

Third, beloved children's books imaginatively fulfill the nostalgist's longing to travel back in time. Children's books seem to transport the reader to her or his childhood. I think here of Vladimir Nabokov's description of the strongly nostalgic pull of revisiting favorite children's books. Reading them, he vividly sees his past:

> I see again my schoolroom in Vyra, the blue roses of the wallpaper, the open window. Its reflection fills the oval mirror above the leathern couch where my uncle sits, gloating over a tattered book. A sense of security, of well-being, of summer warmth pervades my memory. That robust reality makes a ghost of the present. The mirror brims with brightness; a bumblebee has entered the room and bumped against the ceiling. Everything is as it should be, nothing will ever change, nobody will die.

Nabokov's tone conveys a self-awareness—a willingness to reflect—that restorative nostalgists typically lack. So, when a critic points out the racism in Dr. Seuss or Roald Dahl or Mark Twain or Lynne Reid Banks, such readers—and especially White readers—can feel that we are ambushing their childhood memories.[16]

C. Admit Nuance. To diminish the feeling of being ambushed, we might use more nuance. One reason for the affective vehemence is that critics read not my book, but the headlines:

> "'Cat in the Hat' racist, professor says—and so is other kids' lit"
> —*Houston Chronicle*, 25 August 2017
> "Is the 'Cat in the Hat' racist? Yes, as well as other kids books"
> —*The Daily Herald* [Everett, Washington], 19 Sept. 2017

"Is 'The Cat in the Hat' Racist?"

—Education Week, 4 Oct. 2017

In Chapter 1 of this book, I say that the Cat in the Hat bears the influence of blackface minstrelsy, as do so many icons of children's culture. But I do not say that the Cat in the Hat is racist. I will say now—and should have said in Chapter 1—that I do think how his body reencodes racist caricature unconsciously prepares imaginations to accept more overt versions of that caricature. The Cat is an unwitting participant in White supremacy, but racism thrives via the unknowing reproduction of its imagery and ideas. Racism is the weed that, disguising itself as a flower, gradually infiltrates—and becomes indistinguishable from—the garden. It then thrives by blending in with the other plants.

Nuanced reading makes everyday racism visible. This type of reading can help people (especially White people) understand structural racism by showing them that, for instance, White supremacist imagery ranges from obviously racist caricature to the far more subtle forms of complicity. Obvious examples include actual blackface, the art of E.W. Kemble, Little Black Sambo, and Seuss's own African island of Yerka. Less obvious examples include the whitened Oompa-Loompas (in the revised edition of Dahl's novel, discussed in Chapter 2), who still happily acquiesce to their own enslavement, and the Cat in the Hat.

If we want to educate the skeptics, the distinction between degrees of complicity is necessary. Headlines that proclaim the racism of the Cat in the Hat reduce a complex question to clickbait, causing people to reject the argument before they've had a chance to consider it. Distinguishing between the terms "racism" and "implicit bias," Jelani Cobb writes, "Implicit bias dissociates racism from overt villainy and, as a consequence, engenders less defensiveness in the dialogue." That makes "implicit bias" and the acknowledgement of nuance useful rhetorical strategies.[17]

To be clear: the above three suggestions are *rhetorical* strategies. Implicit bias is still racism, as are other subtly complicit forms. As Chapter 5 explores in greater detail, structural racism thrives by making itself difficult to document. In offering these suggestions, I am thinking about how to steer others toward the awareness that—I suspect—many who pick up this book may already share.

I realize that exposing and opposing racism in children's books will not swiftly defeat racism in the US or anywhere else. As Lawrence D. Bobo wrote in 2017,

> [R]acism is a deeply, deeply rooted feature of US culture, the fashioning of our most basic institutions, of how we conceive of many, many things including what we regard as sources of truth versus falsehood, ugliness versus beauty, purity versus pollution and debasement (West 1982; Hacking 2006). Undoing and thoroughly uprooting a multilayered, social phenomenon of this reach, complexity, and centrality is a project of genuinely daunting scope and difficulty. It is also, therefore, a project of inescapably extremely *longue duree.* A massively destructive civil war, the deadliest conflict in American history by orders of magnitude, did not undo it. A 10- to 15-year period of intensive civil rights struggle followed by conflict-ridden desegregation and affirmative action efforts have certainly not undone it.

As an authoritarianism rooted in White nationalism gains strength in the US and around the world, it can be difficult to be hopeful that our efforts will lead to a more just future—unless we remember that hope is not simply wishful thinking. Hope is rooted in action, and the most reliable form of that action is joining the struggle. We join that struggle knowing that, though our efforts may not succeed in our lifetimes, we have to try. As Howard Zinn writes, "human history is a history not only of cruelty but also of compassion, sacrifice, courage, kindness." So, he counsels, "If we see only the worst, it destroys our capacity to do something." On the other hand, "if we remember those times and places—and there are so many—where people have behaved magnificently, this gives us the energy to act, and at least the possibility of sending this spinning top of a world in a different direction."[18]

In the past couple of years, I have often thought of what Henry Louis Gates, Jr., said the morning after the 2016 presidential election. Gates "felt like Frederick Douglass must have felt in 1876 after the [Rutherford] Hayes-[Samuel] Tilden compromise ended Reconstruction." The period from the civil rights movement to 2016 was, Gates noted, a "second Reconstruction," and the 2016 "election clearly represented a backlash against the progress black people have made since 1965—epitomized, symbolically, by the election and term of a black man in the White House." I think of this observation because it reminds me that progress is never "won." It has to be continually defended and fought for.[19]

Children's stories are a key front in this struggle because children's stories contribute so powerfully to the formation of the self. As Mr. Trump and his allies work to roll back the social progress of the last fifty years, we have our work cut out for us. But, then, we always have.

— Philip Nel, September 2018

NOTES

Introduction

1. We Need Diverse Books is a registered trademark of the organization We Need Diverse Books. To learn more, visit <http://weneeddiversebooks.org/>.
2. Larrick 63. Since it was so influential, I am using Nancy Larrick's essay as representative of a lot of similar writing from the 1960s and early 1970s. Donnarae MacCann and Gloria Woodard collect other important pieces in *The Black American in Books for Children: Readings in Racism* (1972). For a more complete history, please consult that volume and Dorothy Broderick's book, *Image of the Black in Children's Fiction* (1973).

   Throughout this book, I have capitalized the "B" in "Black" and the "W" in "White" when they refer to races; when they refer to colors, I leave the initial letters in lower case. The US Census capitalizes all racial and ethnic categories, including White. As Lori L. Tharps explains, "When speaking of a culture, ethnicity or group of people, the name should be capitalized. Black with a capital B refers to people of the African diaspora. Lowercase black is simply a color" ("The Case for Black with a Capital B").
3. Walter Dean Myers, "Where Are the People of Color in Children's Books?"; Christopher Myers, "The Apartheid of Children's Literature." As was the case with Larrick's article, the prominence of the Myerses' articles prompted me to use them as the representative example, but *many* people have written on the subject—some (but not all) of whom I cite elsewhere in the book. Though this is in no way a fully inclusive list, two important ones are Laura Atkins, "White Privilege and Children's Publishing: A Web 2.0 Case Study" and Zetta Elliott, "Decolonizing the Imagination." I have collected a selection of many more articles in this blog post: "'The Boundaries of Imagination'; or, the

All-White World of Children's Books, 2014," *Nine Kinds of Pie*: <http://www.philnel.com/2014/03/17/boundaries/>.

4. "Children's Books by and about People of Color Published in the United States," Cooperative Children's Book Center; "Racial/Ethnic Enrollment in Public Schools," *The Condition of Education*. Note: Throughout this manuscript, I follow other scholars of children's literature in using "children's books" and "children's literature" synonymously. I am grateful to a reader of the manuscript for pointing out that—to some people—"children's books" also denotes textbooks. I am not including textbooks in the term "children's books."

5. Bernstein, *Racial Innocence*, 51, 18.

6. Fields and Fields 17; Trump; Alexander 183.

7. As Eduardo Bonilla-Silva writes, "Racial discrimination is not just about jobs and housing. Discrimination affects almost every aspect of the lives of people of color. It affects them in hospitals . . . , restaurants . . . , trying to buy cars . . . or hail a cab . . . , driving . . . or flying, or doing almost anything in America. Indeed, 'living while black [or brown]' is quite hard and affects the health (physical and mental) of people of color tremendously as they seem to always be on a 'fight or flight' mode" (210). Michelle Alexander's excellent *The New Jim Crow: Mass Incarceration in the Age of Colorblindness* (2010) chronicles the use of the penal system to systematically deny voting rights to people of color. Only Vermont and Maine permit inmates to vote; the "vast majority of states withhold the right to vote when prisoners are released on parole" (158) and erect barriers to regaining the right to vote. As she notes, "No other country in the world disenfranchises people who are released from prison in a manner even remotely resembling the United States. In fact, the United Nations Human Rights Committee has charged that US disenfranchisement policies are discriminatory and violate international law" (158). In 2015, the North Miami Beach Police Department was using mug shots for target practice. Though the department alleged that those mug shots represented people of all ages and sexes, the six-person sheet they were caught using had *only* Black men's faces on it (Golgowski, "Family Outraged"; Crockett, "Woman Shocked").

In the Voices of Diversity project's study of microaggressions at US universities, Demonde—the only African American man in his program—recalled a White woman in the same program saying things like "You're a good Black person." He would respond, "What do you mean a good Black person?" She would reply, "Like, you're not really Black." As he says, "I felt bad. I want to be Black. I am Black. Just because I'm here, I'm in college, I speak, I guess, proper." Other students said to him, "You don't talk Black. You're this Black, you're not this Black" (Caplan and Ford, "The Voices of Diversity," 42).

For a much longer list of privileges than those chronicled in this paragraph, see Peggy McIntosh's classic and widely reprinted "White Privilege: Unpacking the Invisible Knapsack" (1988).

For data on the publishing industry, see Jason Low, Sarah Park Dahlen, and Nicole Catlin's "Where Is the Diversity in Publishing? The 2015 Diversity Baseline Survey Results." Their survey finds 79 percent of the industry to be White/Caucasian: 86 percent at the executive level are White/Caucasian, 82 percent of editors are White/Caucasian, 83 percent of sales are White/Caucasian, 77 percent of Marketing and Publicity are White/Caucasian. Even 89 percent of Book Reviewers are White/Caucasian.

8. S. Cohen, *States of Denial*, 4–5. There many facts that we don't dwell on, such as the fact that (as Michelle Alexander notes) even though people of all races use drugs at similar rates, "in some [US] states, black men have been admitted to prison on drug charges at rates twenty to fifty times greater than those of white men" (7). As Alexander says, "the racial bias inherent in the drug war is a major reason that 1 in every 14 black men was behind bars in 2006, compared with 1 in 106 white men" (100). If we do not think about the racially biased US justice system, then we also do not consider its effect on families, that (quoting Alexander again) the "mass incarceration of people of color is a big part of the reason that a black child born today is less likely to be raised by both parents than a black child born during slavery" (180). If we do think about this, then we might wonder why there are not more children's books like Jacqueline Woodson and James E. Ransome's *Visiting Day* (2002).

9. Bonilla-Silva 3, 213, 3.

10. Omi and Winant 70–71.

11. Elliott, "Decolonizing the Imagination"; Adichie, quoted in Emenyonu 11; Laymon, *How to Kill Yourself and Others in America*, 12.

12. Ward, *Men We Reaped*, 192, 185, 187, 195; Thurston 25–26.

13. Bernstein, *Racial Innocence*, 73, 71, 72.

14. Sollors 201.

15. Bernstein, *Racial Innocence*, 159; Pilgrim, "The Golliwog Caricature"; Olson, 73–94.

16. Ingram. In the 1970s, I encountered no Black children in Lynnfield, Massachusetts. I remember people talking about the possibility that Jim Rice—a star player for the Boston Red Sox—and his family were moving to Lynnfield. The unspoken implication was both that a celebrity and that a Black family would be moving to town. I do not know whether the Rice family ever did move to Lynnfield, or whether that was simply gossip.

17. *Walt Disney's Story Land: 55 Favorite Stories Adapted from Walt Disney Films*, 172.

18. C. Myers, "Young Dreamers."

19. Sontag 88. Notably, David Pilgrim, the founder and director of the Jim Crow Museum of Racist Memorabilia, calls the museum "in effect, a black holocaust museum. I mean no disrespect to the millions of Jews and others who died at the hands of the maniacal Adolf Hitler and his followers. I hesitate to use the word *holocaust* to describe the experience of Africans and their American descendants because I do not want to compare victimizations. But what word

should I use? . . . Africans and their American descendants experienced a holo-caust in this country" (*Understanding Jim Crow*, 20).

20. Amsden; "Through the African American Lens: Explore Selections from the Permanent Collection."

21. "Site Index," Cooperative Children's Book Center. CCBC includes "Holocaust" under "World War II (Tell Them We Remember: Selected Books for Children and Teens about the Holocaust and World War II)."

22. This paragraph and the next borrow from and build on my "Obamafiction for Children: Imagining the Forty-Fourth U.S. President," which offers a much more complete discussion of President Obama in children's literature.

23. Bobo and Dawson 4; "U.S. Elections: How Groups Voted in 2012."

24. "E-16. Unemployment Rates by Age, Sex, Race, and Hispanic or Latino Ethnicity [Percent]"; Bonilla-Silva 209, 225; Alexander 248.

25. DiAngelo, "White Fragility," 54, 57.

26. Bradford, *Unsettling Narratives: Postcolonial Readings of Children's Literature*, 2, 3; MacCann xxv.

27. C. Myers, "The Apartheid of Children's Literature"; Elliott, "Decolonizing the Imagination."

28. Connolly 2.

29. For a more thorough look at multicultural children's literature see Donna L. Gilton's *Multicultural and Ethnic Children's Literature in the United States* (2007).

30. The notion that, in American literature, Whiteness depends upon Blackness comes from Toni Morrison's *Playing in the Dark: Whiteness and the Literary Imagination* (1992).

Chapter 1

1. Flesch; Hersey.

2. Morgan and Morgan 153; Silvey; Morgan and Morgan 154.

3. Charles Cohen 325; Seuss, quoted in Nel, *Dr. Seuss: American Icon*, 70.

4. Fishkin 135.

5. Newell; Nel, *Dr. Seuss: American Icon*, 18.

6. "Minstrels Add $300 to Fund for Trip"; Dr. Seuss [as Ted], "Highball Thompson Wins from Kid Sambo by a Shade"; Seuss, "SHE—*Out sportin' again, are yo', nigger? Jest wait 'til I lay hands on yo' tonight!*"; Seuss, "Cross Section of the World's Most Prosperous Department Store." These are but a few representa-tive cartoons. For more, see Seuss's "'Stand aside, woman! I'se on mah way to the three hundred and fifty-second semi-annual conclave and gatherance of the Antiquated Order of Loyal and Diversified True-blue Ravens, of which organism ah am a sixty-seventh degree Mahoot, to say nothing at all of mah exalted and revered position and office as corresponding scribe and *ex post*

facto protector and guardian of the sacred scrolls and parchments!'" (*Judge* Sept. 22, 1928, p. 16; reprinted in C. Cohen 212). Cohen reprints others in chapter 22 ("Shunning His Frumious Brand of Sneetch") of *The Seuss, the Whole Seuss, and Nothing But the Seuss*, 206–215.

7. C. Cohen 212.

8. Seuss, "There seems to be a white man in the woodpile!"; Morgan and Morgan 119.

9. Seuss, ". . . But for Grown-Ups Laughing Isn't Any Fun," 2.

10. Morgan and Morgan 173–174, 151.

11. Seuss, *If I Ran the Zoo*; Seuss, "Africa—Its Social, Religious, and Economical Aspects"; Abate; Wells, quoted in Kenny 153; Barthes 53 (emphasis in original).Wells's blithely racist description of McBruiser and Nightingale is quite breathtaking, especially in its confident presentation of bigotry as scientific fact: "Florence Nightingale, as will readily be seen, is developed in the 'upper story,' while the feminine 'McBruiser,' whom we have placed by her side, lives in the basement mentally as well as bodily. The former would be governed by high moral principles, the latter by the lower or animal passions; the one is a natural friend and philanthropist; the other is at war with everybody; the one is forgiving; the other is vindictive; the one is, by sympathy, attracted toward the heavenly and the good; the other is of the earth, earthy, seeking her chief pleasure from things physical and animal" (537–538). Nightingale "is refined by the culture inherited from generation to generation, as well as by personal education," while McBruiser "is rude, rough, unpolished, ignorant, and brutish" (538).

12. Bernstein, *Racial Innocence*, 18, 19; Lott 18; Seuss, "How Orlo Got His Book," in Nel, *The Annotated Cat*, 167.

13. Lott 15; Mahar 209; Seuss, *The Cat in the Hat*, 18, 21.

14. McCloud 30; Ngai 95, 116; *The Cat in the Hat* (dir. Hawley Pratt, storyboard by Chuck Jones, teleplay by Dr. Seuss); Ngai 125.

15. Seuss, *The Cat in the Hat*, 2.

16. Seuss, *The Cat in the Hat*, 25.

17. Lott 62, 60; Seuss, *The Cat in the Hat*, 8, 31; Nel, *The Annotated Cat*, 60, 62.

18. T. J. Clark, quoted in Lott 51; Seuss, *The Cat in the Hat*, 2, 33; *The Cat in the Hat* (television show); Seuss, *The Cat in the Hat*, 33, 12.

19. Seuss, *If I Ran the Zoo*; Seuss, *On Beyond Zebra!*; Seuss, *If I Ran the Circus*; Seuss, *Scrambled Eggs Super!*

20. Harry S. Miller's "The Cat Came Back" has had many recorded versions (including relatively recent cover versions by Tom Paxton and Garrison Keillor), has often been referenced in political cartoons and newspapers, and has remained popular enough to inspire an animated cartoon in 1988.

21. Lighter 367; Benny Goodman, quoted in Nel, *The Annotated Cat*, 36–37; Seuss, *The Cat in the Hat Songbook*.

22. Ian Lewis Gordon, quoted in Heer 11; Heer 13. For a thorough look at Herriman's bi-racial self and his passing (as White), see Michael Tisserand's meticulously researched *Krazy: George Herriman, a Life in Black and White* (2016).

23. Seuss, "Sorry, sister, but you can't get wholesale baptizin' rates unless you got a minimum of twelve chillun'"; Lott 9.

24. Bernstein, *Racial Innocence*, 51.

25. Coover 40, 39, 43.

26. Katz; *Dr. Seuss, LP vs. Penguin Books.*

27. Spivack and Fields; Chan and Peters; Latuff.

28. Martin, *Brown Gold*, 50. See also Capshaw's *Children's Literature of the Harlem Renaissance* (2004, written as Katharine Capshaw Smith) and *Civil Rights Childhood: Picturing Liberation in African American Photobooks* (2014), Rudine Sims Bishop's *Free Within Ourselves: The Development of African-American Children's Literature* (2004), and Mickenberg's *Learning from the Left: Children's Literature, the Cold War, and Radical Politics in the United States* (2006).

29. Fishkin 135; RUN-DMC; Rogers; Nel, *Dr. Seuss: American Icon*, 169.

30. "Racial Fur Flies" 28; "Of Rabbits & Races" 19.

31. Ellison, "Change the Joke and Slip the Yoke," 48–49, 55, 54.

32. Wolosky 174; Coover 43. In addition to Seuss's cartoon featuring the Uncle Sam bird in the tub, two other Seuss cartoons from the Second World War feature a top-hatted man sitting in a bathtub: a man representing Japan, in "Man who draw his bath too hot, sit down in same velly slow" (*PM*, Sept. 4, 1941, p. 5); and a man representing America First, in "The old family bath tub is plenty safe for me!" (*PM*, May 27, 1941, p. 12).

33. Masten 54 (emphasis in original); Fadiman 282; *Freedom Summer.*

34. Dudziak 118–119.

35. DiAngelo, "White Fragility," 66.

Chapter 2

1. Kidd 200; Morrison 46.

2. On Twain as children's literature, see Beverly Lyon Clark's excellent *Kiddie Lit: The Cultural Construction of Children's Literature.*

3. "That's Not Twain," A26; Turley; Ravitch; Bell.

4. Christopher Lofting, 152–153.

5. Gubar 124; Kohl 16.

6. Bernstein, *Racial Innocence*, 33; Younge; Alexander 118; Gabrielson, Jones, and Sagara.

7. Lester, "Morality and *Adventures of Huckleberry Finn*," 200; Wallace 23.

8. Du Bois 45; Cullen 833; Woodson, *Brown Girl Dreaming*, 82.

9. Costello.

10. Fielder; Sultan; Hughes; Coates, *Between the World and Me*, 71, 9.

11. Omi and Winant 65, 66; Alexander 180.

12. Griswold xii, xiv, xv; Bernstein, "Signposts on the Road Less Taken" 97–98.

13. Gribben, 9–10; Arac 38, 39.

14. Lester, "Morality and *Adventures of Huckleberry Finn*," 201; Rampersad 223; Oehlschlaeger 117.

15. Gribben 13; Hosea Easton, quoted in Kennedy 5; Stowe 592; Arac 29; Kennedy 21. Furthermore, as Jonathan Arac notes, even *after* Huck's crisis of conscience he continues to say the word: "If Huck has such moral insight that he is willing to go to hell for Jim's sake, why does he not find new ways of saying his new sense of the world? Why not stop using a word that is part of the system he is, we suppose, rejecting?" (32).

16. Bonilla-Silva 3–4; Springer xv; Griswold xiii, xiv; Bonilla-Silva 53. Lofting's racism was genteel but real, as evidenced in his Afterword to Annie Vaughan Weaver's *Frawg* (1930), in which he praises racial caricature as realism. Noting that the "pictures she [Vaughan] draws best are pictures of coloured people," Lofting adds: "And not only can she draw pictures of them but she really knows them. She was brought up among them from the time she was born until only a year or two ago. These little stories you have read are living, moving glimpses of the life, the thoughts and the talk of southern children, just as living and moving as your own face laughing in a mirror" (Weaver 127–128). One of the "moving glimpses of . . . life" is about Frawg's excessive love for watermelon. Standing in the watermelon patch, Frawg and his Pa have a conversation that begins like this:

> "Sonny," said Pa as they stood there, "is you EVER had nuff watermillon?"
>
> "Naw sir, Pa," answered Frawg, "I wain't NEVER had nuff watermillon."
>
> "Wal, sonny, terday you sho gwine have ernuff," and Pa began pulling off the biggest ones he could find.
>
> "Frawg, how many millons kin you eat?" asked Pa. (36–37)

Weaver bases this story on a Black child's fondness for watermelons, and creates a Black family who speaks only in ersatz "Negro" dialect. The book's title page features her drawing of Frawg holding a slice of watermelon. In response, Lofting praises her efforts, claiming that Weaver "really knows" Black people, and in fact draws them "best."

17. Travers, "The Art of Fiction LXIII," 220.

18. Gribben 12; Twain, *The Adventures of Huckleberry Finn* (Norton), 125; Twain, *The Adventures of Huckleberry Finn* (NewSouth), 393; Twain, *The Adventures of Huckleberry Finn* (Norton), 168.

19. Gribben 16; Twain, *The Adventures of Huckleberry Finn* (Norton), 64; Twain, *The Adventures of Huckleberry Finn* (NewSouth), 308; Twain, *The Adventures of Huckleberry Finn* (Norton), 179; Arac 72, 71.

20. Lofting, *The Story of Doctor Dolittle* (Dell), 71; Lofting, *The Story of Doctor Dolittle* (Tom Doherty Associates), 47; Lofting, *The Story of Dr. Dolittle* (Dell), 53; Suhl 1.

21. Dahl, *Charlie and the Chocolate Factory* (1973), 73, 75, 73, 73, 76; Cameron, "A Reply to Roald Dahl"; Bradford, "The End of Empire?," 200.

22. Travers, *Mary Poppins* (Harcourt Brace Jovanovich), 92; Travers, *Mary Poppins* (Collins), 103; Travers, *Mary Poppins* (Harcourt Brace), 89.

23. Mack 383.

24. Kohl 5.

25. Lofting, *Doctor Dolittle* (Tom Doherty Associates), 60; Twain, *Huckleberry Finn* (Norton), 72.

26. Travers, *Mary Poppins* (Harcourt Brace Jovanovich), 178, 53, 127.

27. Travers, *Mary Poppins* (Harcourt Brace Jovanovich), 98; Travers, *Mary Poppins* (Harcourt Brace), 97; Travers, handwritten note on front of file folder (Travers Papers); Travers, *Mary Poppins* (Harcourt Brace), 199, 52. Inasmuch as "more Poppinish" may mean "more nonsensical," this logic belies the fact that nonsense is not inherently subversive or oppositional, as many critics often claim: as Celia Catlett Anderson and Marilyn Fain Apseloff write, "The experience of reading nonsense-literature inoculates the child against narrow-mindedness" (99), or, as Susan Stewart writes, "In nonsense, hierarchies of relevance are flattened, inverted, and manipulated in a gesture that questions the idea of hierarchy itself—a gesture that celebrates an arbitrary and impermanent hierarchy" (209). In contrast to these optimistic allegations, *Mary Poppins*—like any work of literature—bears the ideologies of the culture in which it originates.

28. Ngai 1, 8; Fields and Fields 72.

29. Nussbaum 11, 207; Nico Frijda, quoted in Kim 21; Nussbaum 173, 163.

30. Bradford, "The End of Empire?," 216; Dahl, *Charlie and the Chocolate Factory* (Knopf, 1964), 79–82.

31. Dahl, *Charlie and the Chocolate Factory* (Knopf, 1964), 82.

32. Lorde.

33. Ward, *Men We Reaped*, 207.

34. *Iconoclasts, Season 6, Episode 2: Dave Chappelle and Maya Angelou*; Nussbaum, *Upheavals of Thought*, 298–302.

35. Matsuda, Lawrence, Delgado, and Crenshaw 13; Rosoff. Rosoff makes this argument in the context of not lying to children, two years prior to her famous (and curious) claims that, contrary to all evidence, there are plenty of diverse books: "there are not too few books for marginalised young people. There are hundreds of them, thousands of them," she wrote, alleging that "you don't have to read about a queer black boy to read a book about a marginalised child" (quoted in Flood).

36. Martin, *Brown Gold*, 147, 149.

37. Curtis, *Elijah of Buxton*, 164, 100, 98; Julius Lester, *To Be a Slave*, 62.
38. Marilyn Nelson, *The Freedom Business*, 30–31.
39. King and Monkman; Bradford, *Unsettling Narratives*, 29, 27; Tan; Marsden and Tan.
40. National Coalition Against Censorship; Mendlesohn.
41. Davis; Kennedy 63.
42. Arac 17; Lester, *To Be a Slave*, 85; Farai Chideya, quoted in Kennedy 22.

Chapter 3

1. Tedeschi; Machell.
2. Colman.
3. Brunkard, Namulanda, and Ratard 3; Campanella 714; Frost.
4. Rome; "Mary Katherine Joyce."
5. Rome.
6. Hade, "Reading Children's Literature Multiculturally," 119; Hade, "Reading Multiculturally," 249.
7. Hutcheon; Lerner, quoted in Hutcheon; Mason.
8. Boym xviii, 41, 49.
9. Dyer 1; Bernstein, *Racial Innocence*, 8.
10. "Shreveport City: Segregation: Neighborhood Exposure by Race"; "New Orleans City: Segregation: Neighborhood Exposure by Race." Creating characters who are "authentically" Black is a vexed question. As Donna L. Gilton points out, "cultural authenticity is not as straightforward as it appears. While members of cultural groups are usually much more knowledgeable about their own cultures than outsiders, they vary greatly in their general opinions, as well as in how they evaluate a work" (83). Also, "not all group members know or identify with all aspects of their own culture, and some may perpetuate stereotypes of their own" (83). In other words, the artist or author should strike a balance between cultural specificity and individual idiosyncrasies.
11. Adichie; Elliott, "Decolonizing the Imagination."
12. Giroux 309; Dyson 211–212.
13. Rhodes 90; Lamana 68; Dyson 5–6; Woods 63; Philbrick 104–109, 152–154; Tamara Ellis Smith 40. Though Denise Lewis Patrick's *Finding Someplace* (2015) downplays racism's central role in the disaster, it does note structural racism elsewhere, as when Miss Martine Simon asks the protagonist Reesie, "Do you think this country was ready for anybody colored—trying to make a living off words—to be famous? I wrote my heart out. Yes, and got one book published. Never made much money off any of it" (59). By ending eight months after Katrina, Patrick's novel also grants itself space to address survivors' trauma—those "memories that hid in the shadows when [Reesie] tried

to sleep. Those vivid thoughts that hung like bats in the back of her mind during algebra" (131).

14. Don Brown, *Drowned City: Hurricane Katrina and New Orleans*, 8, 11.

15. Ward, *Salvage the Bones*, 227, 227, 232, 237, 251; Jerng.

16. Laymon, *Long Division*, 83.

17. Martin, "Hushpuppy, Hauntings and Hurricanes: Black Girls Braving Storms, Inside and Out"; hooks.

18. Culp 523.

19. Dyer 38.

20. Hateley 11.

21. Delgado 176; DiAngelo, "White Fragility," 54, 60.

22. Morin; Ireland.

23. Metta.

Chapter 4

1. Kinnamon, quoted in Young, " 'Quite as Human as It Is Negro': Subpersons and Textual Property in *Native Son* and *Black Boy*," 80. For a thorough examination of the Book-of-the-Month Club's role in textual revisions to *Native Son*, see Young's full essay in *Publishing Blackness: Textual Constructions of Race since 1850*, edited by Young and George Hutchinson.

   For a parallel but different example, White publishers printed the literature of the Harlem Renaissance, presenting the works in ways that frustrated some authors. Langston Hughes disliked Mexican artist Miguel Covarrubias's cover for his *The Weary Blues* (Hughes's first book, published in 1926), which featured a Black piano player, whose stylized features (prominent lips, thick fingers) echo racial caricature (Danky 356).

2. Le Guin, *A Wizard of Earthsea* (Bantam, 1984), 39.

3. The source for much of this paragraph is Scholastic editor Cheryl Klein's "Black and White and Read All Over: Diversity and Inequity in Children's Publishing," delivered at Kansas State University in 2010, and published on her blog in 2014. There is not an abundance of hard data to support the assumptions of marketing departments, but according to *SIMBA Children's Publishing Market Forecast 2011*, 13 percent of children's book buyers are Hispanic, 8.2 percent are Black, 3.2 are Asian, and 74 percent are White. If these numbers are accurate, then people of color *do* buy fewer books than White people—but, of course, many factors may explain this, including publishing's lack of diverse titles.See also Donna L. Gilton's observations on structural impediments to increasing the numbers of diverse children's books. In her *Multicultural and Ethnic Children's Literature in the United States* (2007), she points to Joel Taxel's diagnosis of "changes in the industry, including the

replacement of independent bookstores with chains and online vendors, the acquisition of small publishers by large multimedia conglomerates, and the replacement of traditional literary-oriented managers with more bottom line-oriented executives from retailing." These changes, she notes, have "led to a shift from an editorial focus to marketing and financial growth strategies and more emphasis on the bottom line than the public good" (90). At the time she wrote that, independents were still on the decline, but, as John B. Thompson's *Merchants of Culture: The Publishing Business in the Twenty-First Century* (2nd ed., 2012) notes, the decline of independents stopped at about that time: "By 2007 there were probably only 400 independent booksellers left that were of real importance for trade publishers in the US. But by this time the decline of the independents appeared to have levelled off, as those that remained had succeeded in finding a strategy that would enable them to survive in the face of intense competition from the chains and other outlets" (33). So chains still outnumber the independents, but the latter are no longer in decline.

4. Elliott, "Stranger than Fiction: Depicting Trauma in African American Picture Books, or One Hot Mess." For more on systemic racism within the publishing industry, see chapter 5 of this book.

5. Milliot, "The PW Publishing Industry Salary Survey 2015: A Younger Workforce, Still Predominantly White"; Low, Dahlen, and Catlin; Neary; Alexander Chee, quoted in Aiello; Jacob.

6. Trenton Lee Stewart 32; Schutte. All examples in this paragraph come from Schutte's article.

7. Le Guin, "Some Assumptions about Fantasy."

8. "Adult Literacy: Literacy by Race/Ethnicity"; Ari.

9. Hurston 118; Beauvais. As Martha Nussbaum writes in her critique of higher education's increasing emphasis on allegedly profitable research and coursework, "the unfettered pursuit of [economic] growth is not conducive to sensitive thinking about distribution or social inequality" (*Not for Profit: Why Democracy Needs the Humanities*, 22).

10. Dolamore 9, 105, 75, 123, 105, 70.

11. Mendelsund 41.

12. Collins 98, 8; Dodai Stewart; Bernstein, *Racial Innocence*, 8; Dodai Stewart; Lipsitz 369. Collins mentions Rue's skin color more than once: she is also described as having "dark skin" (126).

13. Laura Miller.

14. Kaufman and Libby 3.

15. Bruce, "Whitewashing Book Covers: What Do Kids Think? Part I"; Bruce, "Whitewashing Book Covers: A Trip to Barnes & Noble. Part II"; DasGupta.

16. Larbalestier, *Liar*, 74; Larbalestier, "Ain't That a Shame (updated)."

17. Larbalestier, "Ain't That a Shame (updated)."

18. Carson 258, 243, 242.

19. Carson 241, 242, 251, 250, 395–398.
20. Perkins, "Straight Talk on Race: Challenging the Stereotypes in Kids' Books"; Pon 278–279.
21. Pon 167, 167, 171.
22. Larbalestier, *Liar*, 77, 74, 156, 7.
23. Guevara 51; Hamilton, quoted in Bishop xii; Guevara 52.
24. Older, "Do Black Children's Lives Matter if Nobody Writes about Them?"
25. Bruce, "School Librarian Talks to Students about 'Whitewashing' Children's Book Covers."

Chapter 5

1. Agrawal; Rowling, *Harry Potter and the Philosopher's Stone*, 79; Rowling, *Harry Potter and the Prisoner of Azkaban*, 46.
2. Ramaswamy.
3. Milliot, "The PW Publishing Industry Salary Survey 2015: A Younger Workforce, Still Predominantly White"; Low, Dahlen, and Catlin; "Children's Books by and about People of Color." I am using the 2014 CCBC numbers rather than the 2015 numbers because CCBC published a list of the titles for 2014, but not for 2015. However, CCBC's 2015 diversity numbers are comparably disappointing: 15 percent of children's books *about* people of color, and 10 percent of books *by* people of color.
4. Christopher Myers, "Apartheid of Children's Literature"; Zetta Elliott, "Black Authors and Self-Publishing"; Lo; Gregorio.
5. "Children's Books by and about People of Color Published in the United States." The Cooperative Children's Book Center did not list titles for "Asian Pacifics/ Asian Pacific Americans" nor for "Latinos," and it has not listed titles for 2015 in any category.
6. Duyvis; Martin, *Brown Gold*, xviii.
7. Bartle.
8. Fields and Fields 77–78, 84.
9. Young, *Black Writers, White Publishers: Marketplace Politics in Twentieth-Century African American Literature*, 17, 4.
10. Greco, Rodríguez, and Wharton 192; Deahl; "Publishing Certificate Program"; Unger, "A Note from the Director"; Greco, Rodríguez, and Wharton 192; Deahl.
11. Greco, Rodríguez, and Wharton 192, 194; Deahl; Greco, Rodríguez, and Wharton 194; Older, "Diversity Is Not Enough: Race, Power, Publishing"; Greco, Rodríguez, and Wharton 193.
12. Leader-Picone.
13. Alexander 107.

14. Daniel Handler, "Daniel Handler and Watermelon"; Handler, ". . .and not to overshadow their achievements with my own ill-conceived attempts at humor. I clearly failed, and I'm sorry. -DH [2/2]"; Handler, "My remarks on Wednesday night at #NBAwards were monstrously inappropriate and yes, racist. -DH [1/4]."Handler was trafficking in a style of humor sometimes called "hipster racism," in which the White joke-teller satirically invokes a racist trope, presuming that irony will both (a) distance the teller from the racist content and (b) make the remark funny. While it went over well enough at the event, in the world beyond the awards banquet, the joke instead landed as casual racism. As a result, the "watermelon" comment ended up underscoring the invisibility of structural racism to White people in general and to the publishing industry in particular.

15. Woodson, "The Pain of the Watermelon Joke," A17.

16. Devitt 7. As Michelle Alexander has pointed out in a different context, the United States' "formally colorblind criminal justice system achieve[s] such racially discriminatory results" by granting "law enforcement officials extraordinary discretion regarding whom to stop, search, arrest and charge for drug offenses, thus ensuring that conscious and unconscious racial beliefs and stereotypes will be given free rein" (103).

17. Nel, *J. K. Rowling's Harry Potter Novels: A Reader's Guide*, 22; Jacob.

18. Reid; Clayton; Elliott, "Self-Publishing Often the Only Recourse for Authors of Color."

19. "About Us," *House of Anansi*; Martin, *Brown Gold*, 56, 57; Bird.

20. Donald F. Joyce 95.

21. Bishop 42, 73. My history of African American children's literature in this chapter and, indeed, throughout this book, derives primarily from four books, all of which I strongly recommend: Michelle Martin's *Brown Gold: Milestones of African-American Children's Picture Books, 1845–2002* (2004), Rudine Sims Bishop's *Free Within Ourselves: The Development of African American Children's Literature* (2007), and two books by Katharine Capshaw: *Children's Literature of the Harlem Renaissance* (as Katharine Capshaw Smith, 2004) and *Civil Rights Childhood: Picturing Liberation in African American Photobooks* (2014).

22. Katharine Capshaw Smith 233; Bishop 47.

23. Bishop 61–62.

24. Omi and Winant 14, 20.

25. In the first sentence of this paragraph, I am paraphrasing Omi and Winant's words on the Black Power movement's contribution to racial formation: "It was an effort which, interestingly, drew upon the themes of the dominant ethnicity paradigm and the civil rights movement, while simultaneously rejecting their integrationist and assimilationist goals" (102).

26. Maughan. Note that, although all the books mentioned in the previous paragraph except *The Blacker the Berry* (poetry) are realism or historical, *In the Time of the*

Drums is also a folktale. As noted before, all books can be classified into more than one genre.

27. Taylor 184, 185; Bishop 22, 92.The second sentence of this paragraph alludes to Rudine Sims Bishop's observation that "strong emphasis on African American history functions both as a corrective to the historical neglect, distortion, or omission of that history in school curricula and a manifestation of the belief that knowledge of their history will function as anchor, compass, and sail for African American children as they undertake their life journeys" (249).

28. Curtis, *The Watsons Go to Birmingham—1963*, 210; Fields and Fields 158. So far, I count three YA novels that intersect with Black Lives Matter: Kekla Magoon's *How It Went Down* (2014), Jason Reynolds and Brendan Kiely's *All American Boys* (2015), and Angie Thomas's *The Hate U Give* (2017).

29. Johnson 321–322, 20.

30. Ebony Elizabeth Thomas, "The Dark Fantastic: Race and the Imagination in Youth Literature, Media, and Culture."

31. Elliott, "Decolonizing the Imagination."

32. Walter Dean Myers; Ebony Elizabeth Thomas, "The Imagination Gap in #Kidlit and #YAlit: An Introduction to the Dark Fantastic."

33. Ebony Elizabeth Thomas, "The Imagination Gap in #Kidlit and #YAlit: An Introduction to the Dark Fantastic."

34. Atkins 23.

35. Lofting, *The Story of Doctor Dolittle* (Dell, 1988), 152; Bannerman, back cover; Martin, *Brown Gold*, 9, 11.

36. Gay.

Conclusion

1. Ellison, *Invisible Man*, xx.

2. Seuss, "What This Country Needs . . ."

3. Raymond Williams 132.

4. Díaz.

5. Fields and Fields 105, 104–105; Christopher Myers, "Please Don't Agree with Me."

6. Jamison 39–40; Murakawa.

7. Fields and Fields 158; Holmes 22.

8. Vicky Smith, "Unmaking the White Default."

9. "Accomplices Not Allies: Abolishing the Ally Industrial Complex."

10. "Accomplices Not Allies: Abolishing the Ally Industrial Complex"; DiAngelo, "About Me."

11. DiAngelo, "White Fragility," 66; Baldwin 8.

12. Bernstein, "Signposts on the Road Less Taken," 97.

13. Wooldridge, quoted in Botelho and Rudman 4. Bothelo and Rudman added *class* to Wooldridge's list. I added *race* and *sexuality*.
14. In this paragraph, I have adapted ideas from Botelho and Rudman's "Recommendations for Classroom Research," at the end of chapter 2 in their *Critical Multicultural Analysis of Children's Literature*, 34.
15. Larrick 85; "Racial/Ethnic Enrollment in Public Schools."
16. Milliot, "The PW Publishing Industry Salary Survey 2015: A Younger Workforce, Still Predominantly White"; Low, Dahlen, and Catlin; Ken Chen quoted in Neary.
17. Low.
18. To judge from their websites, Columbia's costs $8,365, Denver's costs $7,111, and NYU's is $6,230.
19. Rankine, in Aiello; Pinkney, "A Proud Slice of History"; Ganeshram.
20. Osnos; Beauchamp. For failing to disclose his communications with (and under investigation for accepting payments from) Russia, Flynn resigned on February 13, 2017, after 24 days on the job.
21. Mickenberg 176; Costello; Lee.

Afterword

1. DiAngelo, "White Fragility," 54.
2. Gloria Wekker, *White Innocence*, 147.
3. Wekker, *White Innocence*, 166.
4. Peggy Berarducci Gynn, comment on Maria Puente's "The Debate over Dr. Seuss: When racist themes collide with childhood nostalgia."
5. Helen Mallery, comment on Jocelyn McClurg and Maria Puente's "Are Dr. Seuss' books racist? Experts weigh in on controversy"; Joseph Barndt, *Understanding & Dismantling Racism*, 136.
6. Virginia Gomez, "You should read what people 'think' of your views on "Cat in th [*sic*] Hat" ENJOY THE COMMENTS---YOU PATHETIC FOOL." Personal email.
7. RM, "If Dr. Seuss is tired and racist…" Comment on Liz Phipps Soeiro, "Dear Mrs. Trump."
8. Wekker, *White Innocence*, 158.
9. "Davesci," comment on Stephen Sawchuk, "Is 'The Cat in the Hat' Racist?" *Education Week*, 4 Oct. 2017; "E.Blackadder," comment on Isabel Fattal, "Reading Racism in Dr. Seuss," *The Atlantic*, 15 Aug. 2017.
10. Boym, *The Future of Nostalgia*, xviii, 49, 8, 54.
11. Boym, xvi, 3, 16, 43.
12. Boym, 41, 43, 58-59.
13. Boym, 50.

14. Baldwin, *Notes of a Native Son*, 103.
15. Benjamin, "Children's Literature," 251.
16. Nabokov, *Speak, Memory*, 76-77.
17. Cobb, "Smelling the Coffee," 32.
18. Bobo, "Racism in Trump's America: reflections on culture, sociology, and the 2016 US presidential election," S89-S90; Zinn, "The Optimism of Uncertainty."
19. Scott Timberg, "Henry Louis Gates on Trump: 'That election clearly represented a backlash against the progress black people have made since 1965.'"

BIBLIOGRAPHY

Abate, Michelle. "I Forgot." Message to the author. 18 Apr. 2008. E-mail.

"About Us." *House of Anansi.* 12 May 2015. <http://site.houseofanansi.com/>.

"Accomplices Not Allies: Abolishing the Ally Industrial Complex." *Indigenous Action Media.* 4 May 2014. 30 Oct. 2015. <http://www.indigenousaction.org/accomplices-not-allies-abolishing-the-ally-industrial-complex/>.

Adichie, Chimamanda Ngozi. "The Danger of a Single Story." *TED* July 2009. <https://www.ted.com/talks/chimamanda_adichie_the_danger_of_a_single_story?language=en>.

Adoff, Jamie. *Jimi and Me.* New York: Jump at the Sun/Hyperion, 2005.

"Adult Literacy: Literacy by Race/Ethnicity." *National Center for Education Statistics.* 5 June 2012. <http://nces.ed.gov/ssbr/pages/adultliteracy.asp?IndID=32>.

Agrawal, Nadya. "Some People Are Pissed Off about the Casting of a Black Hermione Granger." *Huffington Post.* 21 Dec. 2015. <http://www.huffingtonpost.com/entry/some-people-are-pissed-off-about-the-casting-of-a-black-hermione-granger_us_5678486fe4b06fa6887e188a>.

Aiello, Antonio. "Equity in Publishing: What Should Editors Be Doing?" *PEN America.* Fall 2016. <https://pen.org/conversation/editorial-roundtable-diversity-equity-publishing>.

Alexander, Michelle. *The New Jim Crow: Mass Incarceration in the Age of Colorblindness.* 2010. Rev. ed. New York: New Press, 2011.

Amsden, David. "Building the First Slavery Museum in America." *New York Times Magazine.* 1 Mar. 2015. <http://www.nytimes.com/2015/03/01/magazine/building-the-first-slave-museum-in-america.html>.

Anderson, Celia Catlett, and Marilyn Fain Apseloff. *Nonsense Literature for Children: Aesop to Seuss.* Hamden, CT: Library Professional Publications, 1989.

Anderson, M. T. *The Astonishing Life of Octavian Nothing, Traitor to the Nation.* Volume 1: *The Pox Party.* 2006. London: Walker Books, 2007.

Anderson, M. T. *The Astonishing Life of Octavian Nothing, Traitor to the Nation.* Volume 2: *The Kingdom on the Waves.* 2008. Somerville, MA: Candlewick Press, 2009.

Arac, Jonathan. *Huckleberry Finn as Idol and Target: The Functions of Criticism in Our Time.* Madison, WI: University of Wisconsin Press, 1997.

Ari. "Covers Matter." Guest commentary. *The Book Smugglers,* ed. Thea James. 26 Feb. 2010. 5 June 2012. <http://thebooksmugglers.com/2010/02/cover-matters-on-whitewashing.html>.

Atkins, Laura. "White Privilege and Children's Publishing: A Web 2.0 Case Study." *Write4Children* 1.2 (2010): 21–33. <http://www.winchester.ac.uk/academicde-partments/EnglishCreativeWritingandAmericanStudies/Documents/w4cis-sue2cApr.pdf>.

Baldwin, James. *Notes of a Native Son.* 1955. With a new introduction by Edward P. Jones. Boston: Beacon Press, 2012.

Baldwin, James. *The Fire Next Time.* 1963. New York: Vintage, 1993.

Bang, Molly. *Ten, Nine, Eight.* 1983. New York: Mulberry, 1991.

Banks, Lynne Reid. *The Indian in the Cupboard.* 1980. Illus. Brock Cole. 1981. New York: HarperCollins, 2003.

Bannerman, Helen. *The Story of Little Black Sambo.* 1899. New York: HarperCollins, n.d.

Barndt, Joseph. *Understanding & Dismantling Racism: The Twenty-First Century Challenge to White America.* Minneapolis: Fortress Press, 2007.

Barthes, Roland. *Mythologies.* 1957. Trans. Annette Lavers 1972. New York: Hill & Wang, 1994.

Bartle, Lisa R. *The Database of Award-Winning Children's Literature.* 3 Sept. 2016. <http://www.dawcl.com/>.

Beasts of the Southern Wild. Dir. Benh Zeitlin. Screenplay by Lucy Alibar and Ben Zeitlin. Perf. Quvenzhané Wallis and Dwight Henry. 2012.

Beauchamp, Zack. "White Riot: How Racism and Immigration Gave Us Trump, Brexit, and a Whole New Kind of Politics." *Vox* 19 Sept. 2016. <http://www.vox.com/2016/9/19/12933072/far-right-white-riot-trump-brexit>.

Beauvais, Clémentine. "Publishing Is Not a Charity." *An Awfully Big Blog Adventure* 28 Nov. 2015. <http://awfullybigblogadventure.blogspot.co.uk/2015/11/publish-ing-is-not-charity-clementine.html>.

Bell, Shannon. "Publisher Will Remove 'N' Word, Huck Finn Will Now Be PC." *RightPundits.com.* 4 Jan. 2011. <http://www.rightpundits.com/?p=8015>.

Benjamin, Walter. "Children's Literature." *Radio Benjamin,* ed. Lecia Rosenthal. London and Brooklyn: Verso, 2014. 251-259.

Bernstein, Robin. *Racial Innocence: Performing Childhood from Slavery to Civil Rights.* New York: NYU Press, 2011.

Bernstein, Robin. "Signposts on the Road Less Taken: John Newton Hyde's Anti-Racist Illustrations of African-American Children." *Journal of Nineteenth-Century Americanists* 1.1 (2013): 97–119.

Bird, Elizabeth. "Jason Low Talks Diversity with Betsy Bird." *School Library Journal.* 5May2014.<http://www.slj.com/2014/05/sponsored/jason-low-talks-diversity-with-betsy-bird-slj-conversations/#_>.

Bishop, Rudine Sims. *Free Within Ourselves: The Development of African-American Children's Literature.* Westport, CT: Greenwood Press, 2004.

Bobo, Lawrence D. "Racism in Trump's America: Reflections on culture, sociology, and the 2016 US presidential election." *British Journal of Sociology* 68.S1: s85-s104.

Bobo, Lawrence D., and Michael C. Dawson. "A Change Has Come: Race, Politics, and the Path to the Obama Presidency." *Du Bois Review* 6.1 (2009): 1–14.

Bonilla-Silva, Eduardo. *Racism Without Racists: Color-Blind Racism and the Persistence of Racial Inequality in the United States.* 3rd ed. New York: Rowan & Littlefield, 2010.

Bontemps, Arna, and Langston Hughes. *Popo and Fifina: Children of Haiti.* Illus. by E. Simms Campbell. 1932. New York: Oxford University Press, 1993.

Botelho, Maria José, and Masha Kabakow Rudman. *Critical Multicultural Analysis of Children's Literature: Mirrors, Windows, and Doors.* New York: Routledge, 2009.

Boym, Svetlana. *The Future of Nostalgia.* New York: Basic Books, 2001.

Bradford, Clare. "The End of Empire? Colonial and Postcolonial Journeys in Children's Books." *Children's Literature* 29 (2001): 196–218.

Bradford, Clare. *Unsettling Narratives: Postcolonial Readings of Children's Literature.* Waterloo, ON: Wilfrid Laurier University Press, 2007.

Broderick, Dorothy M. *Image of the Black in Children's Fiction.* New York: R.R. Bowker Co., 1973.

Brown, Don. *Drowned City: Hurricane Katrina and New Orleans.* New York: Houghton Mifflin Harcourt, 2015.

Brown, Jeff. *Flat Stanley.* Pictures by Tomi Ungerer. 1964. New York: Scholastic, 1972.

Brown, Jeff. *Flat Stanley.* Pictures by Steve Björkman. New York: HarperTrophy, 1996.

Brown, Jeff. *Flat Stanley.* Pictures by Scott Nash. New York: HarperCollins, 2003.

Brown, Jeff. *Flat Stanley.* Pictures by Macky Pamintuan. New York: Harper, 2009.

Bruce, Allie Jane. "School Librarian Talks to Students about 'Whitewashing' Children's Book Covers." *School Library Journal.* 6 May 2014. 22 Nov. 2015. <http://www.slj.com/2014/05/diversity/bank-street-school-librarian-shares-her-year-long-lesson-in-diversity-in-childrens-books/>.

Bruce, Allie Jane. "Whitewashing Book Covers: What Do Kids Think? Part I." *Lee & Low Blog.* 21 Nov. 2013. 11 Nov. 2015. <http://blog.leeandlow.com/2013/11/21/whitewashing-book-covers-what-do-kids-think-part-i/>.

Bruce, Allie Jane. "Whitewashing Book Covers: A Trip to Barnes & Noble. Part II." *Lee & Low Blog.* 22 Nov. 2013. 11 Nov. 2015. <http://blog.leeandlow.com/2013/11/22/whitewashing-book-covers-a-trip-to-barnes-noble-part-ii/>.

Brunhoff, Jean de. *The Story of Babar*. Translated by Merle S. Haas. 1933. New York: Random House, 2002.

Brunkard, Joan, Gonza Namulanda, and Raoult Ratard. "Hurricane Katrina Deaths, Louisiana, 2005." *Disaster Medicine and Public Health Preparedness*. 28 Aug. 2008. <http://new.dhh.louisiana.gov/assets/docs/katrina/deceasedreports/KatrinaDeaths_082008.pdf>.

Butler, Octavia. *Kindred*. 1979. Boston: Beacon Press, 2004.

Cameron, Eleanor. "McLuhan, Youth, and Literature: Part I." *Horn Book*. Oct. 1972. 15 Sept. 2010. <http://www.hbook.com/magazine/articles/1970s/oct72_cameron.asp>.

Cameron, Eleanor. "McLuhan, Youth, and Literature: Part II." *Horn Book*. Dec. 1972. 15 Sept. 2010. <http://www.hbook.com/magazine/articles/1970s/dec72_cameron.asp>.

Cameron, Eleanor. "A Reply to Roald Dahl." *Horn Book*. Apr. 1973. 15 Sept. 2010. <http://hbook.com/magazine/articles/1970s/apr73_cameron.asp>.

Campanella, Richard. "An Ethnic Geography of New Orleans." *Journal of American History* 94.3 (2007): 704–715.

Caplan, Paula J., and Jordan C. Ford. "The Voices of Diversity: What Students of Diverse Races/Ethnicities and Both Sexes Tell Us about Their College Experiences and Their Perceptions about Their Institutions' Progress Toward Diversity." *Aporia* 6.3 (2014): 30–69. <http://www.oa.uottawa.ca/journals/aporia/articles/2014_10/Caplan_Ford.pdf>.

Capshaw, Katharine. *Civil Rights Childhood: Picturing Liberation in African American Photobooks*. Minneapolis: University of Minnesota, 2014.

Carson, Rae. *The Girl of Fire and Thorns*. New York: Greenwillow Books, 2011.

The Cat in the Hat. Dir. by Hawley Pratt. Storyboard Chuck Jones. Teleplay by Dr. Seuss. Music by Dean Elliott. Lyrics by Dr. Seuss. Perf. Allan Sherman, Daws Butler, Pamelyn Ferdin, Tony Frazier, Gloria Camacho, Thurl Ravenscroft, and Lewis Morford. CBS, 10 Mar. 1971. Television.

Chan, Sewell, and Jeremy W. Peters. "Chimp-Stimulus Cartoon Raises Racism Concerns." *New York Times*. 18 Feb. 2009. <http://cityroom.blogs.nytimes.com/2009/02/18/chimp-stimulus-cartoon-raises-racism-concerns/?_r=0>.

"Children's Books by and about People of Color Published in the United States." Cooperative Children's Book Center. University of Wisconsin. 24 Feb. 2015. <http://ccbc.education.wisc.edu/books/pcstats.asp>.

Clark, Beverly Lyon. *Kiddie Lit: The Cultural Construction of Children's Literature*. Johns Hopkins University Press, 2003.

Clayton, Dhonielle. "Author Q&A: Wendy Raven McNair, of the Asleep Awake Trilogy." *Teen Writers Bloc*. 29 Nov. 2010. <http://www.teenwritersbloc.com/2010/11/29/wendy-raven-mcnair/>.

Clifton, Lucille. *The Black BC's*. Illus. Don Miller. New York: E. P. Dutton & Co., 1970.

Coates, Ta-Nehisi. *The Beautiful Struggle: A Father, Two Sons, and an Unlikely Road to Manhood*. 2008. New York: Spiegel & Grau, 2009.

Coates, Ta-Nehisi. *Between the World and Me*. New York: Spiegel & Grau, 2015.

Cobb, Jelani. "Smelling the Coffee." *New Yorker* 4 & 11 June 2018: 31-32. [quotation is on 32]

Cohen, Charles. *The Seuss, the Whole Seuss and Nothing but the Seuss: A Visual Biography*. New York: Random House, 2004.

Cohen, Stanley. *States of Denial: Knowing about Atrocities and Suffering*. Cambridge, UK: Polity, 2001.

Collins, Suzanne. *The Hunger Games*. New York: Scholastic, 2008.

Colman, Dan. "The Fantastic Flying Books of Mr. Morris Lessmore: An Oscar-Nominated Film for Book Lovers." *Open Culture*. 27 Jan. 2012. <http://www.openculture.com/2012/01/the_fantastic_flying_books_of_mr_morris_lessmore.html>.

Columbia Publishing Course. Sept. 4, 2016. <https://journalism.columbia.edu/columbia-publishing-course>.

Connolly, Paula T. *Slavery in American Children's Literature 1790–2010*. Iowa City: University of Iowa Press, 2013.

Coover, Robert. "The Cat in the Hat for President." *New American Review* 4 (1968): 7–45.

Costello, Maureen B. "The Trump Effect: The Impact of the Presidential Campaign on Our Nation's Schools." *Southern Poverty Law Center*. 13 Apr. 2016. <https://www.splcenter.org/20160413/trump-effect-impact-presidential-campaign-our-nations-schools>.

Crockett, Stephen A. Jr. "Woman Shocked to See Brother's Mug Shot Used as Police Target Practice." *The Root*. 16 Jan. 2015. <http://www.theroot.com/articles/culture/2015/01/woman_shocked_to_see_brother_s_mug_shot_photo_used_as_police_target_practice.html>.

Cullen, Countee. "Incident." 1925. *Norton Anthology of Poetry: Shorter Fourth Edition*. Ed. Margaret Ferguson, Mary Jo Salter, and Jon Stallworthy. New York: W.W. Norton & Co., 1997. 833.

Culp, Jerome McCristal Jr. "The Woody Allen Blues: 'Identity Politics,' Race and the Law." *Florida Law Review* 51 (1999): 511–528.

Cummins, June. "The Resisting Monkey: 'Curious George,' Slave Captivity Narratives, and the Postcolonial Condition." *Ariel* 28 (Jan. 1997): 69–83.

Curtis, Christopher Paul. *Elijah of Buxton*. New York: Scholastic, 2007.

Curtis, Christopher Paul. *The Watsons Go to Birmingham—1963*. 1995. New York: Bantam Doubleday Dell, 1997.

Dahl, Roald. *Charlie and the Chocolate Factory*. Illus. Joseph Schindelman. New York: Alfred A. Knopf, 1964.

Dahl, Roald. *Charlie and the Chocolate Factory*. Illus. Joseph Schindelman. New York: Alfred A. Knopf, 1973.

Danky, James P. "Reading, Writing, and Resisting: African American Print Culture." *A History of the Book in America*, Vol. 4: *Print in Motion: The Expansion of Publishing and Reading in the United States, 1880–1940.* Ed. Carl F. Kaestle and Janice A. Radway. Chapel Hill: University of North Carolina Press, 2009. 339–358.

DasGupta, Sayantani. "Why Are We Still Whitewashing?" *AdiosBarbie.* 21 Feb. 2012. <http://www.adiosbarbie.com/2012/02/why-are-we-still-whitewashing/>.

Davesci, comment on Stephen Sawchuk, "Is 'The Cat in the Hat' Racist?" *Education Week,* 4 Oct. 2017: <https://www.edweek.org/ew/articles/2017/10/04/is-the-cat-in-the-hati-racist.html>.

Davis, Geffrey. "On Diversity and Creativity: The Alchemy of Discomfort." Lecture. Kansas State University. 20 Feb. 2015.

Deahl, Rachel. "Why Publishing Is So White." *Publishers Weekly.* 11 Mar. 2016. <http://www.publishersweekly.com/pw/by-topic/industry-news/publisher-news/article/69653-why-publishing-is-so-white.html>.

Delgado, Richard. "Words That Wound." *Harvard Civil Rights—Civil Liberties Law Review* 17 (1982): 133–181.

Denver Publishing Institute. Sept. 4, 2016. <http://www.du.edu/publishinginstitute/>.

Devitt, Amy J. *Writing Genres.* 2004. Carbondale: Southern Illinois University Press, 2008.

DiAngelo, Robin. "About Me." *Robin DiAngelo, Ph.D.* 23 Nov. 2015. <http://robindiangelo.com/about-me/>.

DiAngelo, Robin. "White Fragility." *International Journal of Critical Pedagogy* 3.3 (2011): 54–70.

Díaz, Junot. "MFA vs. POC." *New Yorker.* 30 Apr. 2014. 1 Nov. 2015. <http://www.newyorker.com/books/page-turner/mfa-vs-poc>.

Dolamore, Jaclyn. *Magic under Glass.* New York: Bloomsbury, 2010.

Dorfman, Ariel, and Armand Mattelart. *How to Read Donald Duck.* Translated by David Kunzle. New York: International Publishers, 1975.

Douglass, Frederick. *Narrative of the Life of Frederick Douglass, an American Slave.* 1845. New York: Penguin, 1986.

Dreifus, Claudia. "Perceptions of Race at a Glance: A MacArthur Grant Winner Tries to Unearth Biases to Aid Criminal Justice." *New York Times.* 5 Jan. 2015. <http://www.nytimes.com/2015/01/06/science/a-macarthur-grant-winner-tries-to-unearth-biases-to-aid-criminal-justice.html>.

Dr. Seuss, LP v. Penguin Books. 109 F.3d 1394, US Court of Appeals, Ninth Circuit. 10 Oct. 1996.

Du Bois, W. E. B. *The Souls of Black Folk.* 1903. New York: Penguin, 1982.

Dudziak, Mary L. "Desegregation as a Cold War Imperative." *Stanford Law Review* 41.1 (1988): 61–120.

Duyvis, Corinne. "Diverse Characters: Corinne Duyvis on the Decline of 'Issue' Books." *The Guardian.* 17 Oct. 2014. <http://www.theguardian.com/childrens-books-site/2014/oct/17/decline-of-issue-books-incidental-diversity>.

Dyer, Richard. *White.* New York: Routledge, 1997.

Dyson, Michael Eric. *Come Hell or High Water: Hurricane Katrina and the Color of Disaster*. New York: Basic Books, 2006.

"E-16. Unemployment Rates by Age, Sex, Race, and Hispanic or Latino Ethnicity [Percent]." Labor Force Statistics from the Current Population Survey. Bureau of Labor Statistics. 8 July 2016. 27 Aug. 2016. <http://www.bls.gov/web/empsit/cpsee_e16.htm>.

E.Blackadder. Comment on Isabel Fattal, "Reading Racism in Dr. Seuss," *The Atlantic*, 15 Aug. 2017: <https://www.theatlantic.com/education/archive/2017/08/reading-racism-in-dr-seuss/536625/>.

Elliott, Zetta. "Black Authors and Self-Publishing." *School Library Journal*. 16 Mar. 2015. <http://www.slj.com/2015/03/diversity/black-authors-and-self-publishing/#_>.

Elliott, Zetta. "Decolonizing the Imagination." *Horn Book*. March–April 2010. <http://archive.hbook.com/magazine/articles/2010/mar10_elliott.asp>.

Elliott, Zetta. "Self-Publishing Often the Only Recourse for Authors of Color." *Latin@s in Kid Lit*. 12 June 2014. <http://latinosinkidlit.com/2014/06/12/guest-post-self-publishing-often-the-only-recourse-for-writers-of-color/>.

Elliott, Zetta. "Stranger than Fiction: Depicting Trauma in African American Picture Books, or One Hot Mess." *Fledgling: Zetta Elliott's (other) blog*. 16 June 2012. 19 June 2012. <http://zettaelliott.wordpress.com/2012/06/16/hot-mess/>.

Elliott, Zetta. *A Wish after Midnight*. Las Vegas and New York: AmazonEncore and Melcher Media, 2010.

Ellison, Ralph. "Change the Joke and Slip the Yoke." 1958. *Shadow and Act*. 1964. New York: Vintage, 1972. 45–59.

Ellison, Ralph. *Invisible Man*. 1952. New York: Vintage, 1990.

Emenyonu, Ernest N., ed. *Writing Africa in the Short Story*. African Literature Today 13. Rochester, NY, and Suffolk, UK: Boydell and Brewer, 2013.

"Employment Situation Summary." Bureau of Labor Statistics. 9 Jan. 2015. <http://www.bls.gov/news.release/empsit.nro.htm>.

Fadiman, Clifton. "Professionals and Confessionals: Dr. Seuss and Kenneth Grahame." *Only Connect: Readings on Children's Literature*. Ed. Sheila Egoff, G. T. Stubbs, and L. F. Ashley. Toronto: Oxford University Press, 1980. 277–283.

The Fantastic Flying Books of Mr. Morris Lessmore. Film. Dir. William Joyce and Brandon Oldenburg. Writer: William Joyce. Shreveport, Louisiana: Moonbot Studios, 2011.

The Fantastic Flying Books of Mr. Morris Lessmore. App. Based on the book by William Joyce, and developed by Moonbot Studios. Programming by Twin Engine Labs. Music and Sound Design by BREED. Narration by Mike Martindale. Shreveport, Louisiana: Moonbot Books. 2011.

Feelings, Tom. *Middle Passage*. New York: Dial Press, 1995.

Fielder, Brigitte. "Confronting Racism: The Fun and the Fury" (panel). American Studies Association Annual Meeting. Los Angeles, CA. 9 Nov. 2014.

Fields, Karen E., and Barbara J. Fields. *Racecraft: The Soul of Inequality in American Life*. 2012. Brooklyn and London: Verso, 2014.

Fishkin, Shelley Fisher. *Was Huck Black? Mark Twain and African American Voices.* New York: Oxford University Press, 1993.

Flake, Sharon. *The Skin I'm In.* New York: Jump at the Sun/Hyperion, 1998.

Flesch, Rudolf. *Why Johnny Can't Read—and What You Can Do about It.* New York: Harper & Brothers, 1955.

Flood, Alison. "Meg Rosoff Sparks Diversity Row over Books for Marginalised Children." *The Guardian.* 13 Oct. 2015. <http://www.theguardian.com/books/2015/oct/13/meg-rosoff-diversity-row-books-marginalised-children-edith-campbell-large-fears>.

Freedom Summer. Dir. Stanley Nelson, Jr. Firelight Films, 2014.

Friedberg, Joan Brest. "Garth Williams." *Dictionary of Literary Biography*, Vol. 22, *American Writers for Children, 1900–1960.* Ed. John Cech. Farmington Hills, MI: Gale Group, 1983.

Frost, Joe L. "Lessons from Disasters: Play, Work and the Creative Arts." *Childhood Education* 82.1 (2005). <http://dx.doi.org/10.1080/00094056.2005.10521332>.

Gabrielson, Ryan, Ryann Grochowski Jones, and Eric Sagara. "Deadly Force, in Black and White." *Pro Publica.* 10 Oct. 2014. <http://www.propublica.org/article/deadly-force-in-black-and-white>.

Ganeshram, Ramin. *A Birthday Cake for George Washington.* Illus. Vanessa Brantley-Newton. New York: Scholastic Press, 2016.

Gay, Roxane. "The Worst Kind of Groundhog Day: Let's Talk (Again) about Diversity in Publishing." *NPR: Code Switch.* 28 May 2015. <http://www.npr.org/sections/codeswitch/2015/05/28/410015276/the-worst-groundhog-s-day-time-to-talk-again-about-diversity-in-publishing>.

Gilton, Donna L. *Multicultural and Ethnic Children's Literature in the United States.* Lanham, MD: Scarecrow Press, 2007.

Giroux, Henry A. "Race, Class, and the Biopolitics of Disposability." *Theory Culture Society* 24 (2007): 305–309.

Golgowski, Nina. "Family Outraged after Son's Mug Shot Found Used in Target Practice by Miami Police." *New York Daily News.* 15 Jan. 2015. <http://www.nydailynews.com/news/national/miami-police-defends-mug-shots-target-practice-article-1.2080396>.

Gomez, Virginia. "You should read what people 'think' of your views on "Cat in th [*sic*] Hat" ENJOY THE COMMENTS—YOU PATHETIC FOOL." Personal email. 14 Dec. 2017. Concerned that I might *not* be reading the comments on one of the news articles, Ms. Gomez cut-and-pasted them into an email and sent them to me. So, while these may represent the views of Ms. Gomez, all are all quotes from an unidentified news article and are not her words.

Gonzalez, Audrey, Crystal Brunelle, K. Imani Tennyson, and Jessica, eds. *Rich in Color.* <http://richincolor.com/>.

Goscinny, René, and Albert Uderzo. *Asterix and Cleopatra.* 1965. New York. William Morrow & Company, 1970.

Goscinny, René, and Albert Uderzo. *Asterix and the Great Crossing.* 1975. London: Hodder Dargaud, 1976.

Graham, Lorenz. *South Town*. Chicago: Follett, 1958.

Greco, Albert N., Clara E. Rodríguez, and Robert M. Wharton. *The Culture and Commerce of Publishing in the 21st Century*. Stanford: Stanford Business Books/ Stanford University Press, 2007.

Gregorio, I. W. "One Asian Book Is Quite Enough." *Diversity in YA*. 6 Apr. 2015. <http://www.diversityinya.com/2015/04/one-asian-book-is-quite-enough/>.

Gribben, Alan. "Editor's Introduction." *The Adventures of Tom Sawyer and Huckleberry Finn*, by Mark Twain. Ed. Alan Gribben. Montgomery, AL: NewSouth Books, 2011.

Grimes, Nikki. *Barack Obama: Son of Promise, Child of Hope*. Illus. Bryan Collier. New York: Simon & Schuster, 2008.

Griswold, Jerry. "Introduction." *Doctor Dolittle*. By Hugh Lofting. New York: Signet, 2000. ix–xvii.

Gubar, Marah. "Innocence." *Keywords for Children's Literature*. Ed. Philip Nel and Lissa Paul. New York: New York University Press, 2011. 121–127.

Guevara, Susan. "Authentic Enough: Am I? Are You? Interpreting Culture for Children's Literature." *Stories Matter: The Complexity of Cultural Authenticity in Children's Literature*. Ed. Dana L. Fox and Kathy G. Short. Urbana, IL: National Council of Teachers of English, 2003. 50–60.

Gynn, Peggy Berarducci. Comment on Maria Puente's "The Debate over Dr. Seuss: When racist themes collide with childhood nostalgia." *USA Today* 30 Sept. 2017.

Hade, Daniel D. "Reading Children's Literature Multiculturally." *Reflections of Change: Children's Literature since 1945*. Ed. Sandra L. Beckett. Westport, CT: Greenwood Press, 1997. 115–122.

Hade, Daniel D. "Reading Multiculturally." *Using Multiethnic Literature in the K-8 Classroom*. Ed. Violet J. Harris. Norwood, MA: Christopher-Gordon, 1997. 233–256.

Hamilton, Virginia. *M. C. Higgins, the Great*. 1974. New York: Aladdin Paperbacks, 1993.

Handler, Daniel. "Daniel Handler and Watermelon." http://www.c-span.org/video/?c4515639/daniel-handler-watermelon.

Handler, Daniel. "My job at last night's National Book Awards #NBAwards was to shine a light on tremendous writers, including Jacqueline Woodson. . . -DH [1/2]" Tweet. 20 Nov. 2014. 10:47 am. <https://twitter.com/DanielHandler/status/535474608724787200>.

Handler, Daniel. ". . .and not to overshadow their achievements with my own ill-conceived attempts at humor. I clearly failed, and I'm sorry. -DH [2/2]" Tweet. 20 Nov. 2014. 10:48 am. <https://twitter.com/DanielHandler/status/535474801469837312>.

Handler, Daniel. "My remarks on Wednesday night at #NBAwards were monstrously inappropriate and yes, racist. -DH [1/4]." Tweet. 21 Nov. 2014. 6:29 am. <https://twitter.com/DanielHandler/status/535772077354397696>.

Handler, Daniel. "It would be heartbreaking for the #NBAwards conversation to focus on my behavior instead of great books. So can we do this? -DH [2/4]." Tweet. 21 Nov. 2014. 6:30 am. <https://twitter.com/DanielHandler/status/535772326940655616>.

Handler, Daniel. "Let's donate to #WeNeedDiverseBooks to #CelebrateJackie. I'm in for $10,000, and matching your money for 24 hours up to $100,000. -DH [3/4]." Tweet. 21 Nov. 2014. 6:31 am. <https://twitter.com/DanielHandler/status/535772601906634753>.

Handler, Daniel. "Brown Girl Dreaming is an amazing novel and we need more voices like Jacqueline Woodson. -DH [4/4]." Tweet. 21 Nov. 2014. 6:32 am. <https://twitter.com/DanielHandler/status/535772846489108480>.

Hart, Kate. "Uncovering YA Covers: 2011." *Kate Hart.* 16 May 2012. 5 June 2012. <http://www.katehart.net/2012/05/uncovering-ya-covers-2011.html>.

Hateley, Erica. "Reading: From Turning the Page to Touching the Screen." *(Re) Imagining the World: Children's Literature's Response to Changing Times.* Ed. Yan Wu, Kerry Mallan, and Roderick McGillis. Berlin: Springer-Verlag, 2013. 1–13.

Heer, Jeet. "The Kolors of Krazy Kat." *Krazy & Ignatz: 1935–1936. A Wild Warmth of Chromatic Gravy.* By George Herriman. Ed. Bill Blackbeard. Seattle: Fantagraphics Books, 2005. 8–15.

Hergé. *The Adventures of Tintin: Tintin in America.* 1931–1932. Translation 1978. New York and Boston: Little, Brown, 1979.

Hergé. *The Adventures of Tintin: Tintin in the Congo.* 1930–1931. Translation 1991. Bruxelles: Casterman, 1991.

Hersey, John. "Why Do Students Bog Down on First 'R'?" *Life* 24 May 1954: 136–150.

Holmes, Anna. "Variety Show." *New York Times Magazine.* 1 Nov. 2015: 21–24.

hooks, bell. "No Love in the Wild." *NewBlackMan (in Exile).* 5 Sep, 2012. <http://newblackman.blogspot.com/2012/09/bell-hooks-no-love-in-wild.html>.

Hughes, Jazmine. "What Black Parents Tell Their Sons about the Police." *Gawker.* 21 Aug. 2014. <http://gawker.com/what-black- parents-tell-their-sons-about-the-police-1624412625>.

Hughes, Langston. *The Dream-Keeper and Other Poems.* New York: Knopf, 1932.

Hughes, Langston. "Sharecroppers." 1937. *Tales for Little Rebels: A Collection of Radical Children's Literature.* Ed. Julia L. Mickenberg and Philip Nel. New York: New York University Press, 2008. 62–64.

Hughes, Langston, and Arna Bontemps. *Popo and Fifina: Children of Haiti.* New York: Macmillan, 1932.

Hurston, Zora Neale. "What White Publishers Won't Print." 1950. *Within the Circle: An Anthology of African American Literary Criticism from the Harlem Renaissance to the Present.* Ed. Angelyn Mitchell. Duke University Press, 1994. 118–121.

Hutcheon, Linda. "Irony, Nostalgia, and the Postmodern." *University of Toronto Libraries* 1998. <http://www.library.utoronto.ca.er.lib.k-state.edu/utel/criticism/hutchinp.html>.

Iconoclasts, Season 6, Episode 2: Dave Chappelle and Maya Angelou. Sundance Channel. 30 Nov. 2006.

Ingram, Christopher. "Three-Quarters of Whites Don't Have Any Non-White Friends." *Washington Post.* 25 Aug. 2014. <http://www.washingtonpost.com/

blogs/wonkblog/wp/2014/08/25/three-quarters-of-whites-dont-have-any-non-white-friends/>.

Ireland, Justina. "Aversive Racism and the Traditional Publishing Model." *JustinaIreland.com*. 27 Aug. 2015. <http://justinaireland.com/dammit-this-is-a-blog/2015/8/27/aversive-racism-and-the-traditional-publishing-model>.

Jackson, Jesse. *Anchor Man*. New York: Harper & Brothers, 1947.

Jackson, Jesse. *Call Me Charley*. New York: Harper & Brothers, 1945.

Jackson, Jesse. *Charley Starts from Scratch*. New York: Harper, 1958.

Jacob, Mira. "I Gave a Speech about Race to the Publishing Industry and No One Heard Me." *BuzzFeed*. 17 Sept. 2015. <https://www.buzzfeed.com/mira-jacob/you-will-ignore-us-at-your-own-peril?utm_term=.khdVM8VKb#.wml57M5Dw>.

Jacobs, Harriet. *Incidents in the Life of a Slave Girl*. 1861. Cambridge, MA: Harvard University Press, 1987.

Jamison, Leslie. *The Empathy Exams*. Minneapolis: Graywolf Press, 2014.

Jerng, Mark. Panelist on "Beyond Pleasure Reading: Race and Genre Fiction." American Studies Association Conference. Toronto, ON. 9 Oct. 2015.

Johnson, Alaya Dawn. *Love Is the Drug*. New York: Arthur A. Levine/Scholastic, 2014.

Joyce, Donald F. *Black Book Publishers in the United States: A Historical Directory of the Presses, 1817–1900*. New York: Greenwood Publishing Group, 1991.

Joyce, William. *A Day with Wilbur Robinson*. 1990. New York: HarperCollins, 1993.

Joyce, William. *Dinosaur Bob and His Adventures with the Family Lazardo*. New York: HarperCollins, 1988.

Joyce, William. *The Fantastic Flying Books of Mr. Morris Lessmore*. Illus. William Joyce & Joe Bluhm. New York: Atheneum Books for Young Readers, 2012.

Joyce, William. *George Shrinks*. 1985. New York: HarperCollins, 2000.

Joyce, William. *The Guardians of Childhood: The Man in the Moon*. New York: Atheneum, 2011.

Joyce, William. *The Leaf Men*. New York: HarperCollins, 1996.

Joyce, William. *Santa Calls*. New York: HarperCollins, 1993.

Katz, Alan. *The Cat NOT in the Hat! A Parody by Dr. Juice*. Illus. Chris Wrinn. Beverly Hills: Dove Books, 1996.

Kaufman, Geoff F., and Lisa K. Libby. "Changing Beliefs and Behavior Through Experience-Taking." *Journal of Personality and Social Psychology* 103.1 (2012): 1–19.

Kayne, Eric. "Census: White Majority in U.S. Gone by 2043." *US News/NBC News* 13 June 2013. 25 Oct. 2015. <http://usnews.nbcnews.com/_news/2013/06/13/18934111-census-white-majority-in-us-gone-by-2043?lite>.

Keats, Ezra Jack. *The Snowy Day*. 1962. New York: Puffin Books, 1976.

Kennedy, Randall. *Nigger: The Strange Career of a Troublesome Word*. 2002. New York: Vintage, 2003.

Kenny, Kevin. "Diaspora and Comparison: The Global Irish as a Case Study." *Journal of American History* 90.1 (2003): 134–162.

Kidd, Kenneth. "'Not Censorship but Selection': Censorship and/as Prizing." *Children's Literature in Education* 40.3 (2009): 197–216.

Kim, Sue J. *On Anger: Race, Cognition, Narrative.* Austin: University of Texas Press, 2013.

King, Thomas, and William Kent Monkman. *A Coyote Columbus Story.* Toronto and Berkeley: Groundwood Books/House of Anansi Press, 1992.

Klein, Cheryl. "Black and White and Read All Over: Diversity and Inequity in Children's Publishing." Nov. 2010. Published 2014. <http://static1.squarespace .com/static/56ba20a360b5e94f4cfddf13/t/572f84dcb654f9062911d94c/ 1462731996750/Black+and+White+and+Read+All+Over.pdf>.

Kohl, Herbert. *Should We Burn Babar? Essays on Children's Literature and the Power of Stories.* New York: New Press, 1995.

Krupa, Michelle. "Racial Divides among New Orleans Neighborhoods Expand." *Times-Picayune.* 7 June 2011. <http://www.nola.com/politics/index.ssf/2011/ 06/pockets_of_new_orleans_grow_fa.html>.

Lamana, Julie T. *Upside Down in the Middle of Nowhere.* San Francisco: Chronicle Books, 2014.

Larbalestier, Justine. "Ain't That a Shame (updated)." *Justine Larbalestier.* 23 July 2009. 5 June 2012. <http://justinelarbalestier.com/blog/2009/07/23/aint-that-a-shame/>.

Larbalestier, Justine. *Liar.* New York: Bloomsbury, 2009.

Larrick, Nancy. "The All-White World of Children's Books." *Saturday Review.* 11 Sept. 1965: 63–65, 84–85.

Larson, Kirby, and Mary Nethery. *Two Bobbies: A True Story of Hurricane Katrina, Friendship, and Survival.* Illus. Jean Cassels. New York: Walker & Company, 2008.

Latuff, Carlos. "Uncle Obama's Cabin." 8 Feb. 2010. *IndyMedia UK.* 9 Feb. 2010. <https://www.indymedia.org.uk/en/2010/02/445830.html?c=on>.

Laymon, Kiese. *How to Kill Yourself and Others in America: Essays.* Chicago: Bolden, 2013.

Laymon, Kiese. *Long Division.* Chicago: Agate Publishing, 2013.

Leader-Picone, Cameron. "Black and More than Black: Rearticulating Race in Twenty-First Century African American Fiction." Unpublished manuscript, 2016.

Lee, Paula Young. "The Power of Pop Literature: Why We Need Diverse YA Books More than Ever." *Salon.com.* 30 Sept. 2016. <http://www.salon.com/2016/09/ 30/the-power-of-pop-literature-why-we-need-diverse-ya-books-more-than-ever/>.

Le Guin, Ursula K. "Some Assumptions about Fantasy." 4 June 2004. 5 June 2012. *Ursula K. Leguin* <http://www.ursulakleguin.com/SomeAssumptionsAboutFantasy .html>.

Le Guin, Ursula K. *A Wizard of Earthsea.* Berkeley: Parnassus Press, 1968.

Le Guin, Ursula K. *A Wizard of Earthsea.* 1968. London and New York: Puffin, 1971.

Le Guin, Ursula K. *A Wizard of Earthsea.* 1968. New York: Bantam, 1975.

Le Guin, Ursula K. *A Wizard of Earthsea.* 1968. New York: Bantam, 1984.

Le Guin, Ursula K. *A Wizard of Earthsea.* 1968. Boston: Houghton Mifflin, 2012.

Lester, Julius. *Day of Tears: A Novel in Dialogue.* 2005. New York: Jump at the Sun/ Hyperion, 2007.

Lester, Julius. "Morality and *Adventures of Huckleberry Finn.*" *Satire or Evasion? Black Perspectives on Huckleberry Finn.* Ed. James S. Leonard, Thomas A. Tenney, and Thadious M. Davis. Durham and London: Duke University Press, 1992. 199–207.

Lester, Julius. *To Be a Slave.* Illus. Tom Feelings. New York: Dial Press, 1968.

Lighter, J. E., ed. *Historical Dictionary of American Slang.* Vol. 1: *A–G.* New York: Random House, 1994.

Lipsitz, George. "The Possessive Investment in Whiteness: Racialized Social Democracy and the 'White' Problem in American Studies." *American Quarterly* 47.3 (1995): 369–387.

Lo, Malinda. "There can be a zillion white authors who write [whatever kind of book] but if one marginalized author exists who does it, that's enough." Tweet. 17 Mar. 2015. <https://twitter.com/malindalo/status/577870204387991553>.

Lo, Malinda, and Cindy Pon, eds. *Diversity in YA.* <http://www.diversityinya.com/>.

Lofting, Hugh. *The Story of Doctor Dolittle.* 1920. New York: Tom Doherty Associates, 1998.

Lofting, Hugh. *The Story of Doctor Dolittle.* New York: Dell, 1988.

Lorde, Audre. "The Uses of Anger: Women Responding to Racism." Speech given at Women's Studies Association Conference, Storrs, CT. June 1981. <http://www .blackpast.org/1981-audre-lorde-uses-anger-women-responding-racism>.

Lott, Eric. *Love and Theft: Blackface Minstrelsy and the American Working Class.* New York: Oxford University Press, 1993.

Low, Jason. "Diversity's Action Plan." American Library Association. 27 June 2015. 27 Oct. 2015. <https://www.youtube.com/watch?v=4EDraVXrxro>.

Low, Jason, Sarah Park Dahlen, and Nicole Catlin. "Where Is the Diversity in Publishing? The 2015 Diversity Baseline Survey Results." *Lee & Low Blog.* 26 Jan. 2016. <http://blog.leeandlow.com/2016/01/26/where-is-the-diversity-in- publishing-the-2015-diversity-baseline-survey-results/>.

MacCann, Donnarae. *White Supremacy in Children's Literature: Characterizations of African Americans, 1830–1900.* New York and London: Garland, 1998.

MacCann, Donnarae, and Gloria Woodard. *The Black American in Books for Children: Readings in Racism.* Metuchen, NJ: Scarecrow Press, 1972.

Machell, Ben. "How the Fantastic Flying Books of Mr Morris Lessmore Took Off." *The Times* (London). 23 July 2011. <http://www.thetimes.co.uk/tto/arts/ books/childrensbooks/article3101464.ece>.

Mack, Lori. "A Publisher's Perspective." *Horn Book* 64.3 (1988): 382–384.

Mahar, William J. *Early Blackface Minstrelsy and Antebellum American Popular Culture.* Urbana: University of Illinois Press, 1999.

Mallery, Helen. Comment on Jocelyn McClurg and Maria Puente's "Are Dr. Seuss' books racist? Experts weigh in on controversy." *USA Today* 6 Oct. 2017.

Marsden, John, and Shaun Tan. *The Rabbits*. 1998. Sydney: Lothian Children's Books, 2010.

Martin, Michelle H. *Brown Gold: Milestones of African-American Children's Picture Books, 1845–2002*. New York: Routledge, 2004.

Martin, Michelle H. "Hushpuppy, Hauntings and Hurricanes: Black Girls Braving Storms, Inside and Out." Children's Literature Association Conference. Biloxi, MS. 14 June 2013. Full-length version forthcoming in *Children's Literature Association Quarterly*, 2016.

"Mary Katherine Joyce." *Legacy.com*. <http://www.legacy.com/obituaries/shreveporttimes/obituary.aspx?pid=142501679#fbLoggedOut>. Published in *Shreveport Times*. 5–8 May 2010.

Mason, Michael A. "The Cultivation of the Senses for Creative Nostalgia in the Essays of W. H. Hudson." *Ariel* 20.1 (1989): 23–37.

Masten, Helen Adams. "The Cat in the Hat." *Saturday Review*. 11 May 1957: 54.

Matsuda, Mari J., Charles R. Lawrence III, Richard Delgado, and Kimberlé Williams Crenshaw. *Words That Wound: Critical Race Theory, Assaultive Speech, and the First Amendment*. Boulder, San Francisco, and Oxford: Westview Press, 1993.

Maughan, Shannon. "Christopher Myers and Random House Partner for New Imprint." *Publishers Weekly*. 7 July 2016. <http://www.publishersweekly.com/pw/by-topic/childrens/childrens-industry-news/article/70848-christopher-myers-and-random-house-partner-for-new-imprint.html>.

McCloud, Scott. *Understanding Comics: The Invisible Art*. 1993. New York: HarperCollins, 1994.

McIntosh, Peggy. "White Privilege: Unpacking the Invisible Knapsack." 1988. *White Privilege: Essential Readings on the Other Side of Racism*. Ed. Paula S. Rothenberg. 5th ed. New York: Worth, 2016. 151–155.

Mendelsund, Peter. *What We See When We Read*. New York: Vintage Books, 2014.

Mendlesohn, Farah. "Nothing Sweet about A Birthday Cake for George Washington." *Guardian*. 27 Jan. 2016. 28 Jan. 2016. <http://www.theguardian.com/world/2016/jan/27/nothing-sweet-about-a-birthday-cake-for-george-washington>.

Metta, John. "I, Racist." *Medium.com*. 6 July 2015. <https://medium.com/@johnmetta/i-racist-538512462265>.

Mickenberg, Julia L. *Learning from the Left: Children's Literature, the Cold War, and Radical Politics in the United States*. New York: Oxford University Press, 2006.

Miller, Harry S. "The Cat Came Back." Arr. By Otto Bonnell. Chicago: Will Rossiter, 1893. Sheet music.

Miller, Laura. "Can You Identify?" *Salon.com*. 16 May 2012. 5 June 2012. <http://www.salon.com/2012/05/17/can_you_identify/>.

Milliot, Jim. "Publishing's Holding Pattern: 2014 Salary Survey." *Publishers Weekly*. 19 Sept. 2014. 21 Oct. 2015. <http://www.publishersweekly.com/pw/by-topic/industry-news/publisher-news/article/64083-publishing-s-holding-pattern-2013-salary-survey.html>.

Milliot, Jim. "The PW Publishing Industry Salary Survey 2015: A Younger Workforce, Still Predominantly White." *Publishers Weekly.* 16 Oct. 2015. <http://www.publishersweekly.com/pw/by-topic/industry-news/publisher-news/article/68405-publishing-industry-salary-survey-2015-a-younger-workforce-still-predominantly-white.html>.

Minear, Richard. *Dr. Seuss Goes to War: The World War II Editorial Cartoons of Theodor Seuss Geisel.* New York: New Press, 1999.

"Minstrels Add $300 to Fund for Trip." *Springfield Union.* Morning ed. 30 Apr. 1921, p. 6.

Montgomery, L. M. *Anne of Green Gables.* 1908. London: Puffin, 1994.

Morgan, Judith, and Neil Morgan. *Dr. Seuss and Mr. Geisel: A Biography.* New York: Random House, 1995.

Morin, Rich. "Exploring Racial Bias among Biracial and Single-Race Adults: The IAT." *Pew Research Center.* 19 Aug. 2015. <http://www.pewsocialtrends.org/2015/08/19/exploring-racial-bias-among-biracial-and-single-race-adults-the-iat/>.

Morrison, Toni. *Playing in the Dark: Whiteness and the Literary Imagination.* Cambridge, MA, and London: Harvard University Press, 1992.

Murakawa, Naomi. "Naomi Murakawa and Eddie Glaude in Conversation—The First Civil Right." *Princeton Community Television.* Recorded at Labyrinth Books. 12 Mar. 2015. <https://vimeo.com/123203080>.

Myers, Christopher. "The Apartheid of Children's Literature." *New York Times.* 16 Mar. 2014. <http://www.nytimes.com/2014/03/16/opinion/sunday/the-apartheid-of-childrens-literature.html?_r=o>.

Myers, Christopher. "Please Don't Agree with Me: The Need for Disagreement in Debates about Literature for Young People." Lecture, Alumni Center, Kansas State University. 22 Oct. 2015.

Myers, Christopher. "Young Dreamers." *Horn Book.* 6 Aug. 2013. <http://www.hbook.com/2013/08/opinion/young-dreamers/>.

Myers, Walter Dean. "Where Are the People of Color in Children's Books?" *New York Times.* 16 Mar. 2014. <http://www.nytimes.com/2014/03/16/opinion/sunday/where-are-the-people-of-color-in-childrens-books.html?smid=fb-share&_r=o>.

National Coalition Against Censorship. "A Birthday Cake for George Washington: The Problem with Banning Books." *National Coalition Against Censorship.* 22 Jan. 2016. <http://ncac.org/press-release/a-birthday-cake-for-george-washington-the-problem-with-banishing-books>.

Nabokov, Vladimir. *Speak, Memory.* 1967. New York: Vintage Books (Random House), 1989.

Neary, Lynn. "To Achieve Diversity in Publishing, a Difficult Dialogue Beats Silence." *All Things Considered.* 20 Aug. 2014. 23 Oct. 2015. <http://www.npr.org/sections/codeswitch/2014/08/20/341443632/to-achieve-diversity-in-publishing-a-difficult-dialogue-beats-silence>.

Nel, Philip. *The Annotated Cat: Under the Hats of Seuss and His Cats.* New York: Random House, 2007.

Nel, Philip. *Dr. Seuss: American Icon.* New York: Continuum, 2004.

Nel, Philip. *J. K. Rowling's Harry Potter Novels: A Reader's Guide.* New York and London: Continuum, 2001.

Nel, Philip. "Obamafiction for Children: Imagining the Forty-Fourth U.S. President." *Children's Literature Association Quarterly* 35.4 (2010): 334–356.

Nelson, Kadir. *We Are the Ship: The Story of Negro League Baseball.* New York: Jump at the Sun/Hyperion, 2008.

Nelson, Marilyn. *The Freedom Business including A Narrative of the Life and Adventures of Venture, a Native of Africa.* Art by Deborah Dancy. Honesdale, PA: Wordsong/Boyds Mills Press, 2008.

Neufeld, Josh. *A.D.: New Orleans after the Deluge.* New York: Pantheon, 2009.

Newell, Peter. *The Hole Book.* New York: Harper & Brothers, 1908. n.p. Morse Department of Special Collections, Hale Library, Kansas State University, Manhattan, Kansas.

"New Orleans City: Segregation: Neighborhood Exposure by Race." *CensusScope.org.* 28 July 2013. <http://www.censusscope.org/us/s22/p55000/chart_exposure.html>.

New York University Summer Publishing Institute. 4 Sept. 2016. <http://www.scps.nyu.edu/academics/departments/publishing/academic-offerings/summer-publishing-institute.html>.

Ngai, Sianne. *Ugly Feelings.* Cambridge, MA: Harvard University Press, 2005.

Nussbaum, Martha C. *Not for Profit: Why Democracy Needs the Humanities.* Princeton: Princeton University Press, 2010.

Nussbaum, Martha C. *Upheavals of Thought: The Intelligence of Emotions.* Cambridge, UK, and New York: Cambridge University Press, 2001.

Oehlschlaeger, Fritz. "'Gwyne to Git Hung': The Conclusion of *Huckleberry Finn.*" *One Hundred Years of "Huckleberry Finn": The Boy, His Book and American Culture.* Ed. Robert Sattelmeyer and J. Donald Crowley. Columbia: University of Missouri Press, 1985. 117–127.

"Of Rabbits & Races." *Time.* 1 June 1959: 19.

Older, Daniel José. "Diversity Is Not Enough: Race, Power, Publishing." *BuzzFeed.* 17 Apr. 2014. <https://www.buzzfeed.com/danieljoseolder/diversity-is-not-enough?utm_term=.xu9k2pkzP#.ir8ZVeZEW>.

Older, Daniel José. "Do Black Children's Lives Matter if Nobody Writes about Them?" *The Guardian.* 6 Nov. 2015. <http://www.theguardian.com/commentisfree/2015/nov/06/do-black-childrens-lives-matter-if-nobody-writes-about-them?CMP=share_btn_fb>.

Olson, Marilynn. "Turn-of-the-Century Grotesque: The Uptons' Golliwogg and Dolls in Context." *Children's Literature* 28 (2000): 73–94.

Omi, Michael, and Howard Winant. *Racial Formation in the United States from the 1960s to the 1990s.* 2nd ed. New York: Routledge, 1994.

"Ormond's History." *Ormond Plantation*. 2015. 23 Jan. 2015. <http://www.plantation.com/about>.

Osnos, Evan. "President Trump's First Term." *New Yorker*. 26 Sept. 2016. <http://www.newyorker.com/magazine/2016/09/26/president-trumps-first-term>.

Patrick, Denise Lewis. *Finding Someplace*. New York: Henry Holt & Co., 2015.

Perkins, Mitali. *Mitali's Fire Escape*. <http://www.mitaliblog.com/>.

Perkins, Mitali. "Straight Talk on Race: Challenging the Stereotypes in Kids' Books." *School Library Journal*. 1 Apr. 2009. <http://www.schoollibraryjournal.com/article/CA6647713.html>.

Philbrick, Rodman. *Zane and the Hurricane: A Story of Katrina*. New York: Blue Sky Press (Scholastic), 2014.

Pilgrim, David. "The Golliwog Caricature." 2000. Rev. 2012. *The Jim Crow Museum of Racist Memorabilia*. 4 Jan. 2014. <http://www.ferris.edu/jimcrow/golliwog/>.

Pilgrim, David. *Understanding Jim Crow: Using Racist Memorabilia to Teach Tolerance and Promote Social Justice*. Toronto and Oakland: PM Press, 2015.

Pinkney, Andrea Davis. *Hand in Hand: Ten Black Men Who Changed America*. Illus. Brian Pinkney. New York: Jump at the Sun/Hyperion, 2012.

Pinkney, Andrea Davis. "A Proud Slice of History." *On Our Minds: Scholastic's Blog about Books and the Joy of Reading*. Jan. 2016. 28 Jan. 2016. <http://oomscholasticblog.com/post/proud-slice-history>.

Pon, Cindy. *Silver Phoenix*. New York: Greenwillow, 2009.

"Publishing Certificate Program." Publishing Certificate Program, City University of New York. 9 Sept. 2016. <https://www.ccny.cuny.edu/english/pcpdirectornote>.

Racebending.com. <http://www.racebending.com/>.

"Racial/Ethnic Enrollment in Public Schools." *The Condition of Education*. Ed. Peggy G. Carr. National Center for Education Statistics. Last updated May 2016. 27 Aug. 2016. <http://nces.ed.gov/programs/coe/indicator_cge.asp>.

"Racial Fur Flies." *Newsweek*. 1 June 1959: 28.

Ramaswamy, Chitra. "Can Hermione Be Black? What a Stupid Question." *The Guardian*. 21 Dec. 2015. <https://www.theguardian.com/books/shortcuts/2015/dec/21/hermione-granger-black-noma-dumezwani-harry-potter-cursed-child>.

Rampersad, Arnold. "*Adventures of Huckleberry Finn* and Afro-American Literature." *Satire or Evasion? Black Perspectives on Huckleberry Finn*. Ed. James S. Leonard, Thomas A. Tenney, and Thadious M. Davis. Durham and London: Duke University Press, 1992. 216–227.

Ransome, Arthur. *Swallows and Amazons*. 1930. Boston: David R. Godine, 2010.

Rappaport, Doreen. *Martin's Big Words*. Illus. Bryan Collier. 2001. New York: Hyperion, 2007.

Ravitch, Diane. "Ravitch: The Chutzpah of Rewriting Mark Twain (and How It Relates to 'The Wire')." *Washington Post*. 11 Jan. 2011. <http://voices.washingtonpost.com/answer-sheet/guest-bloggers/ravitch-the-chutzpah-of-rewrit.html>.

Red Hot Chili Peppers. "Yertle the Turtle." *Freaky Styley*. EMI, 1985.

Reid, Calvin. "From Comics to Prose: Jerry Craft on Self-Publishing." *Publishers Weekly*. 3 Feb. 2014. <http://www.publishersweekly.com/pw/by-topic/authors/pw-select/article/60907-from-comics-to-prose-jerry-craft-on-self-publishing.html>.

Rey, H. A. *Curious George*. 1941. Houghton Mifflin Harcourt, 1973.

Rhodes, Jewell Parker. *Ninth Ward*. 2010. New York and Boston: Little, Brown, 2012.

RM, "If Dr. Seuss is tired and racist…" Comment on Liz Phipps Soeiro, "Dear Mrs. Trump," *Horn Book* 26 Sept. 2017 <https://www.hbook.com/2017/09/blogs/family-reading/dear-mrs-trump/>. Comment made 28 Sept. 2017, 2:45 pm.

Rogers, Sean. "A Conversation with Lynda Barry." *The Walrus Blog*. 17 Nov. 2008. <http://www.walrusmagazine.com/blogs/2008/11/17/a-conversation-with-lynda-barry/>.

Rome, Emily. "Oscar Shorts: 'Morris Lessmore' Has Hybrid Animation, iPad App." *Los Angeles Times*. 23 Jan. 2012. <http://latimesblogs.latimes.com/movies/2012/01/oscars-short-films-fantastic-flying-books-morris-lessmore-animation.html>.

Rosoff, Meg. "You Can't Protect Children by Lying to Them—the Truth Will Hurt Less." *Guardian*. 20 Sept. 2013. <http://www.theguardian.com/lifeandstyle/2013/sep/21/cant-protect-children-by-lying>.

Rowling, J. K. *Harry Potter and the Philosopher's Stone*. London: Bloomsbury, 1997.

Rowling, J. K. *Harry Potter and the Prisoner of Azkaban*. London: Bloomsbury, 1999.

RUN-DMC. "Peter Piper." *Raising Hell*. Profile/Arista Records, 1986.

Schutte, Annie. "It Matters If You're Black or White: The Racism of YA Book Covers." *The Hub: Your Connection to Teen Collections (YALSA)*. 10 Dec. 2012. 10 Nov. 2015. <http://www.yalsa.ala.org/thehub/2012/12/10/it-matters-if-youre-black-or-white-the-racism-of-ya-book-covers/>.

Seuss, Dr. "Africa—Its Social, Religious, and Economical Aspects." *Judge*. 23 Mar. 1929: 14.

Seuss, Dr. ". . . But for Grown-Ups Laughing Isn't Any Fun." *New York Times Book Review*. 16 Nov. 1952: 2.

Seuss, Dr. *The Cat in the Hat*. New York: Random House, 1957.

Seuss, Dr. *The Cat in the Hat Comes Back*. New York: Random House, 1958.

Seuss, Dr. *The Cat in the Hat Songbook*. New York: Random House, 1967.

Seuss, Dr. "Cross Section of the World's Most Prosperous Department Store." *Judge*. 1 June 1929: 24.

Seuss, Dr. "Four Places Not to Hide while Growing Your Beard." *Life*. 15 Nov. 1929: 19.

Seuss, Dr. [as Ted]. "Highball Thompson Wins from Kid Sambo by a Shade." *Jack-o-Lantern*. 2 Apr. 1923: 26. Repr. in Charles Cohen, *The Seuss, the Whole Seuss and Nothing but the Seuss*, 207.

Seuss, Dr. *Horton Hears a Who!* New York: Random House, 1954.

Seuss, Dr. *How the Grinch Stole Christmas!* New York: Random House, 1957.

Seuss, Dr. "How Orlo Got His Book." *New York Times Book Review*, 17 Nov. 1957: 2, 60. Repr. in Nel, *The Annotated Cat*, 167–69.

Seuss, Dr. *If I Ran the Circus*. New York: Random House, 1956.

Seuss, Dr. *If I Ran the Zoo*. New York: Random House, 1950.

Seuss, Dr. "Latest Modern Convenience: Hot and Cold Running Subs." *PM*. Jan. 22, 1942: 22.

Seuss, Dr. *On Beyond Zebra!* New York: Random House, 1955.

Seuss, Dr. *Scrambled Eggs Super!* New York: Random House, 1953.

Seuss, Dr. "SHE—Out sportin' again, are yo', nigger? Jest wait 'til I lay hands on yo' tonight!" *Judge*. 15 Sept. 1928: 2. Repr. Cohen, *The Seuss, the Whole Seuss and Nothing but the Seuss*, 212.

Seuss, Dr. "The Sneetches." *Redbook* July 1953: 77. Repr. in Mickenberg and Nel, *Tales for Little Rebels: A Collection of Radical Children's Literature*. New York University Press: 2008. 207.

Seuss, Dr. *The Sneetches and Other Stories*. New York: Random House, 1961.

Seuss, Dr. "Sorry, sister, but you can't get wholesale baptizin' rates unless you got a minimum of twelve chillun.'" *Judge*. 12 Jan. 1929: 6. Repr. in Charles Cohen, *The Seuss, the Whole Seuss and Nothing but the Seuss*, 213.

Seuss, Dr. "There seems to be a white man in the woodpile!" *PM*. 8 July 1942: 22. Repr. Minear, *Dr. Seuss Goes to War*, 60.

Seuss, Dr. "What This Country Needs Is a Good Mental Insecticide." *PM*. 10 June 1942: 22. Repr. Minear, *Dr. Seuss Goes to War*, 57.

Seuss, Dr. "Yertle the Turtle." *Redbook*. April 1951: 46–47.

Seuss, Dr. *Yertle the Turtle and Other Stories*. New York: Random House, 1958.

"Shreveport City: Segregation: Neighborhood Exposure by Race." *CensusScope.org*. 28 July 2013. <http://www.censusscope.org/us/s22/p70000/chart_exposure.html>.

Siegelson, Kim L. *In the Time of the Drums*. Illus. Brian Pinkney. New York: Jump at the Sun/Hyperion, 1999.

Silvey, Anita. "How the Cat Got His Smile." Narr. Lynn Neary. *Morning Edition*. National Public Radio. 1 Mar. 2007.

"Site Index." Cooperative Children's Book Center. School of Education. University of Wisconsin–Madison. 21 Jan. 2015. <http://ccbc.education.wisc.edu/siteIndex/>.

Smith, Katharine Capshaw. *Children's Literature of the Harlem Renaissance*. Bloomington: Indiana University Press, 2004.

Smith, Lane. *Abe Lincoln's Dream*. New York: Roaring Brook Press, 2012.

Smith, Lane. *The Big Pets*. New York: Viking, 1991.

Smith, Tamara Ellis. *Another Kind of Hurricane*. New York: Schwartz & Wade Books, 2015.

Smith, Vicky. "Unmaking the White Default." *Kirkus Reviews*. 4 May 2016. <https://www.kirkusreviews.com/features/unmaking-white-default/>.

Sollors, Werner. *The Temptation of Despair: Tales of the 1940s*. Cambridge, MA: Harvard University Press, 2014.

Sontag, Susan. *Regarding the Pain of Others*. New York: Farrar, Straus, & Giroux, 2003.

Spivack, Loren, and Patrick Fields. *The Cat and the Mitt by Dr. Truth*. Illus. Leandro Martins Moraes. Amherst, MA: Free Market Warrior Publications, 2012.

Springer, Nancy. "Afterword." *The Story of Doctor Dolittle*. By Hugh Lofting. New York: Tom Doherty Associates, 1998.

Squires, Catherine R. *The Post-Racial Mystique: Media and Race in the Twenty-First Century*. New York: New York University Press, 2014.

Stewart, Dodai. "Racist Hunger Games Fans Are Very Disappointed." *Jezebel*. 26 Mar. 2012. <http://jezebel.com/5896408/racist-hunger-games-fans-dont-care-how-much-money-the-movie-made>.

Stewart, Susan. *Nonsense: Aspects of Intertextuality in Folklore and Literature*. Baltimore and London: Johns Hopkins University Press, 1979.

Stewart, Trenton Lee. *The Mysterious Benedict Society*. 2007. New York and Boston: Little, Brown and Company, 2008.

Stowe, Harriet Beecher. *Uncle Tom's Cabin; or, Life among the Lowly*. 1852. Ed. Ann Douglas. New York: Penguin, 1986.

Suhl, Isabelle. "The Real Doctor Dolittle." *Interracial Books for Children* 2.1–2 (1968): 1, 5–7.

Sultan, Aisha. "Black Moms Tell White Moms about the Race Talk." *UExpress*. 29 Sept. 2014. <http://www.uexpress.com/parents-talk-back/2014/9/29/black-moms-tell-white-moms-about>.

Swift, Hildegarde Hoyt. *North Star Shining: A Pictorial History of the American Negro*. Illus. Lynd Ward. New York: William Morrow & Co., 1947.

Tan, Shaun. "The Rabbits." *ShaunTan.net*. 28 Mar. 2015. <http://www.shauntan.net/books/the-rabbits.html>.

Taylor, Mildred. *Roll of Thunder, Hear My Cry*. 1976. New York: Puffin Books, 1991.

Tedeschi, Bob. "For the iPad, Books That Respond to a Child's Touch." *The New York Times*. 30 July 2011: B9. <http://www.nytimes.com/2011/06/30/technology/personaltech/30smart.html>.

Tharps, Lori L. "The Case for Black with a Capital B." *New York Times*. 19 Nov. 2014. A25. <http://www.nytimes.com/2014/11/19/opinion/the-case-for-black-with-a-capital-b.html>.

"That's Not Twain." Editorial. *The New York Times*. 6 Jan. 2011: A26. <http://www.nytimes.com/2011/01/06/opinion/06thu4.html>.

Thomas, Ebony Elizabeth. "The Dark Fantastic: Race and the Imagination in Youth Literature, Media, and Culture." Book manuscript under development for New York University Press, Postmillennial Pop series (Series Editors: Karen Tongson and Henry Jenkins). 2016.

Thomas, Ebony Elizabeth. "The Imagination Gap in #Kidlit and #YAlit: An Introduction to the Dark Fantastic." *The Dark Fantastic: Race and the Imagination in Children's & YA Books, Media, and Fan Cultures*. 10 June 2014. <http://thedarkfantastic.blogspot.com/2014/06/the-dark-fantastic-notes-toward.html>.

Thomas, Joyce Carol. *The Blacker the Berry*. Illus. Floyd Cooper. HarperCollins/Amistad, 2008.

Thompson, John B. *Merchants of Culture: The Publishing Business in the Twenty-First Century*. 2nd ed. New York: Penguin, 2012.

"Through the African American Lens: Explore Selections from the Permanent Collection." *Smithsonian National Museum of African American History and Culture*. 7 July 2016. <https://nmaahc.si.edu/explore/exhibitions/through-african-american-lens>.

Thurston, Baratunde. *How to Be Black*. New York: HarperCollins, 2012.

Timberg, Scott. "Henry Louis Gates on Trump: 'That election clearly represented a backlash against the progress black people have made since 1965.'" *Salon.com* 12 Nov. 2016: <http://www.salon.com/2016/11/12/henry-louis-gates-on-trump-that-election-clearly-represented-a-backlash-against-the-progress-black-people-have-made-since-1965/>.

Tisserand, Michael. *Krazy: George Herriman, a Life in Black and White*. New York: HarperCollins, 2016.

Travers, P. L. "The Art of Fiction LXIII." Interview by Edwina Burness and Jerry Griswold. *The Paris Review* 86 (Fall 1982): 210–229.

Travers, P. L. Handwritten note on front of file folder. Travers Papers. Mitchell Collection, State Library of New South Wales, Sydney. Notes supplied by Teya Rosenberg.

Travers, P. L. *Mary Poppins*. Illus. Mary Shepard. 1934. New York: Harcourt Brace Jovanovich, 1962.

Travers, P. L. *Mary Poppins*. Illus. Mary Shepard. London: Collins, 1967.

Travers, P. L. *Mary Poppins*. Illus. Mary Shepard. 1981. New York: Harcourt Brace, 1997.

Trump, Donald J. "Donald Trump Transcript: 'Our Country Needs a Truly Great Leader.'" *Wall Street Journal*. 16 June 2015. <http://blogs.wsj.com/washwire/2015/06/16/donald-trump-transcript-our-country-needs-a-truly-great-leader/>.

Turley, Jonathan. "Publisher Announces Intention to Edit Huckleberry Finn to Remove N-word." *Res ipsa loquitur*. 4 Jan. 2011. <http://jonathanturley.org/2011/01/04/publisher-announces-intention-to-edit-huckleberry-finn-to-remove-n-word/>.

Twain, Mark. *The Adventures of Huckleberry Finn*. Ed. Scully Bradley, Richmond Croom Beatty, E. Hudson Long, and Thomas Cooley. 1961. New York: W. W. Norton, 1977.

Twain, Mark. *The Adventures of Tom Sawyer and Huckleberry Finn*. Ed. Alan Gribben. Montgomery, AL: NewSouth Books, 2011.

Uhlberg, Myron. *A Storm Called Katrina*. Illus. Colin Bootman. Atlanta: Peachtree, 2011.

Unger, David. "A Note from the Director." Publishing Certificate Program. City University of New York. <https://www.ccny.cuny.edu/english/pcpdirector-note>. Sept. 9, 2016.

Upton, Florence Kate. *The Adventures of Two Dutch Dolls and a Golliwogg*. 1895. Boston: De Wolfe, Fiske, & Co., 1897.

"U.S. Elections: How Groups Voted in 2012." Roper Center: Public Opinion Archives. University of Connecticut. 22 Jan. 2014. <http://www.ropercenter.uconn.edu/elections/how_groups_voted/voted_12.html>.

Van Allsburg, Chris. *Probuditi!* Boston: Houghton Mifflin Company, 2006.

Wallace, John H. "The Case Against *Huck Finn*." *Satire or Evasion? Black Perspectives on Huckleberry Finn*. Ed. James S. Leonard, Thomas A. Tenney, and Thadious M. Davis. Durham and London: Duke University Press, 1992. 16–24.

Walt Disney's Story Land: 55 Favorite Stories Adapted from Walt Disney Films. Racine, WI: Golden Press, 1974.

Ward, Jesmyn. *Men We Reaped: A Memoir*. 2013. New York and London: Bloomsbury, 2014.

Ward, Jesmyn. *Salvage the Bones*. 2011. New York: Bloomsbury, 2012.

Watkins, Tony. "Cultural Studies, New Historicism, and Children's Literature." *Literature for Children: Contemporary Criticism*. Ed. Peter Hunt. New York: Routledge, 1992. 173–195.

Watson, Renée. *A Place Where Hurricanes Happen*. Illus. Shadra Strickland. New York: Random House, 2010.

Weatherford, Carole Boston. *Moses: When Harriet Tubman Led Her People to Freedom*. Illus. Kadir Nelson. New York: Jump at the Sun/Hyperion, 2006.

Weaver, Annie Vaughan. *Frawg*. New York: Frederick A. Stokes, 1930.

Weems, Mason L. *The Life of George Washington*. 1808. Cambridge, MA: Harvard University Press, 1962.

Wekker, Gloria. *White Innocence: Paradoxes of Colonialism and Race*. Durham and London: Duke University Press, 2016.

Wells, Samuel R. *New Physiognomy; or Signs of Character as Manifested Through Temperament and External Forms*. 1866. New York: Fowler & Wells Co., 1891.

"White-Black Segregation." *CensusScope.org*. 28 July 2013. <http://www.nola.com/politics/index.ssf/2011/06/pockets_of_new_orleans_grow_fa.html>.

Wilder, Laura Ingalls. *Little House in the Big Woods*. 1932. Rev. 1953. Illus. Garth Williams. New York: HarperCollins, 1981.

Wilder, Laura Ingalls. *Little House on the Prairie*. 1935. Rev. 1953. Illus. Garth Williams. New York: HarperCollins, 1981.

Wilder, Laura Ingalls. *The Long Winter*. 1940. New York: HarperCollins, 1981.

Williams, Garth. *The Rabbits' Wedding*. New York: Harper, 1958.

Williams, Raymond. *Marxism and Literature*. Oxford: Oxford University Press, 1977.

Williams-Garcia, Rita. *One Crazy Summer*. New York: HarperCollins/Amistad, 2010.

Williams-Garcia, Rita. *P.S. Be Eleven*. New York: HarperCollins/Amistad, 2013.

Winter, Jonah. *Barack*. Illus. A. G. Ford. New York: Collins, 2008.

Wolosky, Shira. "Democracy in America: By Dr. Seuss." *Southwest Review* 85.2 (2000): 167–183.

Woods, Brenda. *Saint Louis Armstrong Beach*. 2011. New York: Penguin, 2012.

Woodson, Jacqueline. *Brown Girl Dreaming*. New York: Penguin, 2014.

Woodson, Jacqueline. "The Pain of the Watermelon Joke." *New York Times*. 29 Nov. 2014: A17. <http://www.nytimes.com/2014/11/29/opinion/the-pain-of-the-watermelon-joke.html>.

Woodson, Jacqueline. "2014 National Book Award Winner, Young People's Literature" (remarks on receiving the award, starting at 4:50). *National Book Foundation*. <http://www.nationalbook.org/nba2014_ypl_woodson.html#.Vly_Q9-rSHo>.

Woodson, Jacqueline, and James E. Ransome. *Visiting Day*. 2002. New York: Puffin, 2015.

Wright, Richard. *Native Son*. New York: Harper & Brothers, 1940.

Young, John K. *Black Writers, White Publishers: Marketplace Politics in Twentieth-Century African American Literature*. Jackson: University Press of Mississippi, 2006.

Young, John K. "'Quite as Human as It Is Negro': Subpersons and Textual Property in *Native Son* and *Black Boy*." *Publishing Blackness: Textual Constructions of Race since 1850*. Ed. George Hutchinson and John K. Young. Ann Arbor: University of Michigan Press, 2013. 67–92.

Younge, Gary. "How Racism Stole Black Childhood." *The Nation*. 29 Oct. 2014. <http://www.thenation.com/article/186577/price-transgression>. Article appears in the 17 Nov. 2014 print issue of *The Nation*.

Zinn, Howard. "The Optimism of Uncertainty." *The Nation* 20 Sept. 2004: <https://www.thenation.com/article/optimism-uncertainty/>

INDEX

CPSIA information can be obtained
at www.ICGtesting.com
Printed in the USA
BVHW030455080321
601859BV00002B/10